ROMANTIC AMERICA

NATURAL BRIDGE OVER CEDAR CREEK, VIRGINIA - 1826

Extended Travels in

ROMANTIC AMERICA

Being a Nineteenth Century Journey through the
most Picturesque Portions of North America,
Reconstructed from Accounts by European
Visitors; the Whole Embellished
with Watercolour Drawings and
Engravings of the Period

Chosen and Displayed by Joseph Jobé
The Passages from the French, German and Italian Languages Translated by D.B. Tubbs

Published by Edita at Lausanne, Switzerland

PREFACE

The weather was grey in Lausanne and I was spending the afternoon, as I often do, in a shop selling old books and prints. Leafing through a portfolio of topographical engravings, old maps and loose pages from travel books, I came upon a print, of about 1830, showing New York City. I am familiar enough with prints of European cities of this period. Usually they are easily identifiable even without a title or a caption—either the city looks today very much as it did more than a century ago or, at the very least, some famous landmark like the Louvre or the Coliseum, or Trafalgar Square unmistakably recalls present-day Paris or Rome or London. But there was nothing familiar whatever about the print that I now held in my hand. A charming countrified landscape, " romantic " in the literary sense of the word, it contained nothing except its title to link it with the streets and sky-line of present-day Manhattan. Suddenly I realised something which, of course, is obvious but which I had never before thought of : history and change have wrought far different patterns in the Old World and the New. Despite the enormous growth and industrialisation that has gone on here, a European today can form a fairly clear idea just by looking around him of what his city or town must have looked like a hundred and fifty years ago. But in America, especially in the great cities, nothing of the kind is possible. For better or for worse, the visual remains of early 19th-century America have largely disappeared.

In the weeks and months that followed I began trying to recreate that lost America, as well as I could, hunting for diaries and drawings in libraries and museums all over Europe (later in the United States, too). What I wanted were the comments and everyday views of the European visitors who flocked to 19th-century America, full of prejudices and misconceptions in some cases, but always eager to record their opinions of the land and its people, and to talk about what they encountered and what they thought of those astonishing and still-to-be-united States. Gradually, after much research and not a little travel on my part, enough material came to light for me to sketch the itinerary of an illustrated journey through the America of a century or more ago, seen through the eyes of European visitors.

This book is the result. All the authors included are European—that is to say either Continental or British, and nearly all the illustrations, too, were done at the time and by European visitors. All the travellers made their journey to the New World in the period between the War of Independence and the War between the States. Each writer describes what he saw of the country and its people in his own way and from his own particular angle. It is rather as though we had managed to send a variety of different camera crews into the past. The picture cannot of course be complete, or even objective, but we think it is both lively and informative. No single author possessed a complete knowledge of the great transformations that then were taking place in America. Apart from Charles Dickens, none of them is really a literary figure. Many of them were, and are, quite unknown, even in their native lands.

In those days, before undertaking a journey to the United States, one had to be if not rich at the very least well-to-do, and to enjoy travel for its own sake—much of the U.S. had none of the conveniences which normally awaited travellers in Europe. Moreover, almost anyone who went to the U.S. had to be imbued with a spirit of adventure. It was adventure alone that sent a junior French diplomat like Achille Poussielgue (p. 87) off to Florida in his chartered schooner and drove the painter Friedrich Kurz (p. 133) to live for years among the Indians. Some of our authors travelled from scientific curiosity, like Maximilian, Prince of Wied and François-André Michaux. Others, like Henri Herz the pianist and the actor Léon Beauvallet, had to earn a living. The only "tourist" in the modern sense, is probably the romantic young Swiss *chocolatier*, Philippe Suchard. Although Charles Dickens was ostensibly travelling for fun he did in fact collect material for two books during the trip: *American Notes* which appeared in 1842, and a novel, *Martin Chuzzlewit* brought out the following year. The only man on our list who can be called a professional explorer is Captain Richard Burton, who received gold medals from the French and English Geographical Societies for leading the expedition which discovered Lake Tanganyika in 1858. A master of thirty-five languages who had been the first white man to visit Mecca and live to write about it, Burton had a passion for strange religions and "Holy Cities". (He also visited Medina disguised as a Pathan pilgrim). It was his desire to add a third "Holy City" to his collection, in fact, that drove him overland to the Great Salt Lake for an encounter with the Mormons. His opinion of them was fair, if one can judge by the following remark: " I have tried to divide the blame in an impartial manner between the Mormons and the non-Mormons, and having done so without acerbity, I have to be prepared to be blamed by both. "

Our book is arranged in four parts, each section devoted to a separate itinerary. Each journey must be taken at its own pace.

On the first route, for instance, (around the north-east from Philadelphia to New York, Boston, and Niagara Falls, down the Ohio as far as Cincinnati and then on to Washington across the Allegheny Mountains) not a great deal of territory is covered. But a traveller's-eye-view is built up from the recollections of many people, since this part of the U.S. was the one most visited by Europeans.

The second itinerary, all the way from the embryonic capital city of Washington to the tumultuous town of New Orleans, unfolds slowly and with sundry romantic digressions — as befits any account touching upon the Old South. Our third route progresses by steamboat up the Mississippi and Missouri rivers, and splits in various directions for encounters with Indian tribes, trappers, buffalo-herds and " mountain men ", alias *voyageurs*. Our fourth, and last, offers a taste of frantic San Francisco during the Gold Rush, and life in the mining camps.

The illustrations are drawn from the great libraries of Europe and the United States. Some have never been published before. Many have hitherto been seen only by a handful of specialists. A few — a very few — have appeared here and there in magazines. Few of the artists rank high in the history of art, but each of them was " drawing from life ", setting down frankly and sharply the scenes that unrolled before him. They were the candid camera men of their day, and if their productions sometimes strike us as naïve, they have the primitive, documentary charm that one finds in an old family album. In recent years, of course, the stream of American visitors to Europe has grown. Lately, too, considerable numbers of Europeans have become able, once more, to visit the United States as tourists with cash and time enough to savour its splendid (and to us) somewhat exotic scenery, to try to assess its spirit and its sometimes rasping vitality. But if travel is easier now, the comments of tourists today do not read as easily, gracefully, or graphically as do those on the following pages. Accordingly we hope that European readers will be as impressed as we have been with the wit and justice of their ancestors' observations, and that American readers will be pleased to see themselves as others saw them long ago.

JOSEPH JOBÉ.

Asterisks in the text refer to Explanatory Notes on page 218. The numbers which follow quotations allow the source of each passage to be identified. The names of the original works, together with brief notes on their authors, will be found on page 213.

NEW-YORK, BROADWAY - 1824

CHAPTER THE FIRST

*In which the Reader, after disembarking at Baltimore
in the State of Maryland,
sojourns in turn at Philadelphia, New York and Boston,
pays a visit to the Springs of Saratoga and the Falls of Niagara and,
after descending the Ohio River to Cincinnati,
traverses the Allegheny Mountains to reach
Washington, Capital of the Union.*

Advice to European Passengers Travelling to the United States of America,

published in Paris, 1818

The cost of a passage from France to the United States, in the best American ships, is approximately 700 francs [400 francs equal U.S. $76.00 of 1818, about the annual income of a French workman at that time].° For this sum each lady passenger enjoys a state-room to herself. If there are no ladies on board these cabins are given to male passengers; they are the best on board, and the least affected by the movements of the ship in bad weather. Excellent fare is provided by the captain: freshly baked bread each morning in fine weather, French wines and Madeira, brandy, beer, cider and liqueurs in great variety. The ship carries a sufficiency of live poultry, sheep and pigs to afford fresh meat throughout the voyage.

The fare for those travelling steerage is between 350 and 400 francs. The accommodation is comfortable but there is no access to the saloon or first-class passengers' quarters.

Steerage passengers have to find most of their own provisions, and each should therefore take aboard: forty-five to fifty pounds of good biscuits (the captain provides excellent salt beef and pork from America, codfish and potatoes in abundance): thirty to forty bottles of red wine; three bottles of brandy; two bottles of rum; two or three bottles of gin; thirty bottles of good beer; twenty bottles of cider; two bottles of vinegar; pickled gherkins; jam; lemons; apples; and a good folding table-knife.

Locks should be provided on every trunk, and two or three small trunks are better than one large. Each must be marked with the owner's name.

Tea and coffee are furnished by the captain; but six pounds of sugar, brown or white, should be provided; preferably brown, as it refreshes and purges the stomach.

The captain also supplies American molasses, which makes an agreeable drink when mixed with water and vinegar, especially for anyone feeling unwell.

Experienced travellers carry a mixture of boiled milk and sugar in tightly sealed bottles, which keeps thus for a considerable time. As it is impossible to take much exercise on board, especially in bad weather, three

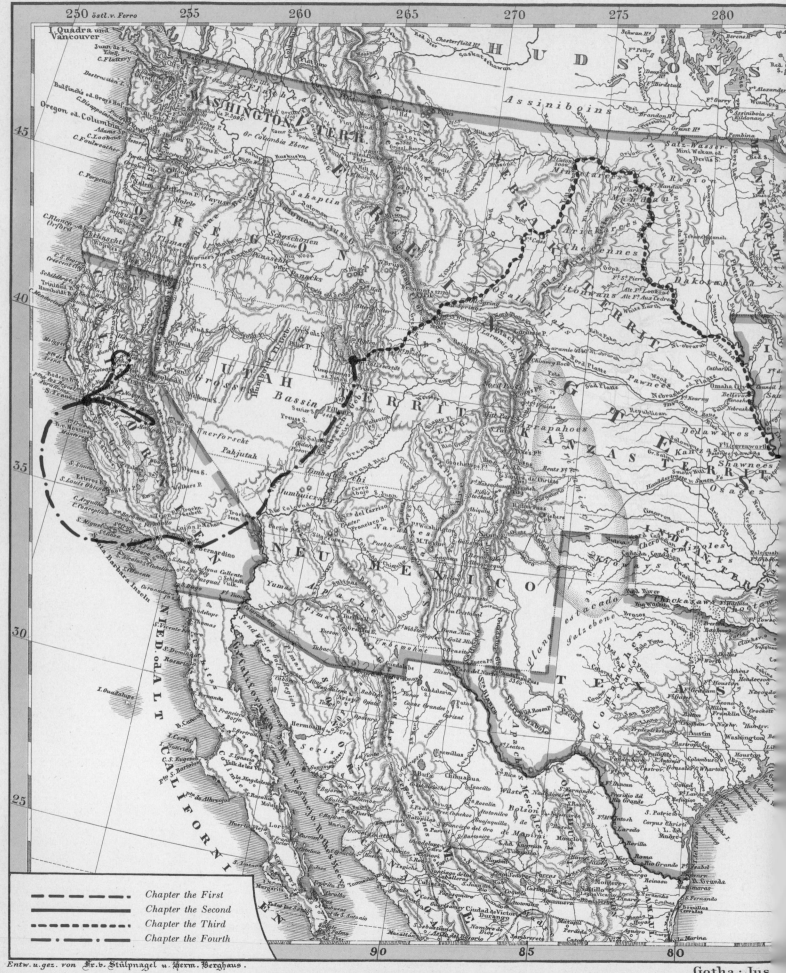

I. Quadra und Vancouver

Juan de Fuca Einf.
C. Flattery

Bulfinch's od. Gray's Haf.
C. Disappointment
Oregon od. Columbia
Adams P.
C. Lookout
C. Foulweather

C. Perpetua

C. Blanco od. Orford

C. S. Georg Crescent City

Trinidad
Humboldt B.

Mendocino
C. Arena

Pto. dos Reyes
S. Francisco

Monterey
C. Año Nuevo

S. Simeon
Estrero B.
S. Louis Obispo

Pta. Arguello
C. Conception

S. Miguel
S. Barbara Inseln
S. Nicolas

WASHINGTON TERR.

Gr. Columbia Ebene

OREGON

UTAH TERRI

NEBRASKA TERR.

Gross

Bassin

Unerforscht

Pahjutah

NEU MEXICO

DAKOTAH TERRIT

Mini tares
Mandan
Arikarees
Cheyennes

KANZAS TERRITORY

Delawares

Shawnees
Osages

Indianer
Choctaws

TEXAS

NIED. od. ALT CALIFORNI

Gotha: Jus.

Entw. u. gez. von Fr. v. Stülpnagel u. Herm. Berghaus.

– – – – –	Chapter the First
————	Chapter the Second
- - - - -	Chapter the Third
–·–·–·–	Chapter the Fourth

On the 13th of July 1824, after a passage of only forty days —a swift crossing for a sailing-ship on the west-bound passage—Philippe Suchard, taking time off from a promising career in the chocolate industry in Neuchâtel (Switzerland) at the age of twenty-eight landed at Baltimore :

Baltimore 1824

With all sails set we entered Chesapeake Bay, passing fairly close to the white tower on Cape Henry that acts as a beacon to shipping. Farther away, on our right hand we could see the lighthouse of Cape Charles, and some distant prairies surrounded by huge forests.

I came on deck and found the city of Baltimore spread before me. Peering through a forest of masts, we could make out church spires and the tops of the poplar trees that are a well-known beauty of the city. The slender spires are marble, and most of the houses are brick-built, the yellow, red and blue of the brightly painted façades looking very pretty against the green of the poplars. Over to our right lay fields ripe for harvest, and from the river bank came the tinkling of cowbells from the cattle feeding there, half hidden from us by fruit-trees. It was now almost light and the first red rays of the sun shed a glow upon the mountains and high ground. [2]

The first impressions of a traveller in a strange land are often valuable not only for what they say about the country but for what they reveal about the traveller himself.

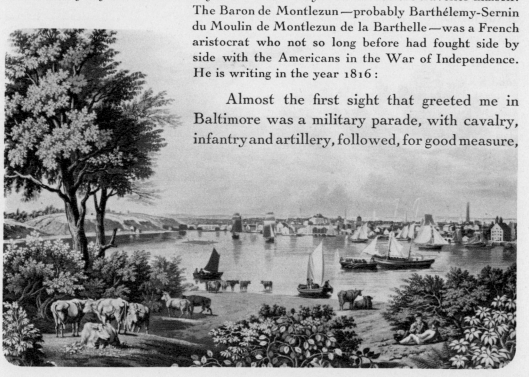

The Baron de Montlezun—probably Barthélemy-Sernin du Moulin de Montlezun de la Barthelle—was a French aristocrat who not so long before had fought side by side with the Americans in the War of Independence. He is writing in the year 1816 :

Almost the first sight that greeted me in Baltimore was a military parade, with cavalry, infantry and artillery, followed, for good measure,

BALTIMORE IN A BUCOLIC SETTING, FROM WHETSTONE POINT - 1830

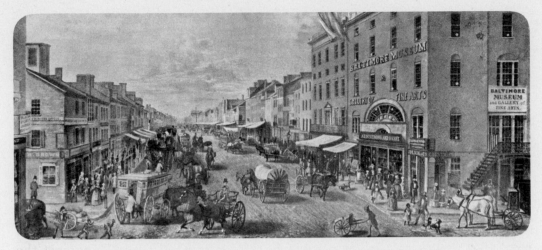

THE BUSY CORNER OF BALTIMORE AND CALVERT STREETS - 1853

by several companies of militiamen in whom, I am bound to confess, I should repose little confidence in time of war, although I should be the last to question their individual valour as fighting men. The weather being kind, the sidewalks of the main street were crowded with women and girls who had come out rather to see and be seen than to enjoy the mournful strains of the military band, and the somewhat ragged drum and fife music that came next, very much as I remembered it from the War of the Revolution. [3]

Philippe Suchard, on the other hand, democratic, and somewhat sentimental like all good Swiss, paints a different picture; he is a real early 19th Century Romantic:

Baltimore 1824

Every morning, even before the rising sun had touched the church spires with light, I was awakened by the sound of voices raised in song. I was curious to discover whence they came, and one morning I set off to explore. The songs came from the harbour. Eight negroes were engaged in unloading a ship's cargo. One of them struck up a sea-chanty, and all their movements kept time with the music. It was a monotonous chant, which rose or fell according to whether the load being handled was light or heavy. The negroes make a habit of singing while they work. It seems that during their first months of captivity the wretched slaves would fall into such a state of melancholy that they became deaf to their masters' exhortations and even indifferent to blows. The only thing that would arouse them was music, and they were accordingly forced to sing. Thus they always sing while at work, and so keep their spirits up. [2]

Some of the recollections of Baltimore left behind by European visitors make quite amusing reading. The French pianist Henri Herz gave a series of concerts there in 1847. As a way of " making the party go ", he would ask members of the audience to suggest a tune, and then improvise variations on it :

*Baltimore
1847*

When the time came for my improvisation turn I used to move amongst the audience, distributing sheets of manuscript for people to write their requests upon. Tunes were then chosen or rejected by majority vote. This used to cause a great hubbub in the hall, because tunes that pleased some would not please others and I often found it hard to discover which the majority wanted. When five or six airs had been chosen in this way, I would arrange them in a fantasia according to the inspiration of the moment and the mood of the audience.

Judging by the applause, I must sometimes have been fortunate in my little musical pleasantries, which seemed very fine and marvellous to the American public of that day. But the best part of the show came when a member of the audience, undeterred by an inability to write music, insisted upon making his preference known. The music-lover would call for silence, solemnly climb upon his seat and whistle, while I, pencil in hand, strove to capture each fugitive air, which was often so vague and formless as to be unrecognisable. Sometimes I made as many as four attempts, at a loss to make sense of it. The audience sat patiently through, and was usually generous in its applause when I finally noted the melody down. I always managed to behave with suitable gravity, but only with great difficulty. Everyone took the whole thing very seriously. [4]

From Baltimore the majority of visitors went inland but many were attracted by the beautiful city of Philadelphia, which the Quakers had made the very model of what a new city should be. Listen to Philippe Suchard, describing the journey to the city of the Quakers :

*To Philadelphia
1824*

Our boat travelled fast, maintaining five miles an hour against the current. The river narrowed continually, and each bank was adorned by pretty country-houses and well-tilled fields. Beyond stretched the limitless forest. At 11 o'clock the boat stopped and everyone had to go ashore. Each passenger was given a ticket bearing the number of one of the coaches which were to carry us across from the Susquehanna River to the Delaware, where another steamboat awaited us. Six fine coaches, each with four sturdy horses, bore us in three hours and a half to Newcastle, on the banks of the Delaware River in the State of Delaware, a journey of about

Baltimore, Maryland — 1834-1835

THE PORT AND CITY FROM FEDERAL HILL

FOUNDERY ON JONE'S CREEK · 1826

with such a steaming and breathing of brandy, gin, and tobacco, as, for my sins, I have seldom encountered before. These miseries were made worse by the half-whispered prosings of sundry berthless passengers — interminable personages, who would neither sleep themselves, nor allow others to sleep. At last, when I had reached a most distracting pitch of restlessness, I got up and tried the open deck, — but a nipping frost soon drove me below again. The tremor from the machinery, the puffing from the wastepipe, the endless thumpings of the billets of wood on their way to the furnace, the bawling of the engineers, the firemen, the pilots, the captains, stewards and stewardesses, to say nothing of children crying, and the irritating pat-pat-pattering of the paddle-wheels, altogether formed an association of head-rending annoyances, for which blessings, forsooth! we are now to thank the inventors of steam-engines and steamboats, the Watts and the Fultons of the past generation![5]

Most visitors to Philadelphia were taken by the charm of the old Quaker city, with its broad flagged streets. Charles Dickens saw it on his first American tour in 1842, when he was thirty — five years after the publication of *Oliver Twist* :

Philadelphia
1842

It is a handsome city, but distractingly regular. After walking about it for an hour or two, I felt that I would have given the world for a crooked street. The collar of my coat appeared to stiffen, and the brim of my hat to expand, beneath its quakerly influence. My hair shrunk into a sleek short crop, my hands folded themselves upon my breast of their own calm accord, and thoughts of taking lodging in Mark Lane over against the Market Place, and of making a large fortune by speculations in corn, came over me involuntarily.

Philadelphia is most bountifully provided with fresh water, which is showered and jerked about, and turned on, and poured off, everywhere. The Waterworks, which are on a height near the city, are no less orna-mental than useful, being tastefully laid out as a public garden, and kept

in the best and neatest order.   The river is dammed at this point, and forced
by its own power into certain high tanks or reservoirs, whence the whole
city, to the top stories of the houses, is supplied at a very trifling expense.

There are various public institutions.   Among them a most excellent
Hospital—a quaker establishment, but not sectarian in the great benefits
it confers ; a quiet, quaint old Library, named after Franklin ; a handsome
Exchange and Post Office ; and so forth. [6]

It was often the little things that emphasized the differences between the two
Continents.   Sometimes people formed quite a wrong impression.   One such was
the Baron de Montlezun, a French aristocrat of the pre-revolutionary regime, who
found neither France after 1815 nor America after the War of Independence to his
liking.   He wrote in 1816 :

The majority of the women here as in other American cities, wear
only black, in order, no doubt, to deepen the prevailing monotony.   The
ladies love to waste their time shopping ; as for the men, there is no occupa-

*Comparison
between Europe
and America
1816*

PHILADELPHIA WATERFRONT WITH THE HUGE " TREATY ELM " - 1800

tion save commerce and anyone not so engaged would find it hard to occupy
his time.   One cannot be reading or writing all day long.

Nearly all the Frenchmen I have met, traders, merchants, travellers
etc., are infected with the revolutionary poison.   The local inhabitants,
save for those few who have moved in good European society, are strongly

tainted with democracy; their manners and customs are essentially different from ours; they are touchy folk, forever at odds with one another. True fanaticism, it would appear, exists only amongst the lower orders; the upper classes are for the most part a band of hypocrites. [3]

Thirty years later Henri Herz, though broader-minded than the Baron, did not think much of American table-manners:

At dinner one day in a hotel, I sat next to a Frenchman with whom I had made acquaintance. When the dessert appeared, there was only one cake remaining on the dish. He handed it to me, and I refused, begging him to take it himself. He insisted that it was mine. The cake looked delicious and I renewed my entreaties.

" For you ", I said.

" I couldn't possibly. . . . "

" Very well, then, if you insist. . . . "

I was about to take it when an American sitting opposite, who had witnessed our exchange of courtesies, grabbed a fork, half rose, reached

PHILADELPHIA, THE FOURTH OF JULY IN CENTER SQUARE - 1812

across and deftly skewered the cake
from under our very noses. Amazingly,
he then proceeded to eat it, apparently
quite unaware that any breach of good
manners had occurred. [4]

"There's gold in them thar hills. . . ."
In 1851, Jean-Jacques Ampère, son of the
famous physicist whose name is preserved in
electrical terminology, was in Philadelphia
and found that even there the effects of the
1849 Gold Rush were making themselves felt:

The Mint at Philadelphia presents
an amazing spectacle, thanks to the
gold now being sent here from California to be made into five-dollar pieces.
Gold literally flows like water. The

CITY TROOPS OF PHILADELPHIA · 1812

newly minted coins are tipped into baskets as though they were so many
groceries. The work of the mint has doubled, so that during the past few
days gold coins to the value of no less than 500,000 dollars have been struck.
When I expressed anxiety about the honesty of the many hands through
which all these riches must pass, I was told: " If someone helps himself
to a coin or two it doesn't matter much and in any case it very seldom
happens. The man who steals a few soon goes on to greater thefts and is
infallibly discovered." How true this is! Self-denial is always easier to
practise than self-control. [7]

It is surprising how early-American life was dominated by machines. In
1824 Philippe Suchard made a special trip to see the marvellous Waterworks at
Philadelphia — an engineering achievement that astounded Europeans:

The hydraulic machine is slightly above one mile distant, on the banks
of the Schuylkill. Some distance upstream from these works, the water
close to the river bank is trapped and led through a conduit to sixteen-foot
water-wheels which drive a double-pistonned pump and raise the water
120 feet into a vast reservoir. The pump supplies 500,000 gallons of water
every twenty-four hours. Until two years ago when this machine was put
into operation a steam engine was used, but now the old method has been put

*Waterworks
at Philadelphia
1824*

aside. From the great reservoir the water runs through pipes and conduits to every quarter of the city, indeed, almost every house, where any desired quantity may be had merely by turning a faucet. There are stand-pipes in every street which can be used as long as need be in case of fire. When the hose from a fire engine is connected to one of these, the water gushes out with double the force provided by an ordinary fire pump. [2]

More interesting still were the Quakers. Every traveller was intrigued by the Society of Friends whose members were known for the austere simplicity of their principles, their affability and devotion to their neighbours. Thus Philippe Suchard:

The Quakers 1824

That there is a certain hardness about members of the Society of Friends, a stiff unrelenting fanaticism, it would be idle to deny. But I must admit also that no Christian sect has, at the same time, so much gentleness, humanity, unselfishness, devotion, and love of truth. . . . They mete out the same affability to all mankind while standing aloof from its follies and passions. They apply the precepts of Christianity literally and strictly, to everyday life, thus appearing odd, uncouth and even ridiculous to those who have been brought up in other ways. They do not argue about forms and dogmas like other Christians; their faith shows in their daily conduct. As a result of childhood training, these habits become an essential part of their lives. Their upbringing, as a result, is certainly very different from most people's and is perhaps unduly strict in many ways; but this very strictness is the surest defense against a light-hearted acceptance of dishonesty and vice in later life. Dancing, music, hunting, gambling and the theatre are forbidden. William Penn's ideas about education seem to me infinitely more noble and wise in themselves, and no less beneficial in their effects, than those of Lycurgus which are now so much the fashion. Anyone who doubts this or cannot understand, has only to visit Pennsylvania, the remotest and most lonely part of America. Here are none of the hypocrisy, vain piety and hidden pride to be found in comparable European sects, but firm conviction, borne out in daily conduct, and soundly based on education and habit. It seems to me that the simplicity and truthfulness, the modesty and honest dealing of the Quakers have had, and continue to have, a great influence on the thinking and conduct of American society, as well as upon the laws and Constitution of the United States. I saw traces of Quaker thinking wherever I went. They deserve the high esteem in which they are everywhere held.

Philadelphia, Pennsylvania — 1834-1835

THE PORT AND CHRIST CHURCH STEEPLE FROM THE DELAWARE

OLD IRON WORKS ON FRENCH CREEK, PHOENIXVILLE, PENNSYLVANIA - C. 1820

The houses are not built with great regularity but the majority of them are in good taste. The covered bridge over the Delaware is particularly fine.

At Princeton, where we changed horses, we met ten coaches filled with well-to-do travellers coming from New York to join the steamboat which we had just left, while we went on to Brunswick to take theirs. A thing which I found more and more surprising every day was the multitude of travellers. It seemed to me that everything was on the move. The hotels had often to accommodate as many guests as one would find at the largest European spa. And to think that only forty or fifty years ago there was nothing here but semi-wilderness!

Princeton, too, seemed a pleasant place, but I was not able to see much of it. For some years now it has been the seat of the most famous university in the United States. At length, after passing through Kingston, we arrived at New Brunswick, pleasantly situated on the Raritan. The river is spanned by a 400-foot bridge made, as usual, with two side-walks on the outside and a pair of carriage roads in the middle.

The weather had turned very hot, and our coaches raised thick clouds of dust. By the time we reached the steamer we were all very travel-stained indeed. But we were met by mulattoes and negroes armed with brushes, towels and pitchers, inviting us into a hall for a wash and brush up. There were even barbers, razor in hand, to rejuvenate the menfolk. Nearly everybody submitted to this purification, which was anyway less painful than the Apostolic razors.° Nowhere in Europe, not even in England or Holland, is the love of cleanliness carried to such extremes. To be clean is regarded as a social duty, to be practised even amongst close friends; at home we are too apt to neglect such niceties. I have dwelt on this deliberately, as an example of the Americans' innate delicacy, which is manifest even in trivial matters.

The country-side in the neighbourhood of New Brunswick was populous and picturesquely varied; as we moved away from that city, the river banks became flatter and indeed they are covered at high water, for the tide comes up as far as Brunswick. On our left stood Perth-Amboy, displaying its trim rows of houses, among which stood out Brighton House, the summer residence of the Brun family of New York, a sort of *château* on top of a little hill, commanding a fine view across the plains. On our right lay Staten Island or Richmond, of which we could see little in passing, but which seemed to grow more and more densely populated as we approached New York. A few more passengers came aboard at Elizabeth-town, on the right bank of the Raritan, and at about six o'clock that evening, in glorious weather, we entered the bay of New York. [2]

THE MORAVIAN CHURCH
FROM ACROSS THE LEHIGH RIVER, BETHLEHEM, PENNSYLVANIA - 1820

In the middle of the nineteenth century New York City had a population of 700,000. Paris at that time boasted 1,600,000 and London 2,800,000. Dickens gave himself a ring-side seat in the old Carlton Hotel looking out on the blinding glitter of Broadway in the horse-drawn age :

New York 1842

The great promenade and thoroughfare, as most people know, is Broadway; a wide and bustling street, which, from the Battery Gardens to its opposite termination in a country road, may be four miles long. Shall we sit down in an upper floor of the Carlton House Hotel (situated in the best part of this main artery of New York), and when we are tired of looking down upon the life below, sally forth arm-in-arm, and mingle with the stream ?

Warm weather ! The sun strikes upon our heads at this open window, as though its rays were concentrated through a burning glass; but the day is in its zenith, and the season an unusual one. Was there ever such a

NASSAU HALL AT THE COLLEGE OF PRINCETON IN NEW JERSEY - 1836

sunny street as this Broadway! The pavement stones are polished with the tread of feet until they shine again; the red bricks of the houses might be yet in the dry, hot kilns; and the roofs of those omnibuses look as though, if water were poured on them, they would hiss and smoke, and smell like half-quenched fires. No stint of omnibuses here! Half a dozen have gone by within as many minutes. Plenty of hackney cabs and coaches too; gigs, phaetons, large-wheeled tilburies, and private carriages—rather of clumsy make, and not very different from the public vehicles, but built for the heavy roads beyond the city pavement.   Negro coachmen and white; in straw hats, black hats, white hats, glazed caps, fur caps; in coats of drab, black, brown, green, blue, nankeen, striped jean and linen; and there, in that one instance (look while it passes, or it will be too late), in suits of livery. Some southern republican that, who puts his blacks in uniform, and swells with Sultan pomp and power.   Yonder, where that phaeton with the well-clipped pair of greys has stopped—standing at their heads now—is a Yorkshire groom, who has not been very long in these parts, and looks sorrowfully round for a companion pair of top-boots, which he may traverse the city half a year without meeting.   Heaven save the ladies, how they dress! We have seen more colours in these ten minutes, than we should have seen elsewhere in as many days.   What various parasols!   What

LOWER MANHATTAN FROM WEEHAWKEN, NEW JERSEY - 1826

rainbow silks and satins!   What pinking of thin stockings, and pinching of thin shoes, and fluttering of ribbons and silk tassels, and display of rich cloaks with gaudy hoods and linings!   The young gentlemen are fond, you see, of turning down their shirt-collars and cultivating their whiskers, especially under the chin; but they cannot approach the ladies in their dress or bearing, being, to say the truth, humanity of quite another sort.

Byrons of the desk and counter, pass on, and let us see what kind of men those are behind ye : those two labourers in holiday clothes, of whom one carries in his hand a crumpled scrap of paper from which he tries to spell out a hard name, while the other looks about for it on all the doors and windows....

The streets and shops are lighted now ; and as the eye travels down the long thoroughfare, dotted with bright jets of gas, it is reminded of Oxford Street or Piccadilly.   Here and there, a flight of broad stone cellar-steps appears, and a painted lamp directs you to the Bowling Saloon, or Ten-Pin alley : Ten Pins being a game of mingled chance and skill, invented when the legislature passed an act forbidding Nine-Pins.   At other downward flights of steps, are other lamps, marking the whereabouts of oyster-cellars — pleasant retreats, say I : not only by reason of their wonderful cookery of

NEW YORK'S CITY HALL AT THE JUNCTION OF BROADWAY AND CHATHAM STREET - 1819

oysters, pretty nigh as large as cheeseplates (or for thy dear sake, heartiest of Greek Professors !), but because of all kinds of eaters of fish, or flesh, or fowl, in these latitudes, the swallowers of oysters alone are not gregarious ; but subduing themselves, as it were, to the nature of what they work in, and copying the coyness of the thing they eat, do sit apart in curtained boxes, and consort by twos, not by two hundreds. [6]

NEW YORK'S GREENWICH AND DEY STREETS,
AS PAINTED FROM BOARDING-HOUSE BY THE BARONESS HYDE DE NEUVILLE · 1810

But what did a newly arrived young Frenchman think of the Great White Way? Listen to Jean-Jacques Ampère:

Broadway 1851-1852

I had been only a few hours in America, but already New York seemed an entire new world. I followed *La Large Rue* (Broadway) for a long while, and, from the number of carriages and omnibuses I almost fancied myself in London, along the Strand. I strolled for an hour looking at the shops. The noise and glitter seemed very strange after eleven days at sea, so I went in search of quieter surroundings; I followed the Hudson River. Here the sounds and activity were of a different sort: a loud noise of hammering came from workshops where steam engines were being built, and the river itself was busy with steamboats heading in every direction. It was a wonderful evening and the light seemed to possess a special quality: my first sunset in the States was truly American, for it was through the masts of shipping that I watched a golden sun go down behind the shipyards.

Penetrating now into silent side-streets I imagined myself back in the original little Dutch town, as calm and phlegmatic as modern New York is bustling and alive, the New Amsterdam so amusingly and imaginatively described by Washington Irving. The illusion of being in Holland was heightened by the brick side-walks and by the trees lining the streets.

Returning to the busier quarters of New York I stopped in front of a shop the like of which was never seen in New Amsterdam, and which perhaps has no counterpart in either London or Paris.

I gazed up and counted five storeys and seventy-five windows; and I was not alone in my admiration. Turning around what should I see but two savages in full costume with feather head-dresses and painted faces. There, on Broadway, in front of the great shop they stood : the natural owners of the soil. Now they are strangers, almost as out of place in the land of their ancestors as a Chinaman would be in the streets of Paris. It summed up the whole history of the two races. Had I beheld the most redoubtable Indian chief amid his native forests, he could not, I am sure, have played more strongly upon my imagination than did those two strollers from the desert in the main street of New York. [7]

A friend who was with him as they walked down Bovery Street made this additional comment :

" Take a good look at this street : it's the one that divides New York into two classes. Those who have not made good money on the east side of Bowery Street, those who have crossed over to the west. What happens if you are ruined ? You just cross back to the east." [7]

For many Europeans the America of 1850 was—and long remained—a country where anything was possible; a land where fortunes could be made or remade in a few weeks or months. And it was not only business men who made the trip : France's great tragic actress Rachel was talked into an American tour in 1855, and although not actually a flop, it was less profitable than the company expected.[°] Rachel was already so weakened by her last illness that she wrote no impressions of the U.S.A.; but Léon Beauvallet, a member of her company, made a few snide comments about New York City :

New York
1855

Walk? You haven't a chance ! They don't put macadam in the streets as we do at home, they just have rocks and pebbles off the beach.

When you go for a walk it's like doing a balancing act on hard-boiled eggs. *Very* hard boiled. A quarter of an hour's walking on those sharp pointed stones is more than enough; there's nothing in the world more tiring except a non-stop tight-rope act.

" What's that you say ? Don't they have side-walks ? " Sure they have side-walks. They have too many side-walks, considering the way they're built and the state they are in—all broken and fallen through and filled with water so that the puddles are so big you can't step across them without falling in and getting wet. There's only one thing for it : the omni-

Philadelphia, Pennsylvania — 1812

CHIMNEY-SWEEPS AND MASTER BEFORE CHRIST CHURCH

NEW YORK'S CITY HALL PARK AND PARK ROW
WITH CARRIAGES, BARREL-SHAPED WATER-WAGON, AND GOOSENECK FIRE ENGINES - 1830

Always, in fact, something going on somewhere, to daze the European visitor. Basil Hall finds it hard to suppress his amazement:

Moving House at New York 1827-1828

Everyone has heard of moving wooden houses; but the transportation of a brick dwelling is an exploit of a different nature. I shall describe simply what I saw, and then tell how the details were managed. In a street which required to be widened, there stood two houses much in the way, their front being twelve feet too far forward. These houses, therefore, must either have been taken down, or shifted back. Mr. Brown undertook to execute the less destructive process. They were both of brick, and built together, one being forty feet deep, and twenty-five feet front; the other thirty-two feet deep, and twenty-two feet front. They were of the same height, that is to say, twenty-two feet, from the ground to the eaves, above which stood the roof and two large stacks of brick chimneys; the whole forming a solid block of building, having two rows of six windows each, along a front of forty-seven feet by twenty-two. This was actually moved, in a compact body, without injury, twelve feet back from the street. [5]

NEW YORK HARBOUR FROM BROOKLYN FERRY SLIP
WITH THE TOP OF MANHATTAN AND TRINITY CHURCH SPIRE - 1848

In spite of all this bustle, New York in 1837 was still relatively small and close to the open country. Vast numbers of boats sailed on the Hudson; West Point, still very rural, made a popular excursion, and the banks of the Passaic in New Jersey were a rendezvous for "amateurs of the picturesque", especially Europeans inspired by the Romantic poets. Listen to Captain Frederick Marryat, a British naval officer who had won sudden fame by his novels of seafaring life, and who wrote in his diary published in 1839 :

A more beautiful wild spot can hardly be conceived; and to a European who has been accustomed to travel far in search of the picturesque, it appears singular that at so short a distance from a large city, he should at once find himself in the midst of such a strange combination of nature and art. Independent of their beauty, they are, perhaps, the most singular Falls that are known to exist. The whole country is of trap formation, and the black rocks rise up strictly vertical. The river, which at the Falls is about one hundred and twenty yards wide, pours over a bed of rock between hills covered with chestnut, walnut, pine and sycamore, all mingled together, and descending to the edge of the bank; their bright

Surroundings of New York 1839

HALF OF A PENNSYLVANIA CHURCH MEETING HOUSE IS
HAULED AWAY TO A NEW SITE AFTER A RELIGIOUS SCHISM IN THE CONGREGATION ! - CA. 1817

and various foliage forming a lovely contrast to the clear rushing water. The bed of black rock over which the river runs, is at the Fall, suddenly split into two, vertically, and across the whole width of the river. The fissure is about seventy feet deep, and not more than twelve feet wide at any part. Down into this chasm pour the whole waters of the river, escaping from it, at a right angle, into a deep basin, surrounded with perpendicular rocks from eighty to ninety feet high. You may therefore stand on the opposite side of the chasm, looking up the river, within a few feet of the Fall, and watch the roaring waters as they precipitate themselves below. In this position, with the swift, clear, but not deep waters before you, forcing their passage through the rocky bed, with the waving trees on each side, their branches feathering to the water's edge, or dipping and rising in the stream, you might imagine yourself far removed from your fellow-men, and you feel that in such a beauteous spot you could well turn anchorite, and commune with Nature alone. [9]

Away from the towns life was simpler and more rugged; people's amusements grew out of their daily tasks, and varied with the seasons : Basil Hall stopped on his way from New York to Boston at Stockbridge, Mass., where they were celebrating the fourth anniversary of the Agricultural Society. The first event was a ploughing match :

*Ploughing Match
1827*

As the first exhibition, a ploughing match took place so near the house, that we could see it pretty well without going over the threshold; we satisfied ourselves for some time with the view from thence. But I was soon tempted, by the growing interest of the scene, to make my mind up for a ducking, and sallied forth in the face of the storm. The ploughmen, who showed a great deal of spirit in this amusing competition, all drove oxen, excepting one man, on whose ridge horses were used. I have such an obscure idea of what good ploughing is, that I cannot tell how this trial ought to rank with similar exhibitions elsewhere; in truth I soon ceased to watch the details of the match, in the personal interest I was led to take in one of the competitors, whose vehement anxiety to win the prize enlisted the sympathy of most of the spectators on the field. He was a small and rather handsome negro, who drove a team of oxen as diminutive, in proportion, as himself. His whole soul was absorbed in the enterprise—he looked neither to the right nor to the left, nor anywhere indeed, but to the heads of his cattle, whose slightest deviation from the straight line, he watched with a quickness, which excited the admiration and sometimes applause of the bystanders. In his hand he wielded a little whip, or more generally he laid it across the plough, using it only when his voice failed to direct his team. Even then he merely touched one or the other of the oxen with the end of

PICNIC SITE NEAR PASSAIC FALLS AND PATERSON, NEW JERSEY - 1826

the lash, not rudely, and with a volley of angry reproaches, but gently, and more as a hint, apparently, to the animals, than as a punishment. Accordingly, as in duty bound, they seemed to enter fully into their master's anxiety, and tugged and panted along in gallant style!

After the match was over, the umpires kept us a long time in suspense before they decided which ridge was the best ploughed; for it appears that expedition in these matters is only one of many points which determine the real merit of the work done. But the judges at last decided in favour of our sable friend,—a result with which the whole field seemed satisfied. Poor blackie, indeed, has very seldom such occasions of triumph, for even in these non-slave-holding States of America, this fatal shade, by marking out the negro as a totally different race, gives him little—or I might say no chance—of placing himself upon any permanent equality with the white lords of the creation, who, on their part, would as soon think of sitting down to eat Indian corn leaves, or chopped pumpkins, with their cattle, as of entering into social intercourse with a " negur "; with whom, however, it would seem they have no objection to engage in many, but temporary competitions. [5]

Besides travelling by boat and stage-coach, Charles Dickens used the railroad. His first encounter was with the line between New York and Boston, which he found quite different from railways in Britain :

By Railroad 1842

I made acquaintance with an American railroad, on this occasion, for the first time. As these works are pretty much alike all through the States, their general characteristics are easily described.

There are no first and second class carriages as with us; but there is a gentlemen's car and a ladies' car : the main distinction between which is that in the first, everybody smokes; and in the second nobody does. As a black man never travels with a white one, there is also a negro car; which is a great blundering clumsy chest, such as Gulliver put to sea in, from the kingdom of Brobdignag [*sic*]. There is a great deal of jolting, a great deal of noise, a great deal of wall, not much window, a locomotive engine, a shriek, and a bell.

The cars are like shabby omnibuses, but larger : holding thirty, forty, fifty, people. The seats, instead of stretching from end to end, are placed crosswise. Each seat holds two persons. There is a long row of them on each side of the caravan, a narrow passage up the middle, and a door at

Paterson, New Jersey — 1800

VIEW ALONG THE TWO-LANE ROAD FROM NEWARK

both ends. In the centre of the carriage there is usually a stove, fed with charcoal or anthracite coal, which is for the most part red-hot. It is insufferably close; and you see the hot air fluttering between yourself and any other object you may happen to look at, like the ghost of smoke.

In the ladies' car, there are a great many gentlemen who have ladies with them. There are also a great many ladies who have nobody with them : for any lady may travel alone, from one end of the United States to the other, and be certain of the most courteous and considerate treatment everywhere. The conductor or check-taker, or guard, or whatever he may be, wears no uniform. He walks up and down the car, and in and out of it, as his fancy dictates; leans against the door with his hands in his pockets and stares at you, if you chance to be a stranger; or enters into conversation with the passengers about him. A great many newspapers are pulled out, and a few of them are read. Everybody talks to you, or to anybody else who hits his fancy. If you are an Englishman, he expects that that railroad is pretty much like an English railroad. If you say " No ", he says " Yes ? " (interrogatively), and asks in what respect they differ. You enumerate the heads of difference, one by one, and he says " Yes ? " (still interrogatively) to each. Then he guesses that you don't travel faster in England; and on your replying that you do, says " Yes ? " again (still interrogatively), and it is quite evident, don't believe it. After a long pause he remarks, partly to you and partly to the knob on the top of his stick, that " Yankees are reckoned to be considerable of a go-ahead people too; " upon which *you* say " Yes, " and then *he* says " Yes " again (affirmatively, this time); and upon your looking out of window, tells you that behind that hill, and some three miles from the next station, there is a clever town in a smart lo-ca-tion, where he expects you have con-cluded to stop. Your answer in the negative naturally leads to more questions in reference to your intended route (always pronounced rout); and wherever you are going, you invariably learn that you can't get there without immense difficulty and danger, and that all the great sights are somewhere else. [6]

Obviously Henri Herz could not make a respectable concert tour of the U.S.A. without playing in Boston. The city was almost a home from home for visiting artists and musicians. Here he is on arrival :

A porter took charge of my light baggage; I lit a cigar and followed him, but I had not gone more than a dozen steps before a policeman stopped me.

*No Smoking
in Boston's Streets
1846*

" No smoking on the street ", he said severely.

" You must be joking, officer. "

" I never joke. It is forbidden to smoke on the street. If you can't do without a smoke, go home. "

" But yesterday I saw at least twenty people smoking with their legs in the air. Is one allowed to smoke only in that delightful attitude ? "

BOSTON, FANEUIL HALL - 1838

" One is allowed to smoke in any position, but only indoors. The Law strictly forbids smoking on the street. It is especially shocking and serious to break this law on the Sabbath, which is dedicated to the Glory of God. "

" In what way can the smoke of my cigar interfere with the meditations of people reading the Bible ? "

" It is unrighteous and it is against the Law. "

This seemed to me a somewhat tyrannical restriction in the Land of Liberty, but I had no choice but to obey. Nowadays, I gather, one can smoke anywhere in Boston and on any day of the week. This is " progress ", according to some people, " irreverence " according to others. To me it is the simplest and most natural thing in the world. [4]

From smoking to long, cool drinks. When Basil Hall visited Boston Harbour he made a discovery of great interest to him if one can judge from his remarks in his diary:

In the course of the day, a gentleman gave us a very interesting account of a species of commerce peculiar, at least on so great a scale, as far as I know, to the United States—I mean the transport by sea of large quantities of ice. This trade is carried on chiefly to the Havannah [*sic*] in the

*Boston Harbour
1827-1828*

BOSTON, THE VIEW UP STATE STREET TOWARDS THE OLD STATE HOUSE - 1837

West Indies, and to Charleston in South Carolina. Upwards of twenty years ago, a gentleman of most praiseworthy enterprise hit upon this idea, which he has pursued ever since with great activity, and, eventually, with success, though in its progress he had many difficulties to encounter. There is no particular care taken to preserve the ice on board, except that the ship is cased inside with planks to prevent it coming in contact with the ceiling. The ice, cut into cubes 18 inches each way, is carefully packed by hand. The loss by melting on the voyage is sometimes one-third of the whole, though it often arrives with no perceptible diminution. My informant told me, that when the ice is embarked in winter, with the thermometer at zero, or below it, and the ship has the good fortune to sail with a brisk, cold, northerly wind, not a single pound of the cargo is lost. As the temperature of the ice on shipping is sometimes 30 degrees below the point at which it begins to melt, a considerable expenditure of cold must take place, and consequently a certain amount of time elapses before it begins to lose weight; so that, if the voyage be short, the entire cargo is saved. On the other hand, if it be embarked from the ice-house of Boston in July, with the thermometer at 80 or 90, the melting process will have already commenced, and if the ship be then met by a southerly wind against her, or get drifted into that immense current of hot water flowing out of the great Bay of Mexico, known by the name of the Gulf Stream, the whole slippery cargo is apt to find its way overboard — via the pumps — before the voyage is half over. [5]

Rachel and her theatrical company were in Boston during the elections. Léon Beauvallet thought he knew something about politics, having weathered the revolution in France in 1848, the " Year of Revolutions "; but Boston could still show him a thing or two :

Elections in Boston 1855

The French elections of '48 were nothing to this. . . . The posters, the letters, the electoral bulletins, the billboards, the ballyhoo! One thing I love about the candidates is their naïvety. Can you imagine! They

BOSTON FROM SOUTH BOSTON BRIDGE LINKING DORCHESTER NECK WITH THE CITY - 1826

VOLUNTEER '' NATIONAL LANCERS ''
DRILLING ON BOSTON COMMON WITH THE NEW STATE HOUSE BEYOND - 1837

have their portraits done on transparent hangings, and they think this will win them votes. Their own *portraits*, I ask you! Ropes are slung across the streets from house to house, and from these dangle the candidates' noble features larger than life, all swaying in the breeze. They look like the big heads in a carnival. It's all very gay and amusing. What is not so funny is the American habit during elections of talking with knife or gun in hand. You see in the paper that " Mr X . . . was buried this morning. Yesterday he was accidentally shot through the heart. . . . " Just that. They carefully do not mention any inquest. What does the law care if a citizen or two get a bullet through the chest? The fella should have stayed home. . . .![8]

On the other hand, Boston hotels made a great impression upon at least one visitor around the mid-century. William Ferguson:

An American hotel, as all who have read any recent book of travels in the United States must know well, is a very different affair from an English one. We strode through a marble-paved hall to an office in one corner, and writing our names in a book which lay open for that purpose, the numbers 133, 134 and 135 are placed opposite them, and we are free of the house. Three or four porters, of whom there is always a supply waiting in the hall, laid hold of our baggage and carried it up-stairs to the rooms

Boston Hotels 1856

indicated by the numbers placed opposite our names. We are now possessed of a bedroom, of which we carry the key. It contains every convenience which a traveller requires, down to writing materials; whilst in some conspicuous place is put up a note of the hours at which meals are served, and other particulars useful to know. Henceforth we have no more trouble. Our bedroom is our private sitting-room; there are public parlours luxuriously fitted up—those for ladies especially so—and at the fixed hours there are sumptuous meals on the table in the eating-hall. There is no trouble in ordering dinner; you come and go just as you find it convenient. In addition to this, each room has a box assigned to it in the office, and numbered to correspond, into which letters or cards which may be left for you are put. These boxes or pigeon-holes are arranged in a conspicuous place, so that you can at a glance tell, without requiring to ask, whether there is anything for you or not. You miss, too, the long rows of bells which disfigure an English hotel hall. The wires leading to each room sound one bell, and uncover at the same time a number arranged below it. The person waiting reads off the number to one of the attendants, who answers the call, and the cover of the number is replaced by touching a spring. Such are some of the more striking of the novel features of an American hotel; and when I add that the parlours were carpeted with Brussels, and the chairs and sofas covered with cut velvet, and that the eating-hall is a magnificent apartment, floored with black and white marble, and decorated with white and gold, so as to have a very cheerful look, I think I have said enough upon the subject of American hotels. It was exquisite luxury, after the confinement of our close state-rooms, to plunge into a warm bath, and afterwards complete one's toilette without having to catch at something to keep you from falling, or go heeling about the floor. [10]

" Taking the waters " was too popular at that time for any good European to lose a chance to see an American spa, even though a trip to Saratoga Springs from Boston meant crossing the whole of Massachusetts by stage-coach and entering the State of New York. Philippe Suchard arrived on the 16th of August 1824 after spending the night at Schenectady:

Saratoga
1824

The surroundings of Saratoga seem very wild. The town itself has but a single street, wide and so far not paved; uprooted tree trunks here and there show that this was until recently forest. Bears are still to be seen on the outskirts.

It is only ten years since a party of hunters discovered the mineral springs. Four years ago the building of palatial hotels commenced, and of these there are already ten. The finest, without question, is the Congress Hall; next come the United Staten [*sic*] Hall and the Pavilion. The number of guests at this establishment at the time of my arrival amounted to 1,230 persons, hailing from every part of the U.S.A., with some from South America, and even a sprinkling from Europe.

There must be twenty springs in and around Saratoga, of which I sampled the most important with my Quaker friend. We were shown where the " cure " is supposed to begin, and where it ends. Some of the warm-water springs taste like those of Baden in the Aargau, others like those of Seltz; it was Balston Spring, five miles from Saratoga which reminded me most of Schwarzbrünnli, in the Canton of Berne. For the most part people do not bathe in the waters, but merely drink them. In the morning this embryo township is thronged with people. At each spring there are children who dip water from the well. Each child has a rod and line with a little wire basket on the end containing three glasses, in which the water is passed round. Amongst those taking the waters at present is the ex-King of Spain, Joseph Bonaparte. He appears to be much happier as a plain citizen of a free country than he was in the days of his

CHURCH IN BALLSTON SPA, NEAR SARATOGA, NEW YORK · 1838

splendour. He is a little above the normal height, with a plump expressive face
and pleasanter, softer features than those of his brother, the great Napoleon.

So far everything at Saratoga is still in the rough planning stage.
Only the most pressing work has been done. There are no board-walks
yet for the visitors, but the surroundings are very agreeable, although
encircled by hills and forests. From a hilltop not far out of town one can
see all the way to Lake St. George. [2]

Away from the cities on the Atlantic seaboard the pioneer spirit of America was
even more impressive. Everything had still to be made, or else was in the throes of
construction : houses, clearings, railroads, highways, canals. Philippe Suchard enjoyed a
close view of America at work when he travelled from Albany to Buffalo along the Erie
Canal — as yet so new that parts of it were not yet open :

The Erie Canal
1824

This masterpiece of American enterprise deserves to be better known.
Just think for a moment : this Canal is 270 miles in length, it is crossed by
five hundred and fifty-six wooden bridges, and there are forty-seven locks,
each with a lift of seven feet (this representing the difference in altitude
between the waters of Lake Erie and those of the Hudson River), and
besides all this there are several aqueducts to carry the canal over the
marshes and small lakes. The longest aqueduct, near Rochester, is built
entirely of stone, including the towpath. The whole immense achievement
has taken no more than two years. . . .

One of the remarkable things about the United States, to my way of
thinking, is that the State (Federal Government) takes no hand in the
building of highways, bridges and canals. However much our own politicians may shake their heads, the American system has served its people
well. There are some very good roads ; local communities are not beset by
corrupt officials enriching themselves or trying to do so at the public
expense ; there is no question of forced labour ; and the cost is infinitely
lower, because there is no Department of Bridges and Highways to pay
for, with all its inspectors, superintendents, cashiers, book-keepers, records,
copy clerks and the like. Whenever a new highway or bridge is needed a
group of stockholders forms a corporation, and the corporation agrees a
price for carrying out the best plan. Usually the owners of real estate
bordering upon the proposed highway or canal comprise most of the stock-
holders, because as the transportation of goods becomes easier, their farm-
produce becomes easier to sell and the value of the whole property is
enhanced. When construction comes to an end the accounts for the work

New York — 1834-1835

MANHATTAN ISLAND FROM WEEHAWKEN, ACROSS THE HUDSON

and all incidental expenses are submitted to the Government and the latter empowers the stock-holders to levy a toll over a certain length of route, usually seven or fourteen miles. . . .

As we went further the country grew more and more wild, and, apart from a few scattered hamlets, practically uninhabited. Very few of the houses were made of brick, the majority being cabins made from roughly hewn logs. These are called " blockhouses ". They are easy to build and cheap as nature provides more than enough wood for all.

A young couple settling in these new territories often has nothing in the world beyond one or two horses, a bale of linen and one hundred dollars. Armed with these they set off into the wilderness and pick themselves a location, a piece of land that takes their fancy. Fifty acres is all they need. The land costs one dollar or two dollars an acre, which they pay partly in cash and partly by means of a mortgage at six per cent. Then they call upon their neighbours, who may live nine or ten miles away, and tell them when they intend building the house. On the appointed day the neighbours appear, each party bringing horses, oxen, axes and so on, for felling trees and hauling logs. The logs have their branches trimmed off

SARATOGA SPRINGS, SHOWING THE NEW COLONNADED CONGRESS HALL HOTEL - 1826

and their ends mortised and tenoned; they are then laid one on top of another, to form a sort of large cage. Any space between the timbers is filled with stones, moss and earth. Before nightfall, the dwelling is complete and the guests, who are usually fairly numerous, sit down to eat and drink; after which they return home, leaving presents of seed and food-stuffs.

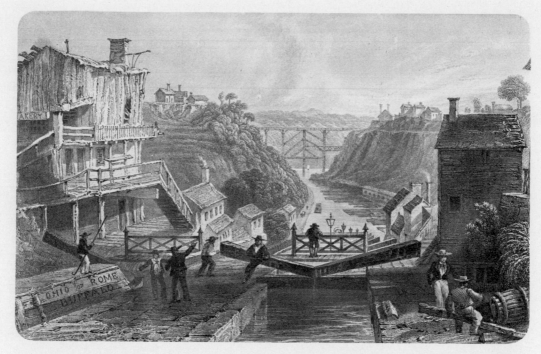

VIEW WEST FROM STONE LOCKS ON THE ERIE CANAL AT LOCKPORT, NEW YORK - 1838

If the distance is too great, they break the journey as the guest of some other settler, for people are always delighted to extend such hospitality.

A young settler who is fairly active and hard-working should, after two or three years, be in a position to build himself a house of brick. This, too, need not be expensive, for there are itinerant brickmakers who exist purely to fill this need. They set up their workshop on the spot where the foundations are to be, and here make and bake bricks, which they sell to the owner at four to six dollars a thousand. The houses have only one storey, and two to four windows on each side. A house with three windows a side requires forty-thousand bricks. In the towns, a house like this is given a coat of paint over its brick walls, and roofed in slate. [2]

In Basil Hall's time (1827) a visitor to Rochester, New York, was literally " let in on the ground floor " as the British say; Hall arrived to see an entire city in course of construction—houses, churches, jails, hotels, and all :

On the 26th of June 1827, we strolled through the village of Rochester, under the guidance of a most obliging and intelligent friend, a native of this part of the country. Everything in this bustling place appeared to be in motion. The very streets seemed to be starting up of their own accord, ready-made, and looking as fresh and new, as if they had been turned out of the workmen's hands but an hour before—or as if a great boxful of new houses had been sent by steam from New York, and tumbled out on the half-cleared land. The canal banks were at some places still unturfed; the lime seemed hardly dry in the masonry of the aqueduct, in the bridges, and in the numberless great saw-mills and manufactories. In many of these buildings the people were at work below stairs, while at top the carpenters were busy nailing on the planks of the roof.

Rochester 1827

Some houses were half painted, while the foundations of others, within five yards' distance, were only beginning. I cannot say how many churches, court-houses, jails and hotels I counted, all in motion, creeping upwards. Several streets were nearly finished, but had not as yet received their names ; and many others were in the reverse predic-

NIGHT SCENE ON THE ERIE CANAL - 1830

ament, being named, but not commenced,—their local habitation being merely signified by lines of stakes. Here and there we saw great warehouses, without window sashes, but half filled with goods, and furnished with hoisting cranes, ready to fish up the huge pyramids of flour barrels, bales and boxes lying in the streets. In the centre of the town the spire of a Presbyterian church rose to a great height, and on each side of the supporting tower was to be seen the dial-plate of a clock, of which the machinery, in the hurry-skurry, had been left at New York. I need not say that these half-finished, whole-finished, and embryo streets were crowded with people, carts, stages, cattle, pigs, far beyond the reach of numbers;—and as all these were lifting up their voices together, in keeping with the clatter of hammers, the ringing of axes, and the creaking of machinery, there was a fine concert, I assure you!

But it struck us that the interest of the town, for it seems idle to call it a village, was subordinate to that of the suburbs. A few years ago the whole of that part of the country was covered with a dark silent forest, and even as it was, we could not proceed a mile in any direction except that of the high-road, without coming full-butt against the woods of time immemorial. When land is cleared for the purposes of cultivation, the stumps are left standing for many years, from its being easier, as well as more profitable in other respects, to plough round them, than to waste time

THE UPPER FALLS OF THE GENESEE RIVER AT ROCHESTER, NEW YORK - 1835

and labour in rooting them out, or burning them, or blowing them up with gunpowder. But when a forest is levelled with a view to building a town in its place, a different system must of course be adopted. The trees must then be removed sooner or later, according to the means of the proprietor, or the necessities of the case. Thus one man possessed of capital will clear his lot of the wood, and erect houses, or even streets, across it; while on his neighbour's land the trees may be still growing. And it actually occurred to us, several times, within the immediate limits of the inhabited town itself, in streets, too, where shops were opened, and all sorts of business actually going on, that we had to drive first on one side, and then on the other, to avoid the stumps of an oak, or a hemlock, or a pine-tree, staring us full in the face.

On driving a little beyond the streets towards the woods, we came to a space, about an acre in size, roughly enclosed, on the summit of a gentle swell in the ground.

" What can this place be for ? "

" Oh, " said my companion, " that is the graveyard. "

" Graveyard—what is that ? " said I, for I was quite adrift.

" Why, surely, " said he, " you know what a graveyard is ? It is a burying-ground. All the inhabitants of the place are buried there, whatever be their persuasion. We don't use churchyards in America. " [5]

After a very uncomfortable night in a hotel at Buffalo, just being rebuilt after a disastrous fire, Jean-Jacques Ampère went to look at Niagara Falls. He was properly impressed, as all good tourists must be :

Niagara Falls 1851-1852

There are people who find Niagara Falls far inferior to what they had imagined. I really must compliment these good folk on their imagination. Perhaps it is that when confronted with such a sight their minds cannot conceive what their eyes are seeing. Niagara, like St. Peter's in Rome, is larger than life; one cannot take in the whole thing at first glance. I have heard other waterfalls compared with Niagara; this is like comparing a lake with the ocean. I have seen many, many waterfalls, in Switzerland, in Scotland, in Norway and in the Pyrenees; but the whole sum of them together would be lost and swallowed up in Niagara—they are as pygmies beside a Titan. To my mind the two greatest things on earth are, amongst monuments raised by the hand of man, the ruins at Thebes; and amongst the works of Nature, the Falls at Niagara. [7]

But now hark to that sentimental Swiss, Philippe Suchard, moved to the depths of his Romantic soul by the Falls, standing in rapture like Jean-Jacques Rousseau before the glories of Nature :

Niagara Falls 1824

The Cataract is in the form of a horseshoe. The eastern side is the more perfect in form, more powerful and more picturesque. As one stands below, the mass of waters surge forth as though falling from the heavens, to be lost in a bottomless gulf. The jutting rocks above seem ready to fly into fragments, crushed by the weight of those liquid columns. The ground shakes and trembles beneath the beholder. Thunder compasses him about while all around Nature is wrapt in stillness, as though mutely astonished. From the depths of the gorge, where boiling chaos reigns, the spindrift rises and sinks back, pursued, attained and engulfed by faëry waters ; while horrendous voices mount from the abyss, o'ertopping the thunder's vasty roar.

From the American shore I crossed to Goat Island, by a long and narrow bridge that boldly spans the rapids. Here is built a charming cabin at which travellers may not only refresh the inner man but, also, a circumstance I found vexatious, nay, disgusting, indulge in the game of billiards ! Here, where all stands dwarfed and humbled before the majesty of the Creator, gaming, that basest of human passions, flaunts its foul demands ! In this noble spot where admiration and meditation should alone hold sway, men require such vulgar pastimes to occupy their thoughts. I could never bring myself to hold converse with a traveller who played billiards in the presence of such a spectacle. He would seem the basest caricature of European civilisation, a depraved, degenerate wretch with the mindless arrogance of a brute. There are places on this Earth not built by human hand more hallowed by mankind of every race and creed, than any fane of stone or bricks and mortar. One cannot stand aside and see them desecrated. [2]

Coming down to earth—and back to Buffalo—Philippe Suchard headed westward, towards Pittsburgh, finding adventures on the way :

Adventures by coach 1824

Since leaving Niagara Falls, I had passed through large tracts of wilderness ; but these were as nothing to those which we met next day between Mercer and Pittsburgh, a journey of fifty miles that is featureless except for the small town of Butler. We often went five or six leagues without seeing so much as a log cabin buried in the woods. Nothing but endless, gloomy forest and only the rarest glimpse of sky.

It may be imagined what the mail route through these fastnesses was like. Despite our four strong horses and the fact that there were only three passengers aboard, our coach made heavy going and during the penultimate stage, indeed, we came near to being dashed to pieces. We were descending a steep hill; Americans do not apply the drag; they let the horses canter—or even gallop—down the hills. This is what our driver did. One of the wheelers had broken its traces and with great skill he was driving the other, which was now all that held the plunging vehicle back. Suddenly we hit a log lying diagonally across the road. Had it lain straight across it would have stopped the coach. As it was the nearside wheels missed the log and the offside ones straddled it, dragging it along. The terrified horses ran away, the bits between their teeth. We took to the air, but at the end of it all came through safe and sound. . . . Three miles out of Buffalo the highway vanished. Our progress continued along the shore of Lake Erie. But what a road—or rather, what lack of road! The poor horses sank up to their hocks, sometimes in sand, sometimes in marshy bog. It was all they could do to draw the coach at a walking pace. I supposed that we had hit a bad patch, and that we should soon be on firmer ground; but our driver politely made known that the " patch " would take us ten hours. The Lake was quite choppy; but this did not deter our brave Phaeton from taking to the water whenever he wished to avoid large boulders or a piece of marshy ground. So long as the wheels of the coach, which were very large, had solid ground beneath them during these aquatic excursions I made no remark. But we came to a place where a long tongue of rock jutted into the lake, and it became necessary to round the headland. The master of our destinies then boldly drove his horses into the water until it closed over their backs; upon which they commenced swimming like dogs, while the wavelets lapped against the panels of our noble carriage. I began to feel ill at ease, and although realising that previous unfortunates had suffered in the same way, felt bound to remark that there were pleasanter forms of travel. The Americans were greatly astonished. It seemed to them perfectly normal and while agreeing perforce, I reflected that every country most decidedly has customs of its own!

We stopped at a lonely house by the lake for a meal and a change of coach and horses. Then the journey continued, if not in pleasanter fashion than during the morning, at least differently. When the horses could go no further owing to quicksands, they were headed not into the water this time, but into the forest bordering the lake. It required great skill to drive the coach *en zigzag* between the trees over fallen logs and across the dry water-courses with which our path was strewn. Finally, however, with no bones broken, we pulled in to Fredonia before nightfall. ²

Charles Dickens, too, found much to marvel at during the trip down the Ohio from Pittsburgh to Cincinnati—not least the boat itself:

*Down
the Ohio River
1842*

The MESSENGER was one among a crowd of high-pressure steamboats, clustered together by the wharf-side, which, looked down upon from the rising ground that forms the landing-place, and backed by the lofty bank on the opposite side of the river, appeared no larger than so many floating models. She had some forty passengers on board, exclusive of the poorer persons on the lower deck; and in half an hour, or less, proceeded on her way.

We had, for ourselves, a tiny state-room with two berths in it, opening out of the ladies' cabin. There was, undoubtedly, something satisfactory in this " location ", inasmuch as it was in the stern, and we had been a great many times very gravely recommended to keep as far aft as possible, " because the steamboats generally blew up forward ". Nor was this an

BUFFALO HARBOUR FROM LAKE ERIE.
WITH LIGHTHOUSE AT RIGHT MARKING JUNCTION OF LAKE WITH BUFFALO RIVER - 1833

unnecessary caution, as the occurrence and circumstances of more than one such fatality during our stay sufficiently testified. Apart from this source of self-congratulation, it was an unspeakable relief to have any place, no matter how confined, where one could be alone; and as the row of little chambers of which this was one, had each a second glass-door besides that in the ladies' cabin, which opened on a narrow gallery outside the vessel, where

PITTSBURGH'S " GOLDEN TRIANGLE " DISTRICT
FROM ACROSS THE MONONGAHELA - 1796

the other passengers seldom came, and where one could sit in peace and gaze upon the shifting prospect, we took possession of our new quarters with much pleasure.

If the native packets I have already described be unlike anything we are in the habit of seeing on water, these western vessels are still more foreign to all the ideas we are accustomed to entertain of boats, I hardly know what to liken them to, or how to describe them.

In the first place, they have no mast, cordage, tackle, rigging, or other such boat-like gear; nor have they anything in their shape at all calculated to remind one of a boat's head, stern, sides or keel. Except that they are in the water, and display a couple of paddle-boxes, they might be intended, for anything that appears to the contrary, to perform some unknown service, high and dry, upon a mountain top. There is no visible deck, even: nothing but a long, black, ugly roof, covered with burnt-out feathery sparks; above which tower two iron chimneys, and a hoarse escape-valve, and a glass steerage-house.   Then, in order as the eye descends towards the water, are the sides, and doors, and windows of the state-rooms, jumbled as oddly together as though they formed a small street, built by the varying tastes of a dozen men; the whole is supported on beams and pillars resting on a dirty barge, but a few inches above the water's edge; and in the narrow space between this upper structure and this barge's deck, are the furnace fires and machinery, open at the sides to every wind that blows, and every storm of rain it drives along its path.   Passing one of these boats at night, and seeing the great body of fire, exposed as I have just described, that rages and roars beneath the frail pile of painted wood; the machinery, not warded off or guarded in any way, but doing its work in the midst of the crowd of idlers and emigrants and children, who throng the lower deck; under the management, too, of reckless men whose acquaintance with its mysteries may have been of six months' standing: one feels directly that the wonder is, not that there should be so many fatal accidents, but that any journey should be safely made. . . .

A fine broad river always, but in some parts much wider than in others: and then there is usually a green island, covered with trees, dividing it into two streams. Occasionally, we stop for a few minutes, maybe to take in wood, maybe for passengers, at some small town or village (I ought to say

COVERED BRIDGE ON THE TRIBUTARY OF NORTHERN OHIO RIVER BELOW PITTSBURGH - 1826

STEUBENVILLE, OHIO,
WITH FERRY LOADING AND KEELBOAT USED BY THE ARTIST FOR TRIP DOWN THE OHIO - 1826

city, every place is a city here); but the banks are for the most part deep
solitudes, overgrown with trees, which, hereabouts, are already in leaf and
very green. For miles, and miles, and miles, these solitudes are unbroken
by any sign of human life or trace of human footsteps, nor is anything seen
to move about them but the blue jay, whose colour is so bright, and yet so
delicate, that it looks like a flying flower. At lengthened intervals a log
cabin, with its little space of cleared land about it, nestles under a rising
ground, and sends its thread of blue smoke curling up into the sky. It stands
in the corner of the poor field of wheat, which is full of great unsightly
stumps, like earthy butchers'-blocks. Sometimes the ground is only just
now cleared: the felled trees lying yet upon the soil: and the log-house
only this morning begun. As we pass this clearing, the settler leans upon
his axe or hammer, and looks wistfully at the people from the world. The
children creep out of the temporary hut, which is like a gipsy tent upon the
ground, and clap their hands and shout. The dog only glances round at us;
and then looks up into his master's face again, as if he were rendered
uneasy by any suspension of the common business, and had nothing more to
do with pleasurers. And still there is the same, eternal foreground. The
river has washed away its banks, and stately trees have fallen down into
the stream. Some have been there so long, that they are mere dry grizzly
skeletons. Some have just toppled over, and having earth yet about their
roots, are bathing their green heads in the river, and putting forth new
shoots and branches. Some are almost sliding down, as you look at them.

MARIETTA ON THE BANKS OF THE OHIO - 1826

And some were drowned so long ago, that their bleached arms start out from the middle of the current, and seem to try to grasp the boat, and drag it under water.   Through such a scene as this, the unwieldy machine takes its hoarse sullen way: venting, at every revolution of the paddles, a loud high-pressure blast; enough, one would think, to waken up the host of Indians who lie buried in a great mound yonder: so old, that mighty oaks and other forest trees have struck their roots into its earth; and so high, that it is a hill, even among the hills that Nature planted round it.   The very river, as though it shared one's feelings of compassion for the extinct tribes who lived so pleasantly here, in their blessed ignorance of white existence, hundreds of years ago, steals out of its way to ripple near this mound; and there are few places where the Ohio sparkles more brightly than in Big Grave Creek. . . .

The night is dark and we proceed within the shadow of the wooded bank, which makes it darker.   After gliding past the sombre maze of boughs for a long time, we come upon an open place where the tall trees are burning.   The shape of every branch and twig is expressed in a deep red glow, and as the light wind stirs and ruffles it, they seem to vegetate in fire.   It is such a sight as we read of in legends of enchanted forests; saving that it is sad to see these noble works wasting away so awfully, alone; and to think how many years must come and go before the magic that created them will rear their like upon this ground again.   But the time will come: and when, in their changed ashes, the growth of centuries unborn has struck its roots, the restless men of distant ages will repair to these again unpeopled solitudes; and their fellows, in cities far away, that slumber now, perhaps, beneath the rolling sea, will read, in language strange to any ears in being now but very old to them, of primeval forests where the axe was never heard, and where the jungled ground was never trodden by a human foot. [6]

Dickens at his most sententious. His " American Notes " came out in 1842. The young Frenchman, Jean-Jacques Ampère was at Cincinnati nine years later, and was much struck by the way that settlers were carving a homeland out of the wilderness. He has a reporter's eye for detail :

Cincinnati 1851-1852

I went down to the river's edge. The *Belle Rivière* was low ; between the water itself and the banks lay a great expanse of ground looking like some marshy foreshore when the sea is out. No embankment beside the river, and too few bridges. Here the bridges are the numerous steamboats that disturb the Sabbath calm as they pant from one bank to the other. I went back into town. The streets are named after trees : Chestnut, Walnut, Pine, etc., recalling the forests they replace. Several of the streets are fine and tree-lined. A dislike of unnecessary frills, and a passion for abbreviation has led to the word " street " being shortened to " St. " on the signboards. The side-walks are paved with large flagstones but are apt to cease abruptly ; this, one feels, is a capital city built in haste and not yet finished. When I went down behind the town I found suburbs in course of construction, and beyond these suburbs hill-tops where felling was still in progress, with half-burned tree-trunks here and there as in forest clearings, and a few trees which the axe had spared : a sad and depressing sight, it was not country any longer—but shortly to become a town.

THE INDUSTRIOUS CITY OF CINCINNATI,
VIEWED FROM A HILL BEHIND COVINGTON AND NEWPORT, KENTUCKY - 1855

RAPIDS ON THE OHIO RIVER - 1826

Cincinnati, with a population of 116,000, is now fifty-eight years old, that is, half a year for every thousand inhabitants ; and included among these is a citizen who is said to have been there longer than the city itself. The place is growing at a great pace, having doubled in the last ten years. Linked by railroad with the Great Lakes and, via the Ohio, with the Mississippi, Cincinnati is the commercial centre of the inland States. They call her the Queen of the West for she is the capital of what was, only twenty years ago, the Far West. Now the West has receded, as civilisation has advanced. . . . Well, yes. I admit that they slaughter and salt a lot of hogs at Cincinnati ; that is one of the reasons that the passing of half a century sees churches, schools, theatres, and even an observatory here, instead of the savages who used to scalp travellers using the Ohio. . . .

Curving gracefully below the rounded, tree-clad hills now in their fiery autumn livery, the blue waters of the Ohio looked lovely in the evening light. Beyond, to my right, rose steeper hills from which one evening I looked down upon the city, spread out before me like an amphitheatre, as the rays of the setting sun gilded the slender white steeples, transforming them into the minarets of some Oriental city. The background was all dark, and a heavy raincloud menaced one side of the sunlit town. I went down to the river again. The clouds had gone, and the golden leaves shed a dappled pattern on the ground. The evening was calm, the landscape serene. A barge drawn by horses glided silently over the clear smooth water; smart spindly-wheeled open cabriolets bowled homewards with families returning from a day in the country. The whole scene reflected quiet satisfaction: the kind of satisfaction that springs from a quiet life; ease without luxury, unostentatious wealth and equality of well-being—for all the carriages, and I would say nearly all the families, looked alike. I could have gone on forever walking beside the Ohio River, with its hills and lovely trees, and its happy-seeming people, but it was getting late, and as I sauntered home I reflected: "It was pigs that produced all this!"[7]

There had indeed been big changes along the Ohio. The French naturalist F. A. Michaux, who was there soon after 1800 had quite another story to tell:

More than one-half of those now dwelling on the banks of the Ohio are original inhabitants, or, as they are called in the United States, First

*Along
the Ohio River
1802*

Settlers, a race of men who cannot bear to linger upon the land they have reclaimed, but must always be moving on in search of richer soil, healthier climes or finer hunting-grounds. Thrusting forward in this way they reach the farthest frontiers of the white man and there make their home; nor do they halt even there, but press on, braving the savage in his own territory. Their treatment of the Indians causes constant

AMERICAN LOG HOUSE - 1826

ill-feeling, which frequently flares into bloodshed—and the Indian is always the loser, rather from shortage of numbers, be it said, than lack of courage.

The settlers on the Ohio spend much time in hunting deer and bears, the skins of which they sell. Their taste for this way of life is not conducive to good husbandry; they tend to neglect their newly-acquired lands, which normally comprise between one hundred and four hundred acres, of which not more than eight or ten have been cleared. The crops from this land, with the milk from their cows, are more than sufficient for them and their families, which are usually fairly numerous, with seldom less than six or seven children. Their houses stand close to the river, nearly always in a pleasant situation with a view; but their construction belies the beauty of  the site; they are no more than miserable log huts, with no windows, and so small that two beds fill most of the room. One of these hovels can be built by two men in less than three days, although from the size and meanness of the finished article one would never guess that they came from a land of forests where timber can be had for the asking. The people do not object to receiving strangers; they give them shelter, which means that they allow them to sleep on the floor wrapped in blankets. They eat corn-bread, smoked ham, milk and butter, but seldom anything else; here, and throughout the West, one spends little on food. [11]

About twenty years later another French-speaking traveller, Philippe Suchard, again passed through Ohio en route to the Swiss settlement of New Vevay. Ohio was developing fast and he found the folk most hospitable:

*On the Ohio River
1824*

In Ohio they grow mainly corn, fruit, wheat, barley, oats, potatoes, etc., and the harvests are always good. The soil is astonishingly fertile. One has only to look at the forest to realise this. One seldom sees trees of such size in Europe. Their trunks are smooth, without moss or lichen, and they rise straight up, with no branches or boughs until the very top. The ground beneath them is a smooth grassy sward, unencumbered by the brushwood one finds at home. One sees few willows beside the streams. The most remarkable tree is the sycamore, from the thickness of its trunk. I heard some incredible tales of great sycamores. I myself saw one that contained a grocery, hardware and liquor store, complete with doors and windows. Once a sycamore attains a thickness of a foot in diameter it starts to go hollow in the centre, which is why it is used for making barrels. One has only to saw it into lengths and fill in the ends. Sycamores like a cool, dampish situation and heavy soil.

The method of collecting maple-syrup is fairly well known. This is how Westerners do it, between the middle of March and the middle of April. A child takes a horse and sled around each morning with a barrel on it for the sap that has run down from holes bored in the trees. In favourable conditions, that is when the weather is fine and cool, each tree may yield as many as twelve pots of syrup without coming to any harm. Settlers usually make 150 or 200 pounds of crude or powdered sugar in this way for house-hold use; commercial producers may make as much as twenty quintals [i.e. 4,400 pounds] a year. It sells for three dollars the quintal. [2]

Leaving the sweetstuffs, *chocolatier* Suchard here goes Romantic again:

A Reader who has not travelled entirely alone for several days virtually cut off from human kind, through trackless wastes, uncertain how he will emerge from the leafy labyrinth and sometimes even in fear of his life, cannot conceive the joy of once more finding himself safe within the confines of a hut, and surrounded by friendly faces.

I looked about me the better to make the acquaintance of my host's family. I counted ten children; the eldest boy about fifteen years old, the youngest still at its mother's breast. This good lady enquired whether I should prefer tea or coffee for supper, and what sort of poultry I should like. She cut me slices of pie and some ham, which she roasted in butter. Next came a fricassee of chicken, a radish salad, fresh butter, stewed plums with hot cakes in place of bread. I describe this supper menu not to explain what a settler's cabin can offer the unexpected guest but because this is what people usually have for supper in the West. Luncheon follows very much the same pattern.

Here, as always, the napery was of the whitest linen, the crockery, including the plates and dishes, made of *terre anglaise*. The lady of the house, looking very clean and tidy, sits alone, the better to serve her guest. The meal usually starts by her asking "Do you take milk and sugar in your tea?" The guest takes what he fancies from the food set  before him but the hostess urges him to take more, saying "Do help yourself." Only when the guest has finished do papa and the children sit down. Not that the children address their father and mother as Papa and Mama; in even the humblest abode it is always "Sir" and "Ma'am".

The room, which did duty first as kitchen, then as dining-room, is now transformed into a *salon*. This time, as on previous visits to America, I was astonished to hear simple farmers discoursing so well on political economy, constitutional matters and the nationalities of Europe. This interest in public affairs is one of the mainstays of American democracy and patriotism; it is due very largely to the universal habit of reading the newspapers. [2]

Kentucky, although admitted to the Union in 1792, was still part of the Frontier during the first quarter of the nineteenth century. As there were no large towns or monuments to visit, travellers decided, with Alexander Pope, that " the proper study of mankind is man ". François-André Michaux is writing when the State of Kentucky was only ten years old :

Kentucky 1802

The boats in which the flour is sent down to Lower Louisiana cost about one hundred piastres [$28]; each boat carries two hundred to three hundred barrels, and has a crew of five. The skipper is paid one hundred piastres a trip and the other men fifty piastres each. The journey to New Orleans from Louisville, where nearly all the loadings are done takes thirty-five days. They reckon 450 miles (one hundred and forty leagues) from Louisville to the junction with the Ohio and around one thousand miles (three hundred and thirty-three leagues) from there to New Orleans, making a total journey of fourteen hundred and thirty-five miles, or about four hundred and seventy-eight leagues [Michaux seems to employ a somewhat elastic " league "] and the boats have to travel some eight or nine hundred miles on the river without seeing any human habitation. A proportion of the men travel back to Lexington by the overland route, a distance of eleven hundred miles (three hundred and seventy leagues), in forty to forty-five days. This journey is extremely onerous, and those who prefer not to face its rigours return by sea ; they take ship from New Orleans to New York or Philadelphia, make their way thence to Pittsburgh, and from Pittsburgh down the Ohio to Kentucky.

Every year, during March or April the inhabitants set fire to the grass, which at this time of year is so long and dry that for three weeks or so the cattle are unable to reach the new growth that is just sprouting. The custom is widely condemned, and rightly so for by burning off the dry and partly withered grass too early, the new grass is left unprotected against the spring frosts and its growth is retarded in consequence. The custom of firing the prairies originated with the Indians, who used formerly to come hunting in Kentucky, and is still practised by them in other parts of North

America, where there exist savannahs of enormous extent. Their object was to attract deer, buffalo etc., to the burned areas, where game can be seen from a greater distance. Unless one has witnessed one of these terrible fires it is impossible to form any idea of them. The flames often extend over a front of several miles and are sometimes driven by the wind with such rapidity that men, even mounted men, have fallen victim to the flames. American hunters, and the Indians, take refuge from this danger by a ruse that is as simple as it is ingenious : they deliberately set fire to the grass in their immediate vicinity and retreat on to the burned portion, where the flames, finding nothing to consume, are unable to follow ; a process known to Canadian hunters as *faire leur brûlé*—burning their own.

In the neighbourhood of their homesteads the settlers are much troubled by squirrels, which do great damage in the corn-fields. This species, *Sciurus carolinianus*, is grey, and a little larger than the European squirrel. They are so numerous that children are sent into the fields several times a day to scare them. At the slightest sound they take refuge in the trees, but come down again the next moment. The squirrels, like the bears of North America are migratory ; at the approach of winter they invade Kentucky in such numbers that the settlers form special hunting-parties.

HARPERS FERRY ON THE POTOMAC - 1813

Squirrel-hunting is a popular sport. The hunters usually go out in pairs, and two guns may kill as many as thirty or forty in a morning. A man on his own, however, would probably not kill more than one or two, because as it climbs the squirrel contrives to keep the tree-trunk between itself and the hunter. I was present at one of these great shooting parties; afterwards we assembled at a pre-arranged place in the woods and more than sixty squirrels were roasted for dinner. The flesh is white and extremely good. This way of preparing them is preferable to all others.

Of the domestic animals, pigs have multiplied best. Every settler raises hogs, several of them owning 150 to 200. The animals live entirely in the woods, where they find ample nourishment, especially in autumn and winter. They turn very wild and always go about in packs. When attacked by a dog or wild animal they run away rapidly or form themselves into a circle for defense. They are stocky, medium-sized animals, with short legs and straight ears. Each settler recognises the hogs belonging to him by the way in which their ears are slit. Sometimes they disappear into the depths of the forest and may not be seen for months, but they are trained to come home from time to time by being given corn once or twice a week. In view of the vastness of the country, its huge forests, the scarcity of population and the lack of predatory animals, it is surprising that the pigs have not multiplied even more rapidly and gone completely wild. [11]

Philippe Suchard, on his return from New Vevay at the beginning of October 1824, took the GENERAL PIKE as far as Cincinnati. From there he rode on horseback to Gallipolis, by way of Washington, Kentucky, Maysville and West Union. On the 18th October he set out from Point Pleasant to ride, sometimes on one bank of the Ohio and sometimes on the other, through Marietta, Newport, Fishing Creek and Elisabethtown to Wheeling, a distance of 130 miles, which took him four days. After Wheeling he made his first acquaintance with American turnpike roads; in four hours he rode from Wheeling to Geneva, by way of Braunville and Uniontown. Next day he reached Smithfield. He crossed the Alleghenies by the Laurel Hill Pass and came down into Cumberland on the Potomac. From this point Suchard pressed on to Baltimore en route for Europe. He sailed on November 15 and arrived at Le Havre December 11, making it possible for him to keep his promise of spending Christmas with his family at Neuchâtel. So we take leave of this pleasant Romantic young tourist and rejoin Charles Dickens in Washington:

Washington 1842

It is sometimes called the City of Magnificent Distances, but it might with greater propriety be termed the City of Magnificent Intentions; for it is only on taking a bird's-eye view of it from the top of the Capitol, that

Niagara Falls, New York — 1812

THE CANADIAN SIDE BY MOONLIGHT

one can at all comprehend the vast designs of its projector, an aspiring Frenchman. Spacious avenues, that begin in nothing, and lead nowhere; streets, mile-long, that only want houses, roads, and inhabitants; public buildings that need but a public to be complete; and ornaments of great thoroughfares, which only lack great thoroughfares to ornament are its leading features. One might fancy the season over, and most of the houses gone out of town for ever with their masters. To the admirers of cities it is a Barmecide Feast; a pleasant field for the imagination to rove in; a monument raised to a deceased project, with not even a legible inscription to record its departed greatness.

Such as it is, it is likely to remain. It was originally chosen for the seat of Government, as a means of averting the conflicting jealousies and interests of the different States; and very probably, too, as being remote from mobs: a consideration not to be slighted, even in America. It has no trade or commerce of its own: having little or no population beyond the President and his establishment; the members of the legislature who reside there during the session; the Government clerks and officers employed in the various departments; the keepers of the hotels and boarding-houses; and the tradesmen who supply their tables. It is very unhealthy. Few people would live in Washington, I take it, who were not obliged to reside there; and the tides of emigration and speculation, those rapid and regardless currents, are little likely to flow at any time towards such dull and sluggish water. . . .

The hotel in which we live, is a long row of small houses fronting on the street, and opening at the back upon a common yard, in which hangs a great triangle. Whenever a servant is wanted, somebody beats on his triangle from one stroke up to seven, according to the number of the house in which his presence is required: and as all the servants are always being wanted, and none of them ever come, this enlivening engine is in full performance the whole day through. Clothes are drying in this same yard; female slaves, with cotton handkerchiefs twisted round their heads, are running to and fro on the hotel business; black waiters cross and recross with dishes in their hands; two great dogs are playing upon a mound of loose bricks in the centre of the little square; a pig is turning up his stomach to the sun, and grunting " that's comfortable! "; and neither the men nor the women, nor the dogs, nor the pig, nor any created creature, takes the smallest notice of the triangle, which is tingling madly all the time.

I walk to the front window, and look across the road upon a long, straggling row of houses, one story high, terminating, nearly opposite, but a little to the left, in a melancholy piece of waste ground with frowzy grass, which looks like a small piece of country that has taken to drinking, and has quite lost itself.   Standing anyhow and all wrong, upon this open space, like something meteoric that has fallen down from the moon, is an odd, lopsided one-eyed kind of wooden building, that looks like a church, with a flag-staff as long as itself sticking out of a steeple, something larger than a tea-chest.   Under the window, is a small stand of coaches, whose slave-drivers are sunning themselves on the steps of our door, and talking idly together.   The three most obtrusive houses near at hand, are the three meanest.   On one—a shop, which never has anything in the window, and never has the door open—is painted in large characters, THE CITY LUNCH.   At another, which looks like the backway to somewhere else, but is an independent building in itself, oysters are procurable in every style.   At the third, which is a very, very little tailor's shop, pants are fixed to order : or, in other words, pantaloons are made to measure.   And that is our street in Washington. . . .

The principal features of the Capitol are, of course, the two Houses of Assembly.   But there is, besides, in the centre of the building, a fine rotunda, ninety-six feet in diameter and ninety-six high, whose circular wall is divided into compartments, ornamented by historical pictures.   Four of these have for their subjects prominent events in the revolutionary struggle.   They were painted by Colonel Trumbull, himself a member of Washington's staff at the time of their occurrence ; from which circumstance they derive a peculiar interest of their own.   In this same hall Mr. Greenough's large statue of Washington has been lately placed.   It has great merits of course, but it struck me as being rather strained and violent for its subject.   I could wish, however, to have seen it in a better light than it can ever be viewed in, where it stands.

There is a very pleasant and commodious library in the Capitol ; and from a balcony in front, the bird's-eye view, of which I have just spoken, may be had, together with a beautiful prospect of the adjacent country. In one of the ornamented portions of the building, there is a figure of Justice ; whereunto the Guide Book says, " the artist at first contemplated giving more of nudity, but he was warned that the public sentiment in this country would not admit of it, and in his caution he has gone, perhaps, into the

THE WASHINGTON RESIDENCE OF FRENCH MINISTER, BARON DE NEUVILLE,
NEAR F AND 15TH STREETS PAINTED IN 1818 BY THE BARONESS

opposite extreme." Poor Justice! She has been made to wear much
stranger garments in America than those she pines in, in the Capitol. Let
us hope that she has changed her dress-maker since they were fashioned,
and that the public sentiment of the country did not cut out the clothes she
hides her lovely figure in, just now.

The House of Representatives is a beautiful and spacious hall, of
semi-circular shape, supported by handsome pillars. One part of the gallery
is appropriated to the ladies, and there they sit in front rows, and come in,
and go out, as at a play or concert. The chair is canopied, and raised
considerably above the floor of the House; and every member has an easy
chair and a writing desk to himself: which is denounced by some people out
of doors as a most unfortunate and injudicious arrangement, tending to long
sittings and prosaic speeches. It is an elegant chamber to look at, but a
singularly bad one for all purposes of hearing. The Senate, which is smaller,
is free from this objection, and is exceedingly well adapted to the uses for
which it is designed. The sittings, I need hardly add, take place in the day;
and the parliamentary forms are modelled on those of the old country. [6]

In 1829 an Italian Jesuit, Giovanni Grassi published an account of his stay in
America. He was mainly concerned with religious matters, but did find the time to
visit the Patent Office in Washington:

Lack of man-power has forced American engineers to find ways of
replacing the human hand by machinery. To encourage this form of
industry an institution known as the Patent Office has been set up in

*The Patent Office
in Washington
1829*

Washington, by which the Government grants inventors exclusive rights to use or sell their inventions, models of which they have to present to the Patent Office where they are preserved and placed on public exhibition. There is no denying that amongst the great abundance of models on view (many claiming novelty when they are in fact ancient inventions) there are some that are highly ingenious. Especially noteworthy is a water-driven saw, so designed that once a tree trunk has been placed in position it will be sawn up into planks without again being touched by human agency. Equally admired is a machine that cuts steel wire into lengths, bends them as necessary and thrusts them into leather belting, thus quickly producing the finest imaginable wool-carder. The spinning mules are also most ingeniously thought out, so as to eliminate almost all fatigue. I cannot leave this subject without recounting a curious incident. A countryman came in to apply for a patent, bringing a model of his device with him, which proved to be nothing other than an Archimedean screw. When told that his invention was not new and shown a picture of it in an old book the good fellow could only reply with every appearance of sincerity, that he had never known that the Archimedean screw existed, that he had thought it out on his own, and that no one but himself was party to his invention.

Last year, according to the newspapers, someone even invented a machine for teaching Latin. [12]

THE CAPITOL BUILDING, WITH DOME STILL INCOMPLETE - C. 1860

THE SOUTH FRONT OF THE WHITE HOUSE - 1815

Until 1932 the President of the United States used to keep open house on New Year's Day. Jean-Jacques Ampère went along on January 1st, and found the White House reception almost bewilderingly democratic:

New Year's Day in Washington 1852

On the first of January one goes and calls on the President. The door is open to all comers. This makes a pretty fair crush but it is no more crowded than a special meeting at the *Institut* at home. No particular costume is laid down but I saw no one who was not properly clad. I had read somewhere in a book of American travels that these receptions were terribly crowded, and among other stories the author described how the father of some little girls had had the happy thought of setting them on the mantelpiece to give them a better view. I saw nothing of this sort. Once past the throngs outside and in the entrance hall, one is ushered into an ante-room, and from thence into the room in which the President is standing. One shakes hands with him and bows to his Lady, then one passes into a third, very spacious *salon* and remains there for a while. I stayed there an hour and saw nothing that failed to conform with the strictest standards of propriety. It was nobody's fault, except my own, if somewhere in the crowd outside I had my pocket picked and lost my watch. I only mention this trifling matter so that any foreign visitors finding themselves in Washington on the first of January, and proposing to attend the Court may take proper precautions. [7]

HUNTING IN FLORIDA - 1851

CHAPTER THE SECOND

In which, after leaving Washington D.C.,
the Reader journeys through
the States of Virginia and the Carolinas,
and, taking ship at Charleston,
breaks his journey at divers places in Florida,
before reaching the Mississippi
and New Orleans.

European visitors during the nineteenth century were not very struck by Washington which, although Capital in name was not yet a city in fact. The true, vibrant life of America they thought lay elsewhere. The majority of travellers, however, contented themselves with visiting the towns near the north-eastern seaboard, ascending the Hudson River and admiring Niagara Falls. But a few bolder and more enterprising spirits realised that this was hardly sufficient. Thus it is that a variety of entertaining writers turn up along the trail from Washington to New Orleans, among them Charles Dickens, always a clear-eyed and realistic observer, the indefatigable botanist François-André Michaux and the engaging young Frenchman, Jean-Jacques Ampère still looking for something entirely new. That embittered aristocrat the Baron de Montlezun, whose quest for countries was in keeping with his *ancien régime* personality, naturally sought out New Orleans and later Havana. Much the same itinerary was followed by Léon Beauvallet, an actor in Madame Rachel's company which was still touring the New World in pursuit of an increasingly chimerical success. In one of Beauvallet's accounts, a member of the company puts a deadly snake to sleep by reciting Racine, remarking that the serpent's boredom is a sure sign he is typically Yankee!

In the course of the journey from the capital down to New Orleans new travellers chime in and new horizons beckon. Achille Poussielgue, for example, a young French diplomat whose passion for sea-voyages and natural history led him in 1851 to charter a schooner and a crew of five for a four-month cruise along the coast of Florida. He took with him enough provisions for six months, five hundred dollars in gold, a draft for 1,000 dollars on a bank in Saint Augustine, Florida, and all necessary equipment for his studies in natural history. Yet his most notable find was a charming specimen of American girlhood, marooned on a lighthouse (see page 87).

With another Frenchman, the painstaking geographer Elisée Reclus who was later to become famous as the author of *Géographie Universelle*, the scene shifted from the open sea to the muddy waters of the Mississippi, as the low-lying territories of Louisiana rose out of the horizon to greet him.

By the time the travellers reach Charleston, not to mention Florida and the little American islands in the Gulf of Mexico, the climate is already warmer—indeed some-

WASHINGTON, E STREET CORNER · 1817

times downright hot and thoroughly disagreeable in its humidity. New crops, like rice, tobacco and cotton, bring unexpected colours to the fields, and new tasks for the husbandman. A certain lethargy prevails, disposing women to thoughts of dress, and imparting to men the airs of the *grand seigneur*. Some travellers prove susceptible to the lingering old-worldly traces of Spanish influence in Florida and of French culture in New Orleans; their feelings upon the subject of Negro slavery vary considerably and betray some embarrassment. It is one thing to hold strong views while closeted in Europe; another to maintain them when confronted with the tangled skein of reality. How is one to believe in a slave's misfortune, the puzzled liberal young man Francis de Castelnau asked himself, when that misfortune stems not from his having been sold, but from having been sold for less than one of his workmates?

From Washington to New Orleans furnishes good company, and takes on the aspect of a pure pleasure trip: the ladies put on their best gowns, all gay with flounces and lace, and make telling play with their tiny parasols. It is a long trip, but the skies are kind, and is there not, in every traveller's heart a secret feeling that Adventure lies just around the corner?

From Washington to Fredericksburg in Virginia, the way to go is by stage-coach. The journey should prove picturesque and piquant—in places, perhaps even dangerous. And the company is charming, for Charles Dickens is one of the party:

Soon after nine o'clock we come to Potomac Creek, where we are to land: and then comes the oddest part of the journey. Seven stage-coaches are preparing to carry us on. Some of them are ready, some of them are not ready. Some of the drivers are blacks, some whites. There are four horses to each coach, and all the horses, harnessed or unharnessed, are there. The passengers are getting out of the steamboat, and into the coaches; the luggage is being transferred in noisy wheel-barrows; the horses are frightened, impatient to start; the black drivers are chattering

By Coach 1842

WASHINGTON AND GEORGETOWN FROM THE ROAD TO ALEXANDRIA, VIRGINIA - 1827

to them like so many monkeys; and the white ones whooping like so many drovers: for the main thing to be done in all kinds of hostlering here, is to make as much noise as possible.   The coaches are something like the French coaches, but not nearly so good.   In lieu of springs, they are hung

TEA-PARTY AT MOUNT VERNON - 1796

on bands of the strongest leather. There is very little choice or difference between them; and they may be likened to the car portion of the swings at an English fair, roofed, put upon axle-trees and wheels, and curtained with painted canvas. They are covered with mud from the roof to the wheel-tire, and have never been cleaned since they were built.

The tickets we have received on board the steamboat are marked No. 1, so we belong to coach No. 1.   I throw my coat on the box, and hoist my wife and her maid into the inside.   It has only one step, and that being about a yard from the ground, is usually approached by a chair: when there is no chair, ladies trust in Providence. The coach holds nine inside, having a seat across from door to door, where we in England put our legs: so that there is only one feat more difficult in the performance than getting in, and

STAGE-COACH - C. 1827

that is, getting out again.   There is only one outside passenger, and he sits upon the box. As I am that one, I climb up; and while they are strapping the luggage on the roof, and heaping it into a kind of tray behind, I have a good opportunity of looking at the driver.

He is a negro — very black indeed. He is dressed in a coarse pepper-and-salt suit excessively patched and darned (particularly at the knees), grey stockings, enormous unblacked high-low shoes, and very short trousers. He has two odd gloves: one of parti-coloured worsted, and one of leather. He has a very short whip, broken in the middle and bandaged up with string.   And yet he wears a low-crowned, broad-brimmed, black hat:

AN AMERICAN DILIGENCE - 1810

faintly shadowing forth a kind of insane imitation of an English coachman! But somebody in authority cries " Go ahead! " as I am making these observations. The mail takes the lead in a four-horse waggon, and all the coaches follow in procession : headed by No. 1.

By the way, whenever an Englishman would cry " All right! " an American cries " Go ahead! " which is somewhat expressive of the national character of the two countries.

The first half mile of the road is over bridges made of loose planks laid across two parallel poles, which tilt up as the wheels roll over them ; and *in* the river. The river has a clayey bottom and is full of holes, so that half a horse is constantly disappearing unexpectedly, and can't be found again for some time.

But we get past even this, and come to the road itself, which is a series of alternate swamps and gravel-pits. A tremendous place is close before us, the black driver rolls his eyes, screws his mouth up very round, and looks straight between the two leaders, as if he were saying to himself, " we have done this often before, but *now* I think we shall have a crash. " He takes a rein in each hand; jerks and pulls at both; and dances on the splash-board with both feet (keeping his seat, of course) like the late lamented Ducrow on two of his fiery coursers. We come to the spot, sink down in the mire nearly to the coach windows, tilt on one side at an angle of forty-five degrees, and stick there. The insides scream dismally; the coach stops; the horses flounder; all the other six coaches stop; and their four-and-twenty horses flounder likewise : but merely for company, and in sympathy with ours. Then the following circumstances occur.

BLACK DRIVER (to the horses). " Hi! "

Nothing happens. Insides scream again.

BLACK DRIVER (to the horses). " Ho! "

Horses plunge, and splash the black driver.

GENTLEMAN INSIDE (looking out). " Why, what on airth—"

Gentleman receives a variety of splashes and draws his head in again, without finishing his question or waiting for an answer.

BLACK DRIVER (still to the horses). " Jiddy! Jiddy! "

Horses pull violently, drag the coach out of the hole, and draw it up a bank : so steep, that the black driver's legs fly up into the air, and he goes back among the luggage on the roof. But he immediately recovers himself, and cries (still to the horses),

" Pill! "

No effect. On the contrary, the coach begins to roll back upon No. 2, which rolls back upon No. 3, which rolls back upon No. 4, and so on, until No. 7 is heard to curse and swear, nearly a quarter of a mile behind.

BLACK DRIVER (louder than before). " Pill! "

Horses make another struggle to get up the bank, and again the coach rolls backward.

BLACK DRIVER (louder than before). " Pe-e-e-ill! "

Horses make a desperate struggle.

BLACK DRIVER (recovering spirits). " Hi, Jiddy, Jiddy, Pill! "

Horses make another effort.

BLACK DRIVER (with great vigour). " Ally Loo! Hi. Jiddy, Jiddy. Pill. Ally Loo!"

Horses almost do it.

BLACK DRIVER (with his eyes starting out of his head). " Lee, den. Lee, dere. Hi. Jiddy, Jiddy, Pill. Ally Loo. Lee-e-e-e-e! " They run up the bank, and go down again on the other side at a fearful pace. It is

Montpelier, Virginia — 1818

HOUSE OF PRESIDENT MADISON IN ORANGE COUNTY

impossible to stop them, and at the bottom is a deep hollow, full of water. The coach rolls frightfully. The insides scream. The mud and water fly about us. The black driver dances like a madman. Suddenly we are all right by some extraordinary means, and stop to breathe. A black friend of the black driver is sitting on a fence. The black driver recognises him by twirling his head round and round like a harlequin, rolling his eyes, shrugging his shoulders, and grinning from ear to ear. He stops short, turns to me, and says :

" We shall get you through sa, like a fiddle, and hope a please you when we get you through sa. Old 'ooman at home Sir : " chuckling very much.

" Outside gentlemen sa, he often remember old 'ooman at home sa, " grinning again.

"Aye, aye, we'll take care of the old woman. Don't be afraid".

The black driver grins again, but there is another hole, and beyond that another bank, close before us. So he stops short : cries (to the horses again) " Easy. Easy den. Ease. Steady. Hi. Jiddy. Pill. Ally. Loo," but never " Lee ! " until we are reduced to the very last extremity, and are in the midst of difficulties, extrication from which appears to be all but impossible. And so we do the ten miles or thereabouts in two hours and a half ; breaking no bones, though bruising a great many ; and in short getting through the distance, " like a fiddle ".[6]

Virginia, that outpost of southern hospitality, manners and customs, naturally appealed to the Baron de Montlezun who found in the Fredericksburg neighbourhood if not Paradise, at least conditions of life that appeared acceptable . . . to a cooper :

During the middle of the day, while the coach was stopped I walked for several miles, strolling alone through superb woodlands. The weather was wonderful, and I was delighted to find many plants and wild flowers that I had never seen before. I came to a pretty frame house belonging to a cooper, who was hard at work outside making flour-barrels.

Ten years before, he told me, he had purchased 1,000 acres of land covered with standing timber. He paid twelve pounds ten shillings an acre, but now that some of it had been cleared and brought into cultivation, the property was worth four times its original cost. Besides the land he owned two negresses and six negroes, two of whom worked on the farm.

In Virginia
1817

Here was man thoroughly satisfied with his lot; the house was charming, its woodwork painted pale grey. The cooper was his own architect, and he had made most of the furniture. While he was at his coopering, the negroes tilled the farm, his wife looked after the house and everything worked out beautifully in this corner of the wilderness that they had so courageously made their own. I mention these details to give some idea of the country. Some people may not be amused, others may like them; and there may be some who will find them useful. I am not out to write novels, but to describe the world as I find it. [3]

MONTICELLO, PRESIDENT JEFFERSON'S HOUSE - 1821

One of the most famous and revered European visitors in America during this period was General Lafayette who returned to the United States in 1824. He went down to Virginia by coach and was received by two ex-Presidents, Thomas Jefferson and James Madison. According to Charles-Ogé Barbaroux, Lafayette's companion and official historian on that memorable visit, it was a most moving occasion:

Th. Jefferson, J. Madison and the Marquis de Lafayette 1824

Before reaching Orange [about forty miles west of Fredericksburg], he was met by Mr. Madison, who was for many years the First Magistrate of the American Republic and had always been his friend. The County was *en fête*, the inhabitants being bent on showing their gratitude to these two patriarchs of the Revolution, both of whom in their different ways had rendered equal service to the United States. And how much *more* American, if that were possible, became the ovation when ex-President Jefferson joined the procession! He had himself conveyed beyond Charlotteville as far as Monticello, where he received the General. The two friends

embraced warmly, with tears in their eyes.   What storms had passed over
these three venerable heads since their first meeting, what glory had been
theirs since last they met!   Jefferson and Madison, twice raised up by the free
vote of a sovereign people to the highest office in the land; Lafayette, staunch
champion of French liberty through times of change; three great men who had
devoted their lives, in equal measure, to the defense of the same principles.

It was not national principles, however, nor means of transportation, but
local customs which had begun to absorb the attention of the later traveller, Charles
Dickens, by the time he eventually reached Richmond during the first half of 1842:

The next day, and the next, we rode and walked about the town, *Richmond*
which is delightfully situated on eight hills, overhanging James River; a *1842*
sparkling stream, studded here and there with bright islands, or brawling
over broken rocks.   Although it was yet but the middle of March, the
weather in this southern temperature was extremely warm; the peach
trees and magnolias were in full bloom; and the trees were green.   In a
low ground among hills, is a valley known as " Bloody Run ", from a
terrible conflict with the Indians which once occurred there.   It is a good
place for such a struggle, and, like every other spot I saw, associated with
any legend of that wild people now so rapidly fading from the earth, it
interested me very much.

The city is the seat of the local parliament of Virginia; and in its
shady legislative halls, some orators were drowsily holding forth to the
hot noon day.   By dint of constant repetition, however, these constitutional sights had very little more interest for me than so many parochial
vestries; and I was glad to exchange this one for a lounge in a well-arranged
public library of some ten thousand volumes, and a visit to a tobacco

RICHMOND, VIRGINIA, FROM ACROSS THE JAMES RIVER - 1804

manufactory, where the workmen were all slaves. I saw in this place the whole process of picking, rolling, pressing, drying, packing in casks, and branding. All the tobacco thus dealt with, was in course of manufacture for chewing; and one would have supposed there was enough in that one store-house to have filled even the comprehensive jaws of America. In this form, the weed looks like the oilcake on which we fatten cattle; and even without reference to its consequences, is sufficiently uninviting.

Many of the workmen appeared to be strong men, and it is hardly necessary to add that they were all labouring quietly, then. After two o'clock in the day, they are allowed to sing, a certain number at a time. The hour striking while I was there, some twenty sang a hymn in parts, and sang it by no means ill; pursuing their work meanwhile. A bell rang as I was about to leave, and they all poured forth into a building on the opposite side of the street to dinner. [6]

Francis de Castelnau who had crossed the States of the Union from Florida to Lake Michigan passed through the same town some years earlier, in 1840. The visit made him reconsider some of the prejudices and generalisations on slavery that he had brought with him from France:

Slavery 1840

When I first arrived from Europe, my head filled with ideas concerning universal liberty, and saw slaves for the first time, I could not look upon them without pity and a sense of sadness at their lot. Soon however I saw slaves who were gay and to all appearance happy. Bewildered, I wrote in my diary: *a slave can laugh*. One day in Richmond I heard that a slave-auction was to be held. For a while I was undecided; curiosity urged me to go, while my principles held me back. I felt that by attending the sale I should in some way be sanctioning a human sacrifice. However, I had come to study American customs, so I decided to attend. I said to myself, I am about to behold a slave-market, a sale of miserable naked captives. What scenes of horror will shortly meet my gaze; my ear is attuned already to a mother's screams as her child is snatched away. Wives will be torn from their husbands writhing in anguish and despair; and all, all, regardless of their tears, will be sold—sold away for ever, they and their children too!

The slave-market was an auctioneer's shop. In the midst of the throng stood some well-dressed Negroes, chatting and laughing. What brutes, I thought, to laugh, when their fellows are suffering so cruelly! But I waited in vain for slaves, or rather, I learned that the only slaves were those whom I had been blaming for their lack of sympathy! One

Richmond, Virginia — 1796

SHOWING THOMAS JEFFERSON'S NEW STATE CAPITAL

man only was weeping. He at least understood his position; I enquired the reason for his tears. " Massa ", he said, " I only fetched 600 dollars, and James, who ain't so strong as me fetched 700; I'm disgraced. " I felt greatly relieved. Since that day I have seen thousands of slaves sold, but never again have I felt any philanthropic qualms. [14]

Wherever the European traveller went in those days surprise was waiting around the corner. Whilst travelling from Virginia to see the caves at Mammoth, Kentucky, Achille Poussielgue, a young diplomat attached to the French Embassy, admired that marvel of nature which is the famous Natural Bridge, but he was even more astonished at what he saw one evening in a forest in the country:

One evening we emerged from the forest into a space only recently cleared. In the middle stood a huge rustic shed built of logs, and around it, to our astonishment, about a hundred mountain ponies tethered to a ring of posts. From the shed came a murmur of voices.

Beautiful Virginia 1859

It proved to be a co-operative school. Children from six to twelve years of age were seated on benches, and one by one they went up to recite their lessons to a benign-looking master sitting at a table. It was delightful to see these bright young faces in the midst of the wilderness. The lesson was nearly over, and the children were collecting their certificates of attendance. Having obtained his certificate each child would rush out of school, leap upon his steed waving and cheering as he set off for home.

When the children had gone, the master accompanied us to Christiansburg, the village where he lived, and where we were spending the night. He was a most admirable person, the best type of Schoolmaster. On the way he explained that as it was not practical for him to visit each isolated homestead and give private lessons, this shed had been constructed in a central location, and he went there twice weekly to teach writing, reading, arithmetic and history. Children came from fifteen miles around and he told us that they were very seldom late. Primary education in America is very sound; its aim, above all is to produce thinking citizens capable of taking an interest in public affairs. Children are taught to recite the Constitution, and encouraged to study the lives of their eminent compatriots. Accustomed to fending for themselves with horse and gun, inured to long lone rides and to looking after the animals at night, the children accept responsibility at an early age. It would be almost impossible to find a man—or indeed a woman—unable to read, write and figure. There is not a hut, however poor, in which you will not find some books and a political newspaper. [15]

From Richmond, Virginia, to Charleston, South Carolina, the following were the stages of the journeys by train that the Englishman, William Ferguson, took in 1855 : 1) from Richmond to Petersburg, by the Richmond and Petersburg Railway, 22 miles ; 2) from Petersburg to Weldon, by the Petersburg Railway, 64 miles ; 3) from Weldon to Wilmington by the Weldon and Wilmington Railway, 162 miles ; 4) from Wilmington to Kingsville, by the Wilmington and Manchester Railway, 171 miles ; 5) from Kingsville to Charleston, by the South Carolina Railway, 105 miles. Listen to William Ferguson describing this journey :

SCHOOL ON A COUNTRY ROAD - 1820

*By Railway
1856*

The Cape Fear has to be crossed before we get to the Wilmington and Manchester Railway, by which we proceed south. The steamer plies in connection with the railways, and we get tickets to Charleston on board, as well as our traps re-checked.

From the deck of the steamer, we had observed that the east shore of Cape Fear River, on which Wilmington stands, is very low, little if at all raised above the level of the water ; and we now find ourselves on the opposite bank, proceeding through a swamp covered with, to us, a strange jungle of trees, shrubs, and creepers. The railway here, as through many other swamps in its course, is built of frame-work piles. Emerging from the swamp, we cross some rice-fields. These are next thing to a swamp — low flat fields, muddy and wet, close by a riverside, so as to be capable of easy irrigation. Beyond this, we enter the forest, tall pines on each side, with an under-growth of myrtles and bay. I get out upon the end platform of the last carriage, and it is a singular scene which I see. The surface of the country for miles on miles is so flat, that there is neither embankment nor cutting. There is drawn out behind, a long vista, miles long, straigth as an arrow-flight shut in by walls of pines—on and on the train hurries, shortening the great iron line before, and lengthening the great iron line behind—with nothing for

RICE-FIELDS IN SOUTH CAROLINA - 1828

hours together to break the uniformity of the scene. But now the character of the trees is changing. Water-oaks and cedars take the place of pines; and instead of rolling along the solid earth, we find the rails are supported amidst a universal flood on strong piles—we are in the middle of a swamp. The tall, slender, white-barked stems of the cedars spring from a peculiar broad expansion of the root, which seems adapted to give them a fixed hold of the muddy soil. The water is in motion, circling among the trees and eddying round the railway supports. At one point, the swamp opens out into a large sheet of water about a mile broad, and several miles long, and straight across it goes the rail—water on each side nearly as far as we can see, but bounded behind by the wall of wood, unbroken in its outline, save by the narrow gap which marked where we had got an exit from the forest. A few water-birds float on the surface of the lake, undisturbed by the passage of the railway train through their wild domain. But this incident is passed, and we are in the dreary woods again.

This alternation of swamp and forest is the character of the country passed through by this road, throughout nearly its whole extent.

Till we reached Great Pee-Dee River, ninety-five miles from Wilmington, there is very little cleared land near the road. Marion and Sumpterville are the only towns on the

BRIDGE ACROSS THE CONGAREE, SOUTH CAROLINA - 1828

whole line, and contain about five hundred inhabitants each. The population is very scattered. The station buildings are merely a wooden house, or a log cabin or two, sometimes only a depot for turpentine.

The bridge over the Great Pee-Dee River is well worthy of attention. I knew its construction before leaving England, and was on the look-out for it. The Pee-Dee River is not very broad, but it runs through a swamp, and its own bed is sand. It was found impossible to pile it in the ordinary way, and this has been accomplished by sinking great cast-iron cylinders to a depth of eighty feet through the sand and gravel. Each cylinder having been brought to its place in the bed of the river, a receiver was screwed on its uppermost end, and the air extracted by an air-pump. The consequence of this was, that the sand and water rose from below, and the cylinders sank correspondingly by their own weight, as the opposing sand was withdrawn. Compartment after compartment was added to the cylinders, and they were sunk till sufficient stability was gained. Two piers were formed in this way in the bed of the river, supporting the usual form of an unfilled-up tubular bridge of wood. It vibrated as the train passed slowly, but the structure is said to be very sufficient, and it is a beautiful piece of work.

As we were passing along a low embankment in the midst of a jungle forest, all at once the whistle gave vent to a series of the shrillest and most unearthly sounds. Two low hoarse notes were growled out, and then a loud shrill one; and this was repeated several times, to the great astonishment and perhaps fright of some of the passengers, till the object of it was made manifest by seeing some poor cows, which had strayed upon the rail, sprawling, in the highest intensity of fear, among the tangled bushed and fallen trees of the brake. The more they struggled, the worse they entangled themselves. How they got out, we did not wait to see; the whistle had frightened them off the rail, and that was all the engineer cared for.

Manchester, which gives its name to this railway, and finds a place on the map, consists of two wooden houses. The town *is not*, but *to be* built.

About five o'clock we reached Kingsville, the termination of this road. We had to wait nearly two hours here for a train on the Columbia branch of the South Carolina Railway — so we had plenty of time for tea and to look about. At last the train came up. It was a luggage-train and had one passenger-car attached. By dint of the extremest packing, the passengers all got in; but it was a horrible ride. The car was lower in the roof than usual, and narrower, and the seats were too small and too close together to sleep comfortably. After travelling so far, the feeling of fatigue and pain in our bones became almost intolerable. Add to all, there was a wood-fire in the stove, which filled the air with irritating dryness; and as most of the male

Natural Bridge in Virginia — *1835*

SEEN FROM THE BANKS OF CEDAR CREEK

passengers were chewing tobacco, and spitting out oceans of the acrid juice on every side, there were many elements of discomfort.   All this weary distance which had to be traversed in these far from happy circumstances was one hundred and five miles, and was got over at the frustrating rate of but little more than ten miles an hour! [10]

In fifty years the town of Charleston had changed very little if one can judge by the descriptions of two Frenchmen who had visited it, the first, François-André Michaux in 1804, the second, Jean-Jacques Ampère, fifty years later.   An atmosphere very characteristic of the southern countries emanates from these two descriptions : a feeling of live and let live in a mild climate.   Listen to Michaux :

The streets in Charleston are wide but they are not paved, and every time you step off the brick side-walk your foot sinks into sand.   There are more carts and carriages here, in proportion, than in any other American city; as they bowl past, they grind this sand up so finely that the slightest breeze blows it into the stores and makes it very unpleasant for persons on foot.   The streets have pumps at intervals to supply drinking-water, but the latter is so brackish that it is a wonder that strangers ever accustom themselves to it.   Seven tenths of the city is built of wood, the rest is brick.   The last census, made in 1805, showed a population of 10,690 whites and 9,050 slaves. [11]

Charleston 1804

And now listen to Jean-Jacques Ampère, fifty years later :

Charleston stands between two rivers, like New York, but it spreads out laterally instead of coming to a point.   There is some shipping, but the town lacks the liveliness of New York.   The world of Commerce lies behind us in the North and we are unlikely to find such commercial activity again except possibly at New Orleans.   Charleston is a quiet place.   There are trees in the streets and we were surprised to find gardens again.   There are not many gardens in Boston, New York and Philadelphia ; land is too valuable and the speculators too active.   Here you see magnolias growing as well as pomegranates and the azedarach, or Pride of India. Most of the houses have verandahs and many have a tall portico.   The climate dictates the architecture, and clearly affects the life of the people.   Nowhere else have I seen so many stone houses.   During a long walk beside one of Charleston's two rivers, I found something that is lacking in most American cities —tranquillity and silence.   On the other side clumps of trees gave an illusion of woodland.   In Boston, New York or Philadelphia they would have been cut down long ago. The people seem more leisured, less anxious to tear down and rebuild. I enjoy the southern calm of the city and its people. But of course this is only relative; Charleston is the centre of much commercial activity. Of the two million or so bales of cotton exported from the United States, 400,000 are shipped from this town, 800,000 or 900,000 from New Orleans, and the rest from Savannah and Mobile. Of this total almost one million five hundred thousand go to England. [7]

The waspish Baron de Montlezun felt more at home in Charleston than in Philadelphia. He was able to comment romantically about the beauty of the young women. The social life was more like that of France under the Old Regime; no titles, perhaps, but a nice grading by birth and fortune. Everyone was strongly republican, of course, but all the same. . . :

CHARLESTON, SOUTH CAROLINA, LOOKING ACROSS COOPERS RIVER · 1837

Pretty American Girls 1817

In Charleston, as everywhere, beautiful women are rare although one sees some quite pretty young persons. Once past the age of twenty they fade with astonishing rapidity, like northern blossoms transplanted into tropic heat. They seem more graceful than their northern neighbours because their feet are smaller. Strangely enough, although there is nothing in the climate to encourage *embonpoint*, these good ladies are in such terror of growing fat that they have adopted the delightful habit of regaling themselves with chalk and vinegar.

Otherwise they are well-behaved and virtuous, and fully cognisant at all times and ages, even in the fire of youth, of a proper wifely submission to their husbands, to whom they are invariably faithful. A lady's sole pleasure in life, or at least her foremost concern, is to please her husband, and to submit to no will save his.

They all dress smartly and well, without going to the extremes; fashion here is a mixture of the styles of London and Paris, with a marked preference for the latter.

SOUTH CAROLINA MILITIA - 1849-1859

Those whom, despite the Republic, I shall designate " gentlemen ", have a frank, natural air about them, instead of the morose expressions to be found in the North. Their manners have greatly improved. They are always performing acts of disinterested kindness. In the country they are hospitable; sociable and civil in town. They are almost the only Americans to whom laughter comes naturally. I think, too, that they will improve as time goes on.[3]

These were the days before the bombardment of Fort Sumter, when slaves were to be seen in the streets of Charleston. Naturally, travellers' reactions varied all the way from indifference to violent disapproval. As a young French actor on tour, Léon Beauvallet saw the laughing picturesque side, which, as an image of the American negro, has persisted in theatrical and literary productions to this day:

Slavery at Charleston 1855

We are right in the heart of the slave country. You cannot move without treading on a Negro. They are quite well-mannered, here, the blacks. . . . When Sooty meet nice white man he say " Good day ". Nice

CHARLESTON FROM THE SEA - 1817

white man think strange Sooty know him and nearly stop to talk. That make big scandal, believe me!

But they do not look at all badly off. Negroes are happier here than in New York, where they are as free as they would be in a zoo.

They laugh all the time. As for the women, so long as they have a foul old pipe in their mouths that's all they care about

They smoke from morning to night, it's their tic, their hobby; the bee, so to speak, in their bonnets. And do they look hideous with those ugly great things in their mouths!

One nice thing down here is the temperature. Real summer weather. Wherever you look, there are roses, and orange trees covered with fruit. It's delicious! [8]

Jean-Jacques Ampère was in Charleston at about the same time:

SLAVE-DRIVER   I have just witnessed a hideous   BACKWOODSMAN
scene. All arguments against immediate
Abolition have fled from my mind. In broad daylight in the main square at Charleston, I watched the sale by auction of a Negro family. They were brought on a tumbril, as though going to their execution. Close by flew a red flag, the emblem of slavery and crime. The Negroes appeared as indifferent as the spectators. The auctioneer—who, I am told, is not ostracised by society—was playfully extolling the merits of a Negro: "Very intelligent and a first-rate gardener". Buyers pressed forward to examine men, women and children, opening their mouths to look at their teeth.

"Going, going, gone!" They were knocked down to the highest bidder. Ten yards away, a donkey was auctioned off in exactly the same manner. A horse, too. The man fetched sixty-nine dollars; the horse, seventy-one. [7]

At roughly the same time as Dickens and Beauvallet, William Ferguson was also travelling in the vicinity of Charleston, and not without irony describing in his note-book the Cooper River plantations of rice and cotton:

Rice and Cotton Plantations 1856

The Cooper River is a broad winding creek running northwards into the interior, and at a distance sufficiently far up to be beyond the influence of the salt-water; it is bordered by rice plantations. On some of these, cotton is also grown. The windings of the river nearly double the direct distance. It flows through swamps, into which the elevated ground or bluffs project like capes into the sea. . . .

Each plantation has a little pier or jetty—" landing " in the local term. It was the first day of the Easter holidays, and the boat was crowded with families going up to spend April at their plantations. We stopped at every landing, and put ashore whites, blacks, beds, pots, pans, carriages, horses, etc.

The peculiarity of the distribution of their time here prevents the planters from attempting to have their places in the country surrounded by fine pleasure-grounds. They can only reside on the plantations in winter, when everything is bare. In summer, by the 1st of May, swamp-fever drives them away, and they cannot return with impunity till the first black frost sets in. Frost is called black when it produces ice, and a single night of this effectually destroys the fever.

Many of the planters' houses are extremely picturesque. The finest of all is said to be Mepkin. It is the highest bluff on the river, and it is varied with oak-wooded dells and water. We landed at one of the wooden jetties, on a shelf of rock not much above the level of the water. Beyond this, the bluff rises in a cliff of chalk-marl sixteen or seventeen feet vertically. It then slopes gently up till it is probably sixty or seventy feet above the water, receding in table-land. This bank is wooded chiefly with large well-grown live-oaks and other evergreen trees. A little dell, through which a streamlet finds its way to the river, runs from the landing back into the bluff, widening and ascending till it shades off into the table-land. On its left stands the house, fronted by a lawn of some extent, sloping

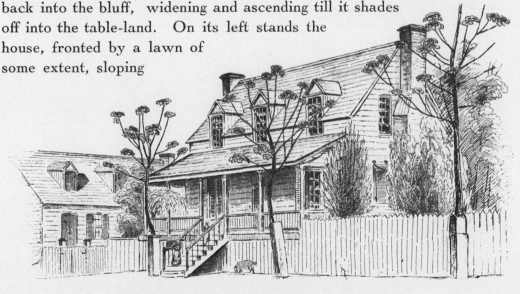

HOUSES IN VILLAGE OF RICEBOROUGH, GEORGIA - 1828

ARCHED BRIDGE OVER THE SAVANNAH RIVER AT AUGUSTA, GEORGIA. - 1842

gently towards the dell, the water in which, collected into a little lake, can just be seen from the windows. Some very magnificent oaks grow on the lawn—huge fellows, which it takes six men to span with outstretched arms. They are " live oaks ", so called because the leaves continue upon the trees, and remain green all winter. They are felling now to give place to fresh ones. The trunks are not lofty, fifteen or twenty feet, at which height they branch. The limbs spread out and the branches bend down, forming a tree of great beauty of outline. They were hung with the mournful-looking tillandsia. . . .

We then got on horseback, and rode round the plantation for about an hour. It had been very cold on the river, but in the woods, it was most

GEORGIA SWAMP PLANTATION ON THE RIGHT BANK OF THE ALATAMAHA RIVER - 1829

pleasant. The sun was shining out, the air was fresh and balmy, and full of the fragrance of the yellow jessamine. Everything was new and interesting. All conspired to make the hour one of great pleasure. We cantered along a fine open avenue, and then turning abruptly off by a bridle-path through the wood, came to a cleared field, in which some negroes were at work, preparing it for corn. The soil is sandy, and so friable that it is easily worked. The instrument used is a hoe. It is large, perhaps about eight inches square, and has a long handle. With this the soil is raked up into ridges, and the corn is planted on the ridges. It is the custom to keep on planting corn, year after year, in the same field; and it shows how rich the soil is, that it continues to produce good crops for years in succession. . . .

We had been rising gradually as we rode along, and now we halted our horses amid fine old pines which crest the cliff, and overhang the river. It is the picturesque site of the plantation graveyard. A small brick enclosure contains the tombs of the whites, with marble memorial-stones. Outside, among pines, lie the blacks—a wooden cross, or board with a diamond-shaped head, marking their resting-place. It was a chapter on the separation of the races. It reaches hither, but no further. Beyond this, all are equal. [10]

We leave Charleston by sea, this time with Achille Poussielgue, on the staff of the French Embassy in Washington, whose main interests in life are hunting, fishing and adventure. He chartered a small schooner to sail down the coast of Florida. Hardly a mile off the Hazard Lighthouse, by the mouth of the St. John River, he descried, through his telescope, a girl waving frantically from the tower. She had a white flag and was signalling. He lowered a boat; what else was a Frenchman to do?

As we came near I marvelled how stone foundations could be laid on those shifting sands. The little island is awash at high tide and the waves beat against the tower; at low tide some steps are uncovered.

WOODEN COVERED BRIDGE OVER THE CHATTAHOUTCHIE AT COLUMBUS, GEORGIA. - 1842

We beached the dinghy and leaped ashore. The steps were so slippery with seaweed that we could hardly stand. We reached the light-house itself and found it polished so smooth by the waves that there was hardly foothold for a lizard. As we stood wondering why we had been summoned only to be kept waiting thus, a rope ladder was lowered from the gallery and a girl's voice called " Make it fast to the stanchions in the stonework and climb up : we need your help ! "

I led the way, and I confess I was glad to reach the balustrade after a sixty-foot climb up that swaying rope ladder. I reached the top and there was nobody there !

JACKSONVILLE, FLORIDA, AND HARBOUR - 1851

Toby [Poussielgue's mulatto servant] had never seen a revolving light before, so I left him to admire it while I went down a spiral staircase that evidently led to the lightkeeper's quarters. After descending one storey I found a door marked " 1 ". I knocked impatiently. No answer. I knocked louder. Still no reply. I redoubled my knocking; there was a light footstep behind me and a charming voice, with a hint of mockery in it, said " I am sorry if I have kept you waiting, sir; you seem a trifle impa-tient." I turned and found myself face to face with the most elegant creature. She made me a low curtsey. Her *toilette* was impeccable: a white dress with cherry-coloured bows, and a wide crinoline; her slender

LIGHTHOUSE ON THE FLORIDA COAST - 1840

hands wore mittens and her magnificent golden hair was adorned with black lace. Altogether a somewhat surprising apparition to find in a lonely lighthouse off the Florida coast. For the moment I could find nothing to say. Later she recounted her story.

Miss Fanny Brandt was the daughter of a master-at-arms in the United States Navy. Her mother died while she was very young and Fanny was brought up in the family of a Presbyterian minister. She received a very good education with a view to becoming a teacher. When Brandt left the service to work in the Navy Yard at Norfolk, Virginia, she went there to visit him and became involved in an affair of the heart—which caused a great stir in a community composed almost exclusively of Naval officers and dockyard employees. Her father did not take kindly to this blot on the family name. With the help of an old shipmate, now Captain of a Coast-guard cutter operating off Florida he spirited his daughter away one dark night from the house where she had taken romantic refuge and carried her, bound and gagged, aboard the cutter, which then deposited them both upon the lonely lighthouse, of which he had had himself appointed keeper.

It may be imagined what life was like for a fashionable young woman out there, with no one for company save her bigoted old seadog papa and his black slave, Peter, the only servant he had brought with him. For the first month Miss Fanny did nothing but weep and seek some means of communicating with the man for whom she had compromised herself—an

OLD SPANISH RAMPART, FLORIDA - 1838

officer of high rank in the Navy. She spent days on the gallery of the lighthouse hungrily watching sails pass on the horizon; but no vessel ever came close to the lighthouse, save the steamboat from Jacksonville to Savannah which called every month, anchoring a mile off the island for the purpose of collecting mail and delivering fresh water and provisions.

Brandt and the Negro possessed a small boat, in which it might have been possible to reach the shore, but when this was not being used for fishing, or collecting supplies from the hamlet of Hazard, five miles away on the mainland, they hoisted it forty feet high against the tower, out of reach of the waves. Even worse, the iron outside staircase leading from the upstairs windows to the ground had been dismantled at Brandt's orders; the old sailor did not trust his daughter. The two men used to descend by means of a knotted rope, and climb back up a rope ladder fixed to the balustrade. They were always careful to untie the lower end and the girl dared not venture upon it.

Miss Fanny possessed her soul in patience, knowing that a lightkeeper's tour of duty lasted only six months. During the other six months of the year keepers were relieved and given a watchman's job in the dockyard. Her father's people hailed from the Key West direction and no doubt he would head there in due course. She resigned herself therefore, put on a cheerful face to her father, and assisted the Negro with the cooking and household chores. She also established a " roof garden " on the

CALVARY CHURCH, SAINT AUGUSTINE - 1851

terrace, where she grew pineapples, strawberries, peas and salad vegetables in earth-filled baskets and planted potatoes and runner-beans around
the balcony. Her sweetness earned the devotion of Peter, the negro, who

brought her presents of birds
and flowers when he went
ashore. Thus passed the first
six months of her exile.

However, Fanny's father
never spoke of leaving, and
the cutter which had brought
them never reappeared on the
horizon. One day while he
was asleep she came across a
letter that had arrived on the
previous day's steamer from
Jacksonville. It bore the letter-
head of the Lighthouse Service
at Key West: old Brandt had
requested permission to perform his duties unaided. The
request was granted. Head-
quarters complimented him
upon his zeal, and announced

CASA DE LA MERCED, SAINT AUGUSTINE - 1851

that, as he would be doing double duty, his pay would be increased, and
that each month spent on the lighthouse in this way would count as two
for purposes of pension.

Fanny, greatly daring, taxed her father with this, and there was a
terrible scene. Brandt declared his intention of remaining until his retire-
ment in twelve year's time. He would give her back her liberty, and she
would be free to seek the man who had made her so many fine promises.
Her feelings may be imagined: only twenty, with someone who loved her,
and to be cooped up for twelve years with a rough old salt and a stupid
Negro! A dozen times she was tempted to throw herself from the gallery
into the sea; but there was something of her father's obstinacy in the poor
girl's character and she refused to give up.

A year passed. Brandt began to suffer from rheumatism in his joints,
the attacks becoming so severe that he was forced to take to his bed.

Fanny nursed him devotedly, hoping all the time that he would apply for a transfer; but the old sailor made no move. There being no alternative, the girl was taught to signal and to look after the light, so that she could take charge while Peter was fishing or fetching supplies. She could of course have escaped by conniving with the Negro, who would have liked nothing better; but she could not bring herself to abandon her father while he was ill, and the Negro, she knew, would never dare return after assisting an escape, for Brandt was quite capable of finding enough strength to blow the slave's brains out as a reward for his compliance. One day she wrote some letters and gave them to Peter to mail on the mainland, where there was a Post Office. One was to the Lighthouse Service, describing her father's state of health, the other to the man she loved, imploring rescue. But Peter never came back; he had turned runaway.

Father and daughter remained there alone; Brandt bed-ridden, the girl without a boat at her disposal.

Two long months went by. Four times the steamer passed within sight of the lighthouse; on two other occasions it hove to waiting for the dinghy, but each time, seeing nobody come, it steamed off at full speed, despite the girl's frenzied entreaties. On the lighthouse all the supplies were running short. There was no more water, only beer remained to quench the girl's thirst and that of the invalid. Soon that too would be gone. Miss Fanny boiled up some Spanish wine mixed with mallow and other medicinal herbs. This was the moment when our schooner appeared and dropped anchor.

GENERAL VIEW OF KEY WEST - 1842

I was greatly touched by the poor girl's story, and by the sad fate of the old lightkeeper, whom I found dying in his miserable bunk with no medicines and no proper medical care. I promised the girl that I would rescue her; but to do her justice, when I proposed taking her to Jacksonville and leaving my two servants to man the lighthouse and care for her father, she stoutly refused to leave. After putting ashore stocks of water, wine, medicines and food, together with my mulatto, Toby, I personally took charge of letters from Miss Fanny, promising to inform the sheriff at Jacksonville of her plight. She clasped my hand and thanked me in the warmest terms. My heart was heavy as I took my leave. Had I dared, I would have sent Constant for help and stayed with her in the lighthouse.

As I write this we have weighed anchor and are standing towards the shore. I have taken a last look at the lighthouse as its top disappears below the horizon. A sad, sad tale indeed. . . . [15]

Two days later Achille Poussielgue went on board the steamer in Savannah, Georgia, and told the captain about Fanny Brandt and her father, and the mulatto Toby. The captain promised to call at the Hazard Lighthouse and take the three personages off, which was done. During the crossing Fanny's father died and was buried at sea. When Poussielgue questioned Toby on the lot of the unfortunate Fanny, Toby merely looked at his master and grinned. And Poussielgue came to this sad conclusion:

I think my heroine was nothing but an adventuress and her father was right to shut her up in a lighthouse.

THE KEY WEST ARSENAL · 1842

The little schooner called in at Saint Augustine, America's oldest city, founded by the Spaniards in 1565. In 1851 it was still Spanish in feeling, lazy and sub-tropical, with a population of 2,000 devoted to the siesta and to the care of visiting invalids :

Saint Augustine
1852

We followed the main street, called, I think, the Calle de la Merced. The houses had only one storey and a single doorway with wrought-iron gate giving on to the street; but in compensation they had a wealth of pinnacles, turrets, colonnades and carved balconies.

It was Sunday, and people were going to Mass, dressed up in their best clothes. They presented an astonishing mixture of types, ranging over the whole gamut of civilisation. Negroes clad only in a pair of tight drawers, trappers, both white and Indian, in mocassins, wolf-skin leggings, and greasy, blood-stained buckskin shirts jostled with planters in white duck and gentlemen from the North in their everlasting black suits. Kerchiefed negresses decked with jewelry, in gorgeously coloured shawls, stalked down the street, their feet and legs bare, and not a petticoat amongst them. The Mulatto women and squaws, their hips swathed in cotton-print *naguas*, their upper garment a camisole with two holes for their bare arms, contrasted with golden haired damsels in Parisian gowns, and proud dark-eyed *señoras* wearing mantilla and yellow-and-white striped *reboso*. The children too presented contrasts : little Negroes and half-caste waifs rolling in the streets, wearing nothing but a straw hat and a lighted cigar, while the sons of non-conformist ministers passed disdainfully in their black suits like regular little men. Wild parrots swooped in and out amongst the waving palm-trees. In the harbour, Indians selling fruit and vegetables from dug-out canoes paddled between the steamboats for all the world like the natives of Hispaniola who greeted Christopher Columbus.

While Eastern Florida slumbers, awaiting Anglo-Saxon initiative from the North, Saint Augustine lives happily on the proceeds of its fruit, and on the money brought in by the great many valetudinarians who thrive in this wonderful climate. [15]

The French theatrical troop, managed by Rachel's brother Félix, put in at Key West, Florida, and tried a little unofficial snake-charming, inspired by the scene in Racine's *Phèdre* where Théramène recounts how young Hippolyte has been devoured by a serpent. Léon Beauvallet :

Key West
1855

The beach here is very damp. It is also covered in sponges, seaweed, live shell-fish and even livelier snakes than we have ever come across before.

As proof of its liveliness one of the latter, bent on upsetting poor Félix's apple-cart, rushed at several members of the company with intent to devour. It felt like having actor for lunch, I suppose.   A greedy reptile.

Old Randoux rose to the occasion with utmost *sang froid*; and in tones that put the ocean itself to shame launched into Théramène's great speech.° And before he was halfway through, the serpent was fast asleep.   From the effect that this piece of literature had upon him it was obvious that the reptile was a genuine U.S. citizen! We meanly took advantage of his slumbers and beat him with our sticks, so that "when he woke up he was dead."[8]

All goods leaving Alabama by sea—mainly cotton—sailed from Mobile.   Jean-Jacques Ampère sailed down the Alabama bound for Mobile and describes the scene :

On the Alabama River 1852

We called at all the landings to pick up bales of cotton from the plantations.   These bales are slid aboard down planks and are then piled one upon the other as masons pile stones when building a wall.   As the wall of cotton rose around our decks I realised why people in New Orleans built ramparts of cotton as defense against British round-shot in the recent war. Sometimes the bales are toppled over the river-bank so that they roll and bounce right to the water's edge.   This proceeding has elements of drama. Some roll down without effort, some halt half-way and have to be restarted ; others describe the most unexpected zigzags, eluding all efforts to catch them and prevent their falling into the water.   This can be difficult and quite risky, for it is best to keep out of their way.   One Negro was especially skilful—far better than the whites working with him.

Occasionally loading takes place at night, by the light of resin torches, but they prefer to load lumber, which is taken aboard at an amazing rate. While this is going on Negroes illumine the scene by means of long poles with glowing braziers at the end.   I was reminded of Egypt, where the Arabs call this kind of torch a *machallah*, for I saw the same flicker of torch-light on black faces beside the Nile as I now beheld on the banks of the Alabama.   It is strange to find such manifestations of industry and commerce upon river-banks which as yet have not even a clearing.   Such is the poetry of modern America.   Gone are the great uncharted wastes that beckoned us twenty years ago : the prosaic Civilisation of twenty years hence is not yet in sight.   This is the half-way stage, enlivening the imagination with memories of life in the wild, and musings upon the orderly times to come.   As I sat on deck, watching the rays of the setting sun reflected on the water and gilding the river-bank itself, it seemed to me that the colours here were already softer than those of the North, although no less brilliant. There was no sound save that of our paddle-wheels and the throbbing of the engines; their stertorous panting echoed across the universal stillness, as though to fill the vast unpeopled Prairies far away. [7]

From Mobile to New Orleans the quickest route was overland; but the sea voyage was much more rewarding—especially for specialists like Elisée Reclus, the great French geographer who visited New Orleans in 1855:

The Mouth of the Mississippi 1855

Suddenly it seemed to me that the colour of the water had changed. This was indeed so. Instead of dark blue it was now yellow, and I could see the line of demarcation running from East to West, crisp and sharp as though drawn with a measuring line. Northwards, a darkish misty smudge heralded the approach of land : we had entered the waters of the Mississipi. Before long our pace slackened and our vessel seemed to be making slow headway. Soon it stopped altogether : our hull had entered the mud. This was the end of the journey; we could do nothing but patiently wait. All night long the ship rocked gently on its bed of noisome ooze, but it was not for me to complain. This mud was what I had travelled two thousand miles to see. . . .

Just before dawn the captain had an idea. He dispatched a pinnace into the estuary to pick up a pilot. The little boat was soon lost in the early morning mist and the sound of its oars grew fainter and fainter until it vanished altogether in a northerly direction. We searched and listened in vain, but the fog had swallowed her up; then, of a sudden she appeared again, suspended, to all appearance, above a curtain of cloud. Having passed through the first thick patch of mist creeping over the sea, which reduced our horizon to a couple of cables' lengths, she emerged into clear dry air, and thus appeared to us beyond the fog, apparently sailing in the sky. These alternate patches of clear air and fog are not uncommon at the mouth of the Mississipi, where currents of salt water and fresh come together, each at different temperatures.

At long last a black dot emerged from the mouth of the Mississipi and was seen to be heading our way; it was a tug coming to take us in tow. She grew larger and I was able to study her closely. I had never before seen an American steamer, and I confess that I was enchanted by her crisp lines, her speed and her businesslike air; she seemed the embodiment of Youth

Mobile, Alabama — 1841

THE WATER-FRONT AND SHIPPING FROM THE MARSH OPPOSITE THE CITY

but in some way heroic, as though dwelling in realms superior to mankind. She came on, listing slightly to one side, the mighty beams of her engines rising and falling through the deck like enormous arms, black smoke belching forth with every pulsation of her machinery. She was indeed a lovely craft—the very epitome of power. She executed a graceful pirouette, came alongside, picked up the cable that we threw her and made fast gunwale to gunwale without the slightest jar.

Almost before she touched a young man leaped down from her wheel-box on to our deck. He kept his hat on, mumbled something by way of greeting to our captain, seized the helm and began issuing orders to our flabbergasted crew. Thirty seconds later, with the tug's assistance, our ship was cleaving its way out of the mud bank. Your true American citizen wastes no time on ceremony. [16]

One tiny spot in the midst of the Mississipi delta caught the attention of the Englishman Basil Hall:

We turned round and went down the south-east Pass to the dreary abode of the Pilots, called the Balize—from the Spanish word Valiza, a beacon. The V in Spanish words, it may be remarked, is often, though improperly, confounded in pronunciation with B. From this wretched place—planted in the midst of a boundless swamp or morass—no firm land is in sight, or is within fifty or sixty miles of it. There are about twenty buildings in all, six of which are dwelling-houses. The intercourse between them is carried on exclusively along paths made of planks and trunks of trees laid over the slime and water. It is impossible, indeed, to walk more than ten yards in any direction, without sinking up to the neck in a mud-hole or a quicksand; so that for all the usual purposes of locomotion, the local inhabitants might just as well be at sea.

In the middle of this half-drowned village, there stands a rickety sort of look-out house, to the top of which we managed to climb with some difficulty. The extensive field of view which this commanded was flat and

In the Delta of the Mississippi 1827

PILOT-TOWN AT THE MOUTH OF THE MISSISSIPPI - 1828

dreary, beyond any imagination to conceive; but still it was not without variety and interest. We could discover several of the passes, and great numbers of bayous or natural canals, creeping amongst the marshes slowly to the sea, which occupied about one-third of the whole horizon in the south. On the east and west, the marshes extended as far as the eye could reach, bristling with roots, trunks, and branches of trees. [5]

As the American city most influenced by France, New Orleans was naturally a place many French travellers wanted to visit. In a long letter to the Paris magazine *L'Illustration*, 27 May, 1848, one of them, L. Xavier Eyma, who was employed in the French Admiralty, described his trip to New Orleans the previous year. Here are some extracts from his letter:

New Orleans 1848

To the Editor: Sir,

. . . After a crossing of two and a half days during which we covered forty-five leagues [about 112 miles] we entered one of the enormous lagoons which Nature so generously delves in mid stream. We as yet saw nothing of New Orleans, because the land in Louisiana is so low-lying that it is hidden, as it were, behind the water, and one does not see the country one is heading for until one runs into it. Scarcely were the masts of shipping in the harbour visible through a telescope before we descried that famous

HOUSE-BOATS AND SHIPPING ON THE MISSISSIPPI AT NEW ORLEANS - 1819

New Orleans landmark, the dome of the Saint Charles Hotel. We sailed on through the outskirts and then, suddenly, the whole city unrolled before us in that magnificent semicircle described by the Mississipi at this point.

I do not believe, Sir, that it is anywhere given to the human eye to contemplate a finer and more majestic spectacle than the harbour of New Orleans, situated on the left bank of the river. The great horseshoe around which the town is built surpasses in proportions anything that the mind

NEW ORLEANS MARKET FOLK - 1819

can conceive. The ships lying three, four, and five abreast at the quay-side form a barrier so dense that even the eye is denied entry, and a forest of masts and yards curves away until lost in the distance, sketching delicate patterns against the sky. One can as yet form no opinion of the city, for only odd corners are visible, glimpsed occasionally through the rigging, and beyond the great steamboats which have a basin to themselves. Tremendous noise and bustle reign throughout the huge harbour. Paddle-steamers pass continually, keeping the waters in perpetual tumult; there is a constant *va-et-vient* of tug-boats with sailing ships lashed to their flanks, while ferry-boats shuttle between New Orleans and Algiers, a little town on the other side.

In popular parlance New Orleans is often referred to as the Queen of the South. The name is well merited, aptly suggesting the beauty, grandeur and high importance of the city. The original town, which has always been the home of the French population is, numerically speaking, the first of the three wards comprising the city, although I must confess right away that in point of importance, wealth and external appearance she occupies second place. This part is popularly known as the Creole Quarter, which I regard as a compliment. The second ward dates from the annexation of Louisiana to the United States. The old French settlers hated the thought of allowing Anglo-Saxons across their threshold; so the said Anglo-Saxons built a new town of their own alongside, which is larger, richer and finer than the old, and bears the American stamp. The third district is quite recent. It is poorer and less important than the others, and barely completed as yet. But a great future lies in store for it, because one day New Orleans may well be the first city of the Union, and this ward, too, will be caught up and swept along on the winds of progress. The person responsible for the new quarter used to be one of the wealthiest men in America; and although he has suffered reverses of late this in no way prevents his standing extremely high in public esteem, for he is renowned for his probity and zeal in the service of his country. I am referring to Monsieur Bernard Marigny, whose name is an honoured one in Louisiana, where his family have been prominent in local affairs since the earliest days of the colony. It was at the Marigny home in Monsieur Bernard's father's time, that the young Duke of Orleans (now King of the French) found haven during his American visit. The King never forgot the truly French hospitality that he received on that occasion; and when M. Marigny later went to Paris, Louis-Philippe repaid his debt of gratitude by admitting him into the Royal Family circle, just as he himself had shared the home life of the Marignys.

Three or four streets in New Orleans are noted for their shops : these are St. Charles, Royale, De Chartres and part of Canal Street. Some of these stores could be picked up and set down again in the heart of Paris, where they would be by no means out of place.

There are two trades in New Orleans which never fail to strike the visitor : the slave trade and the trade in coffins, both of which are carried on quite openly, in broad daylight. There are shops selling both these commodities, which you go out and buy as you would a loaf of bread. One just has to accept it; certainly nobody here makes any objection. It is simply the custom; shop-keepers can sell what they like.

New Orleans has all the amusements to be expected in a large and wealthy city. Theatres, concert-halls and ball-rooms abound; nor are the arts neglected. Splendid masked balls are held, and are patronised by the highest Society. The attraction of these *soirées* can be appreciated only by those privileged to have encountered the witty, graceful and lovely ladies of New Orleans, some of whom are the most splendid creatures ever shaped by God's hand. To the charms of their person moreover are added greatness of heart and nobility of sentiment. Their generous feeling knows no bounds, and they are unselfishness itself.

Nowhere will you find such open warm-hearted generosity as at New Orleans. You are greeted with the most charming smiles. The menfolk are intelligent to talk to, and they could not be more hospitable and obliging. They invite you to meals and even have you to visit in their homes, where you are made the guest of honour. All those who have ever set foot in Louisiana will, I am sure, wish to join with me in paying this tribute to a fine and generous people.

Balize at the Mouth of the Mississippi — 1819

THE PILOT-STATION USED FOR NAVIGATION UNTIL 1870

Nor do the charms and delights of New Orleans herself complete the picture; the surroundings vie with the city herself, Saint Louis Bay, Pascagoula, Mandeville and all the lakeside resorts offering similar attractions throughout the summer season. The Louisianans do not mind how far they go provided there is a dance at the finish. For this reason they frequent the Carrolton pleasure-gardens some ten or fifteen miles out just for the pleasure of dancing. Lake Pontchartrain forms one of the most agreeable of these excursions. It may be reached in three ways. Two paved highways lead there, of which one, called America Drive, is positively swarming with carriages on certain days : sometimes I have counted almost one hundred at a time. The hotel to which it leads is very popular as an after-dinner rendez-vous. A pier runs out far into the lake, where people go to fish, and to dream, and to scan the horizon for shipping.

One can also get there by taking the train to one of the neat little lakeside resorts, much patronised for dinner by visitors from New Orleans. I was taken one day as guest of Mr. Musson, the charming President of the Gulf of Mexico Railroad, to Lake Borgne. The country-side through which it runs gave me the impression of being quite pristine, untouched by the intrusive tilth of civilisation. Its great forests bespeak that virginal quality extolled by M. de Chateaubriand, while lacking, however, some of the flowerier elements that his genius calls attention to. We passed mighty trees, of the most bizarre form and habit, including some whose roots writhe up from the ground and multiply, to become in their turn covered with leaves and branches. We passed through great groves of tall, flower-laden magnolias, so dense that the rays of the sun never lighten their gloom, and no human foot would dare to brave the solitude. A thicket of creepers guards these bosky dells, more intimately entwined than the fibres of a fabric.

But suddenly, wide grass-lands greet the eye, rolling endlessly to the horizon—the Prairies in whose existence I had never really believed when described by Fennimore Cooper. The Prairies of Louisiana are not comparable with those of the West, but they are astonishing none the less ; and I assure you, Sir, that the spectacle is grand indeed, a vast expanse of lofty herbage several miles in extent, stretching away into the unimaginable distance. Deer-stalker and his friends seem almost tangible, for Indian signs and relics are to be seen on every hand. I had no difficulty in re-creating in my mind's eye America as she was before the Paleface came. But the sound of our locomotive and the rapidity of its motion quickly recalled me to civilisation....[17]

Travellers were not interested only in scenery; they were intrigued by the American Way of Life, and by the ideas which played such a part in building the nation. Here is another French citizen, Elisée Reclus, writing from New Orleans:

HOUSE AT NEW ORLEANS - 1828

American Way of Life 1816

In Europe every stone has its history; churches are built on the site of dolmens, and people have repaired to the same spot to worship through the centuries, whether they be called Gauls, Franks or Frenchmen. We obey traditions rather than persons, and let ourselves be ruled more by the dead than by the living. In America there is nothing like this. They have no special veneration for the past or for the place of their birth, and the population is continually in motion, like the waters of a lake that are finding their own level. People are governed solely by economic laws. The young and growing republic has its ruins already, like those of the ancient world; modern life is too active and tempestuous for tradition to carry much weight. Simple old-fashioned patriotism no longer exists. The masses have little feeling for anything except their pecuniary interests, while the nobler citizen, who is as rare in America as elsewhere, entertains thoughts not of " country " but of " liberty ". [16]

Discoursing on another aspect of American liberty, Xavier Eyma, like many another European visitor, was astonished at the absence of policemen:

What strikes me in Louisiana, as in all the States, is the complete absence of police apart from the " watchmen ". The latter exist in great numbers and are perfectly organised. Their task is no light one, for they are concerned not only with tracing nocturnal marauders, but also with keeping a watch for fires. This conspicuous lack of policemen it must be admitted, has had the effect, especially in the southern and western States, of banishing law and order from men's minds, so that they are apt to take the law into their own hands. If a man is insulted or believes himself insulted, he will draw a knife or a pistol and deal with his assailant on the spot, before a hundred witnesses. Nobody dreams of arresting him, and the authorities are far too willing to accept the well-worn plea of self-defense. This type of murder has become more and more frequent since the Louisiana legislature imposed such heavy penalties for duelling. Louisianans are proverbially good shots, and it remains to be seen whether more young men of military age perish under the present law than did so under the duelling code. [17]

Hundreds of ships berthed at New Orleans every year, and the fire hazard was as great in the harbour as it was on shore. Elisée Reclus had not been long there before witnessing one such conflagration :

During one of my first nights in New Orleans there occurred one of those terrible disasters which are so frequent in the United States. Seven great steamships were on fire at the same time. It was a magnificent sight. The seven vessels, moored side by side, resembled so many separate and distinct furnaces afloat upon a sea of flames. Great whirlwinds of fire gushed skywards from their burning holds, white tongues of flame, licking back beneath the promenade decks, revealed the graceful lines of each

*Fire
in the Harbour
1855*

VIEW FROM TREMOLET'S HOTEL, NEW ORLEANS - 1819

floating palace for the last time, with all its crystal windows and ginger-bread work.   But one by one the individual decks were pierced by jets of flame, and soon each vessel with its three tiers of cabins was engulfed in a fiery whirlwind.   Towering above their ships, the tall black funnels stood out dark and sinister amid the eddying flames, while on high the flags at the mast-head could now and then be seen fluttering gaily as at a regatta.   One by one the decks fell in with a horrid crash, and the engines and boilers, bereft of their supports, toppled suddenly causing the whole fiery mass to rock.   Funnels and upper works collapsed one by one, sending showers of debris into the river, so that soon the entire Mississippi seemed on fire. All, all—the houses on the water-front, the surging crowds and merchandise on the quay-side, the great ships lying in harbour; even the town of Algiers, across the water—was bathed in a blood-red glow.   The sky looked inky black by contrast and the stars had disappeared.   The screams of victims in the burning vessels added to the horror.   Forty-two persons were burned alive before rescue operations could be organised.   It is common knowl-edge that from the appearance of the first steamboat on the Mississippi until the present day more than 40,000 people have been burned or drowned in accidents of one sort or another, through explosion, collision or fire; this is an average of one thousand victims a year. [16]

But New Orleans was famous for warmth of another sort.   The Baron de Montlezun went to the White Ladies' Ball in 1816.   Although he could not, of course, resist comparing the festivities with those of Versailles, he was nevertheless enchanted by the care-free gaiety of the people :

Yesterday I went to the White Ladies' Ball, which is so called to distinguish it from that of the coloured women.   It was held in a vast, long, beautiful ball-room, furnished with boxes.   Two hundred candles shed their soft light upon the scene, a pleasant change from the abominable glare of the lamps at present so fashionable in France.   The ball was graced by sixty young ladies, all dressed with elegant simplicity in white.   Nearly all wore white roses in their hair, to set off the plaits and curls and ringlets of their *coiffure*, while calling attention to the alabaster whiteness of their throats and those other roses in their cheeks.

Here, as in every warm climate, dancing is a ruling passion with the ladies, who retain their taste for it until an advanced age.   At the conclu-sion of a waltz the young mother will give her baby the breast, which the freedom of her ball-gown has already come near to setting at liberty. . . .

New Orleans, Louisiana — 1835

VIEW UP MISSISSIPPI TOWARDS ST. LOUIS CATHEDRAL

The ball, although drawn from all that was best in New Orleans society, was distinctly colonial and democratic in tone. A couple of men came to blows, or worse, in the entrance to the ball-room. The men all wore boots in defiance of etiquette, and carried canes stout enough to merit a far more rustic designation. Thick clouds of pipe-smoke contrasted very disagreeably with the delicious perfumes worn by the fair sex.

The band was miserable, of the worst description : a mere half-dozen itinerant musicians who ground out dirge-like renderings of ancient dances. Fortunately their want of spirit was in marked contrast with the enthusiasm of the ladies, so that six quadrilles and as many waltzes succeeded one another without a pause.

The ball opened at eight o'clock and continued until three in the morning. The ladies made no bones about going home on foot as their mothers and grand-mothers had done before them. [3]

Forty years after that dancing session, Henri Herz, the French musician whom we have already met, was brave enough to conduct a concert in New Orleans for sixteen pianists, or nearly sixteen, as it turned out to be. Giving an account of it he wrote :

The piece for sixteen pianists succeeded too well for there to be no encore. We played it again, but this time for the benefit of the community chest. The receipts amounted to no less than fourteen thousand piastres, that is to say twenty thousand francs [equivalent to about 4,000 dollars at that time].

Charity Concert 1846

An amusing episode took place at our last concert. Just as we were going to begin this piece, with the good ladies seated two by two in front of their pianos, I noticed that we were one pianist missing.

It was not so much the lady's fingers that I regretted, but the lack of an elegantly attired female form upon the piano stool. Everybody would notice and it would spoil the effect. What was to be done ? " Desperate ills call for desperate remedies "; and for once the proverb was right.

I scanned the hall and was fortunate enough to see, in one of the boxes, formally attired, a lady to whom I had once been introduced.

I went boldly across and spoke to her. " Madame ", I said " A most dreadful thing has happened and I am lost unless you come to my aid. "

" Come to your aid, Mr. Herz ? In what way ? "

" By taking the place of a pianist who has let us down . "

" But I don't play the piano. "

" Never mind.   So long as you can read music. . . . "

" But I can't. "

" Not at all ? "

" Not a note, I assure you. "

" Never mind.   Perhaps it is just as well.   It will make it all the easier for you to take the lady's place. "

" You are not serious, Mr. Herz ? "

" Never more so. "

" But what would you have me do ? "

" Nothing.   Just run your fingers gracefully up and down the keyboard without actually touching the notes.   People will *think* they can hear you and they will see you, which is the important thing.   In fact you will have all the advantages : you will not play any wrong notes, which is more than can be said for a pianist.   And if I may say so, no one could more elegantly grace the occasion.   There is such a thing in life as music for the eye and in this respect, madame is a virtuoso. "

" My dear Monsieur Herz, what you ask is absolutely impossible. "

" Say rather, nothing could be simpler. "

" I shall be a laughing-stock. "

" There, madame, you do speak of impossibilities. . . . "

" If I could only read music a little. . . . "

BRIDGE ON THE BAYOU ST. JEAN - 1830

VIEW OF THE BAYOU ST. JEAN - 1830

" ... There might be some risk. "

" But what will my friends say ? "

" They will say that you are good to the poor, and that you have spared me much embarrassment. "

" And if afterwards they ask me to play ? "

" You will say you know nothing by heart. "

" And if they hand me the music ? "

" You will say that you play only pieces written for sixteen pianists. "

" I can say that ? "

" One can say anything. But please, madame, time is short. The audience is getting restive. "

" Well, if I bow to your wishes, it is not from any desire to shine in public. It is purely to help you and to benefit the poor. "

" Madame, I kiss your hands. "

The dear sweet creature sat down next to a real pianist, and surprised that lady no little by her silent fingering. She could not have been more conscientious. Her hands ranged gracefully over the keyboard like swallows skimming the ground.

The only thing was, that when there came a pause in the music and everyone else stopped playing she, with praiseworthy zeal, continued, much to some people's surprise.

In short we carried the day. After the concert sixteen gifted pianists, including one who could not play a note, took a number of curtain calls and collected innumerable bouquets. [4]

BIVOUAC ON THE BANKS OF THE MISSOURI · 1833

CHAPTER THE THIRD

In which the Reader,
after leaving New Orleans,
ascends the Mississippi and Missouri Rivers,
to arrive at last in the City of the Saints,
Capital of the Mormons,
latterly known as Salt Lake City.

The traveller bent upon tracing the course of the Mississippi and Missouri rivers or penetrating into the West as far perhaps as the Rocky Mountains, could look forward to a very long, very slow and very arduous journey. For these great territories lay beyond the fringes of civilisation, where the writ of the United States Government did not run. Ever since 1804, when Merriwether Lewis, William Clarke and their friends set out on their expedition to discover a river route linking the Atlantic and Pacific, the valleys of the Mississippi and Missouri had constituted a frontier region inhabited by a motley and extremely mobile population, made up originally of Indians who lived by hunting, and were therefore essentially nomadic—together with increasing numbers of white hunters, trappers, settlers and soldiery. At first the races merely regarded one another with considerable reserve and mistrust bordering on open hostility. But relations grew progressively worse as time went on, until the Black Hawk War of 1832, in which the Sac and Fox nations were driven back beyond the Mississippi, and the massacre of General Custer's forces on the Little Big Horn in 1876.

The hunters and trappers who formed the spear-head of the white advance were, in the main, bold and versatile men. They could wield an axe, set a trap and cast a line with the best; but the rifle was their main means of support. It was they who blazed the trails and they who, by terror or diplomacy, kept the Indians at bay. The settlers followed after them, clearing the land of timber, burning the wood and leaving the stumps to rot. Hunting and fishing gave way to crops of corn and vegetables, and the rearing of pigs and cattle.

After the settlers came a steady trickle of tradespeople and professional men— doctors, lawyers and preachers. The 1830s saw a sharp rise in population, and the dates on which new States were admitted to the Union reflect this westward advance : Louisiana (1812), Mississippi (1817), Illinois (1818), Missouri (1821), Iowa (1846), Kansas (1861). It was into this incredibly raw, changing, strange, vast and frequently splendid world that our European travellers plunged (1800-1860) ; and it was, of course, more in the capacity of explorers than of tourists that the first of the writers whom we shall meet in this chapter made the journey from New Orleans to Salt Lake City, Utah.

Among the already familiar are Basil Hall, Jean-Jacques Ampère, François-André Michaux and Charles Dickens—the novelist being determined not to leave the United States without having pushed beyond the Mississippi, if only for a few miles. New observers include several Frenchmen, L. Xavier Eyma and E. de Girardin, largely unknown except for their writings about the New World, and a number of quite celebrated and seasoned travellers.

Bernhard Karl, Duke of Saxe-Weimar-Eisenach, was 33 when he landed in America during the summer of 1825. He spent some eleven months in the U.S.A., making a circular tour southward and westward from Boston, through Charleston (South Carolina), New Orleans, St. Charles (Missouri), and Pittsburgh, thus fulfilling a childhood dream. He returned to Europe enchanted with his trip, which, he wrote, had taught him a great deal, and would have had still more to teach had he not been obliged to rejoin his unit in the army of the King of Holland.

Another German nobleman, Prince Maximilian zu Wied, had reached the age of 50 when he left his castle in the Rhineland and set out on a great journey lasting two years (1832-1834) which eventually took him from Boston to Saint Louis, and then up the Missouri River all the way to Fort Mackenzie in what is now Wyoming, where he wanted to study at first hand the Indians of the Northwest. The Prince was not only a

great traveller, but an excellent naturalist and anthropologist.   Moreover, he brought
his own private painter, Karl Bodmer, a Swiss artist whose job was " taking views ".
The large volume in which the Prince's travels were eventually described is illustrated
with eighty-one very fine engravings (see pp. 109, 136, 137, 144, 145, 146, 147, 150 and
151) and is today a rare and much sought-after book.   Bodmer's original drawings now
belong to the Northern Natural Gas Company, of Omaha, Nebraska.

Another Swiss artist, the young painter Friedrich Kurz, set off for the Mississippi
convinced that somewhere upon its upper reaches he would find a race of Indians whose
beauty of form would approach the ideals of Ancient Greece.   His journey-log is
decorated with drawings which do in fact, show Indian squaws whose features bring to
mind the school of Raphael—which is not in the least surprising, considering the fact
that beauty is often in the eye of the beholder.

As for the Frenchman, Jules Rémy, we know little, except that he had travelled
extensively in the South Seas before undertaking his journey to Salt Lake City.   His
accounts show him to have been a determined character as well as a man of education. Perhaps this is why he was presented with a striking and original " testimonial "
by one of the Westerners who helped as guide and servant on the expedition.

But first we must be introduced to the famous and picturesque steamboats
which in those days plied the Mississippi River.   Here is Basil Hall's description,
date-lined 1828 :

The steamboats on the Mississippi, which are vessels from two to *Mississippi*
four hundred tons burden, are moved by one engine, generally on the high- *Steamboat*
pressure principle.   As the water in which they have to navigate is always *1828*
smooth, and the winds are seldom violent, they are enabled to adopt two
very commodious devices, which it would be impossible to apply to sea-

going steam-vessels. The
deck is made to extend
on both sides eight or ten
feet beyond the hull, by
which a great additional
width is acquired, while
over this wide space they

THE STEAMBOAT " PHILADELPHIA " LOADING WOOD ON THE MISSISSIPPI - 1829

are enabled to form two tiers of accommodation above the deck. In the lower range the usual luxuries of a packet are provided for passengers who require state-rooms or sleeping-berths and those who have the means of paying for such entertainment have an ample table provided for them. There is in all these boats, also a separate cabin for the ladies in a third suite, which lies below the deck. The upper tier of all is occupied by what are called Deck Passengers, chiefly consisting of the men who, having floated down the Mississippi in their great flats or arks, take advantage of the steamboats to return home again. These deck passengers, of course, pay a much smaller sum than those below stairs, as they provide themselves, and have but rough lodgings allotted them. They generally contract for an abatement of two dollars from their passage-money, on condition of assisting to carry on board the firewood. [5]

By the time Jean-Jacques Ampère boarded one of these steamboats in 1851-52, they already enjoyed a fantastic—indeed almost legendary—reputation. He writes:

*Mississippi
Steamboat
1851-1852*

Here I am on one of the Mississippi steamers that have earned such notoriety by reason of the explosions and disasters attributable to them. Only yesterday I was told of one which blew up in a shower of debris as it left the quay, one fragment killing a bystander at a coffee shop. Everyday the papers tell of similar mishaps. Yesterday's paper reported three, all on the Ohio and Mississippi. It is here that the risks are most serious, intensified as they are by the foolhardiness of the captains. The " rugged individualism " of this country may be said to have its drawbacks.

WOODING STATION ON THE MISSISSIPI - 1829

The Government does practically nothing to guarantee the safety of passengers : it is for them to satisfy themselves as to the staunchness of the vessel and the prudence or otherwise of its skipper.   My good friend M. Gustave de Beaumont quotes a conversation he had with one such officer :

" Your engine is in terrible condition, captain. "

" Sure. "

" How much longer do you think it will last ? "

" Until it bursts. "

Not least among the causes of accident are the races that constantly occur between rival steamboats, which dangerous practice the passengers, so far from opposing, frequently encourage.   Sometimes indeed even women passengers ransack their luggage for items of a combustible nature with which to feed the boilers.   Were it only their own lives at stake, I should find no cause to demur; but these enthusiasts imperil also some hundreds of lives more precious than their own.   One can hardly find terms strong enough to condemn such culpable ostentation.

The evil must eventually provide its own cure.   One half of the steamers built in the Mississippi valley during the last twenty years have already been destroyed, either in collision with other vessels or as the result of explosion. [7]

L. Xavier Eyma would have remained unknown if he had not sent a description of his travels in the United States to the celebrated magazine *L'Illustration* in 1848. It seems that he was sent to the United States by the French Government on a study tour and, perhaps because he looked at the problem statistically, he was far more encouraging than his compatriot Jean-Jacques Ampère :

There has been much talk, Sir, of the accidents in America in which steamers have been involved.   Permit me to remark that there has been some exaggeration in these reports.

However rare such catastrophes may be, they are to be deplored; but let us first examine the facts : accidents are almost unknown except on the Mississippi, and even there it is not always the fault of the captains (whose foolhardiness I am not seeking to excuse) nor of the engines, which are generally good, nor of the boats themselves, which are usually well built.

One has to remember that the most navigable reaches of the Mississippi are dotted with great tree-trunks, the tops of which reach the surface,

Mississippi Steamboat 1848

forming obstruction or " snags " with which steamers often collide, usually with disastrous results.

It must be remembered too, that there are more than 1,000 steamboats plying the Mississippi, each making three or four trips a year, which gives something like 3,500 trips; and on average there is rather less than one disaster a year. Accidents have been an inevitable concomitant to the discovery and application of steam-power. There is a reverse to every medal; a fatal aspect to all progress. [17]

Thus reassured we leave New Orleans with Basil Hall:

Up the Mississippi 1828

On the 25th April, 1828, at six o'clock in the evening, we embarked on board the PHILADELPHIA, one of the largest class of steamboats on the river, and started three hours afterwards on our voyage up the grand Mississippi.

As the steamboats on the river, and indeed all over America, burn nothing but wood, and as their engines are mostly high-pressure, the consumption of this bulky description of fuel is so considerable, that they are obliged to call at least twice a day at the wooding stations on the banks of the stream. The PHILADELPHIA used about one cord of wood an hour, or 128 cubic feet. A cord consists of a pile eight feet long by four feet high. Sometimes, when we were pushing hard, we burnt 30 cords in a day. Each cord cost from 2 ½ to 3 dollars, or from 11 to 12 shillings; but the price varied at different stations—decreasing in price as we went up. The full price of a passage for a deck passenger from New Orleans to Louisville (Ky.), a distance of 1,430 miles, was generally ten dollars at the time of my visit.

When the supply on board began to run short, the pilot cast his eye round, and upon the first convenient opportunity, he steered the boat for one of the numerous piles of firewood which occurred at every league or two during the greater part of the way. When the river is brim-full, or more than full, that is to say, running over, there was nothing left for it but run the boat alongside of the trees, make a hawser fast to one of them, and stop the engine. As soon as this was done, two or three broad, strong planks were thrust over the vessel's side, to form a gangway to the shore, along which the crew and the deck passengers carried the wood. . . .

It was always a lively, bustling scene at these wooding stations; for the grand object being expedition, the Captain stood urging his crew and the passengers to hurry on board as fast as they could with their loads. Few of these stops were longer than a quarter of an hour. . . .

On the 26th April, at the distance of fifty or sixty miles above New Orleans, we had the satisfaction of seeing one of those formidable breaches in the levee, called crevasses, which I have already spoken of.   The river

THE STEAMBOAT " HURON " AT A WOODING STATION - 1830

was tumbling through the opening with a head or fall of four or five feet, in a tumultuous manner, resembling one of the St. Lawrence rapids.   This boiling, or rather surf-like appearance—for it rose and fell in snow-white ridges or short waves—did not spread itself far to the right or left, which at first surprised me, but gushed nearly at right angles to the parent river straightforward, across the cultivated fields, into the forest growing in the boundless morass lying beyond the cleared strip of land.   There was something peculiarly striking in this casual stream—a mere drop from the great Mississippi—which in many other countries might almost have claimed the name of a river, leaping, and writhing, and foaming along, with a sound

THE STEAMBOAT "GRAND TURK" LOADING AT NIGHT - 1827

exactly like that of breakers on a reef, through the middle of a village, amongst trees, over the tops of sugar plantations, and at last losing itself in a great cypress swamp. [5]

Naturally, in that day and age travel on the Mississippi had to be pursued more or less according to the whims of the river itself, always with surprises around the next bend. The halts for furnace-wood gave passengers a chance to go ashore. Listen to Basil Hall again :

*People along the
Mississippi River
1828*

The place where we made fast was a wooding station, owned by what is called a Squatter, a person who, without any title to the land, or leave asked or granted, squats himself down and declares himself the lord and master of the soil for the time being. There is nobody to question his right, and, indeed, according to all accounts, it might not be altogether a safe topic of conversation to introduce. These hardy fellows are sometimes called the Pioneers of the wilderness —and justly so called —for they go ahead of the more orderly and civilised population, and clear away the grounds in the line of march. They are said, but I do not know with what truth, to have no great affection for the niceties of the law; and when the tide of population creeps up to them, they take up their axes and retreat beyond the reach of those odious regulators of other people's affairs— judges and juries.

In such a wild part of the country as we called at on the 1st May, where as yet there had been no regular survey of the land, of course these squatters are just as free to perch on the banks of the river, as the buzzards or vultures are to take possession of the cotton-wood trees growing above them. But even in the States lying to the eastward of the Mississippi, they are often to be found. We encountered many of them also in Georgia, where their nick-name is Crackers—but they are merely honest Squatters— free-and-easy settlers, who are their own law-makers and law-breakers, as the case may be. As these people, after all, do great good to the countries in which they settle, their operations are not discouraged. In process of time, many of them become useful citizens of thickly peopled territories, of which but a few years before they were the only inhabitants, while the idlers and rovers proceed to the westward.

It is the fashion to speak slightly of these Pioneers, Squatters, Crackers, or whatever name it pleases them most to be called by, but I must own that I was well satisfied with almost every one of them whom I encountered. In general, I thought they had less of that frigid, uninviting formality, which characterises the Americans further to the eastward. They were somewhat gruff, indeed, at times; but they seemed to trust themselves and us with more readiness, and some- times understood a joke, which I hardly ever saw exemplified on this side of the Mississippi. [5]

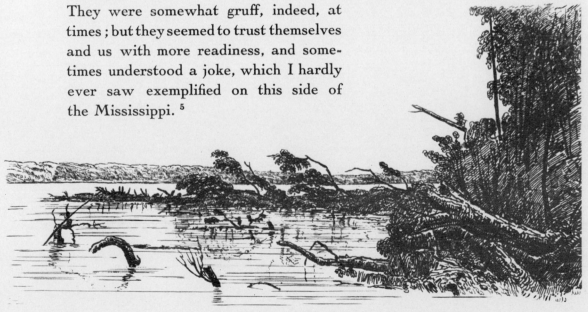

THE MISSOURI AFTER A FLOOD · 1829

But most of the time one just travelled, with nothing much to write home about. *Noblesse oblige*, however, and Prince Bernhard of Saxe-Weimar-Eisenach, travelling uneventfully from New Orleans to Saint Louis in 1826, made a noble effort to keep his observations interesting for people back home in Germany:

Between New Orleans and St. Louis 1826

The following morning, the 28th March [1826] we saw little to report beyond a few turtles floating past on lumps of wood. The river twists and turns in great loops; its banks are for the most part wooded, and so low-lying, to judge by the water-marks on the trees, as to be completely submerged when the river is in flood. On the left bank lay several high " bluffs ", of which the most important appeared to be one named Lofty Heights, on which is a little settlement called Fort Adams, named after a fort which formerly stood there. Large isolated plantations are to be seen; mostly of cotton now, for we have left the sugar country behind. While we stopped for fuel at one of these landings I went briefly ashore.

The soil is dark and appears to be fertile. The trees are mostly ash and aspen, some of the latter measuring sixteen feet in circumference. All the trees are covered with grape-vines and creepers. There are also many acacia trees. The garden of the plantation house contained a large arbour of Champagne roses in full bloom, looking very lovely and smelling delicious. The plantations also keep bees. The vegetation seems to be as forward here as it would be in July at home. The right bank of the river belongs to Louisiana, the left to Mississippi. Just before Fort Adams we passed the place—232 miles from New Orleans—where the wide Red River flows into the Mississippi. [18]

In those days the Mississippi landscape was very wild, and the settlements very far apart. Most people seemed to agree with the French observer François-André Michaux, who was there soon after 1800:

Settlements along the Mississippi 1800

It may not be out of place to remark that the word " town " in the United States is often bestowed on a collection of seven or eight houses, and that building methods are not everywhere the same. In Philadelphia the dwellings are of brick; the other cities and the country around them have mostly frame-houses. Seventy or eighty miles inland, in the central and southern States, especially west of the Allegheny Mountains, seven tenths of the people live in " log houses " otherwise known as cabins.

A log house is made from tree-trunks between twenty and thirty feet in length and four or five inches in diameter laid one upon another and held in place by notches at each end. The roof is formed from lighter logs of similar length brought together from opposite sides; these are " tiled " with shingles, hung on wooden pegs. Two doorways, which act also as windows, are made by sawing away part of the logs forming the fabric of the house. The fire-place, which is always at one end, is built of logs, with only a clay fire-back six inches in thickness between the fire and the wall. Despite this, conflagrations appear to be rare.

The interstices between logs are filled with clay, but so carelessly that daylight shows through everywhere, and in winter the houses are very cold, despite blazing log fires. The doors have wooden hinges and few of them will lock. At night they are merely pushed shut or fastened by means of a stick. Four or five days suffice for two men to build one of these houses,

A RIVERSIDE HOUSE AT NATCHEZ ON THE MISSISSIPPI - 1830

which contain no nails or ironwork of any sort. Two large beds serve the whole family. Often during the summer the children are set to sleep in blankets on the floor, which is raised a couple of feet from the ground and made of boards. Feather beds take the place of mattresses, as sheep are very scarce and what wool there is is needed for stockings. Clothes are hung on the wall, or over a long pole. [11]

After leaving New Orleans on March 26th, 1826, Prince Bernhard touched at Herculaneum, Missouri, and reached Saint Louis on April 7th, a matter of 1,150 miles in less than thirteen days. Herewith the appropriate entry from his log:

Herculaneum and St. Louis 1826

Towards five o'clock in the evening we reached a little place called Herculaneum, on the right-hand bank, where the Joachim River (whose name is here twisted into " Owashing Creek ") joins the Mississippi. The creek divides the place in two. Herculaneum is only a tiny village 30 miles from St. Louis, but there are several decent houses, some quarries and lead-workings near by, and two shot-factories. The bluffs forming the right bank of the river are cleft by the " Owashing ", which flows through a narrow, picturesque little gorge reminding me of the Ilmthal. Seen from the river, Herculaneum is quite charming, standing between its two high crags with tree-girt hills behind. Each crag has its " shot-tower " for casting bird-shot. The rocks also abound in flints. We were some time at Herculaneum, taking on wood.

On April 7th, [1826] at five o'clock in the morning we recommenced our journey, reaching St. Louis around eleven o'clock in the forenoon. We had thus covered 1,150 miles in less than thirteen days, a journey which, before the advent of steamboats, would have taken at least three months. How useful and splendid a discovery is the new-fangled steam-power, what a tribute to the inventive genius of mankind!

We sought lodging at a number of houses, but, finding the accommodation too mean, eventually settled at the Missouri Hotel, a far from aristocratic inn, where we were compelled to make shift with very indifferent and restricted quarters. . . .

St. Louis lies on fairly high, rocky ground and for nearly a mile extends along the right bank of the Mississippi. Most of the houses have terraced gardens sloping steeply down to the river. The city has a population of 4,000. It consists of a long main street parallel with the river, and a number of side-roads leading into the hills where a scatter of houses indicates the line on which a second long street may one day be built. The houses are mostly new two-storey structures in brick; stone has been used in a few cases, and some are built of wood and earth in the Spanish Colonial style like the old houses in New Orleans.

Along the heights encircling the town there was once a wall, now demolished. At the corners stood massive round fortresses, whose walls are still to be seen. Northward of the town are seven artificial mounds disposed in two rows to form a parallelogram. These belong to a much-discussed chain of Indian earthworks and forts extending down the Ohio and Mississippi rivers, and forming a line all the way from Lake Erie to New Mexico. Neither documentary nor traditional evidence exists as to the origin of these works or of the peoples who built them. These tumuli await further excavation. Some have yielded human remains, others nothing at all. The double row of mounds at St. Louis has not been investigated as yet. [18]

Ascending to the junction of the Ohio and Mississippi rivers, we rejoin Charles Dickens, who reached this point in 1842. He was not often impressed by the customs of the New World, but he was mightily astonished by the size of the great river:

Junction of the Ohio and the Mississippi Rivers 1842

But what words shall describe the Mississippi, great father of rivers, who (praise be to Heaven) has no young children like him. An enormous ditch, sometimes two or three miles wide, running liquid mud, six miles an hour: its strong and frothy current choked and obstructed everywhere by huge logs and whole forest trees: now twining themselves together in great rafts, from the interstices of which a sedgy lazy foam works up, to float upon the water's top; now rolling past like monstrous bodies, their tangled roots showing like matted hair; now glancing singly by like giant leeches;

HOUSE AT THE FOOT OF WALLNUT HILL AT VICKSBURG, MISSISSIPPI - 1830

and now writhing round and round in the vortex of some small whirlpool, like wounded snakes. The banks low, the trees dwarfish, the marshes swarming with frogs, the wretched cabins few and far apart, their inmates hollow-cheeked and pale, the weather very hot, mosquitoes penetrating into every crack and crevice of the boat, mud and slime on everything: nothing pleasant in its aspect, but the harmless lightning which flickers every night upon the dark horizon.

For two days we toiled up this foul stream, striking constantly against the floating timber, or stopping to avoid those more dangerous obstacles, the snags, or sawyers, which are the hidden trunks of trees that have their roots below the tide. When the nights are very dark, the look-out stationed in the head of the boat knows by the ripple of the water if any great impediment be near at hand, and rings a bell beside him, which is the signal for the engine to be stopped: but always in the night this bell has work to do, and after every ring, there comes a blow which renders it no easy matter to remain in bed.

The decline of day here was very gorgeous, tinging the firmament deeply with red and gold, up to the very keystone of the arch above us. As the sun went down behind the bank, the slightest blades of grass upon it seemed to become as distinctly visible as the arteries in the skeleton of a leaf; and when, as it slowly sank, the red and golden bars upon the water grew dimmer, and dimmer yet, as if they were sinking too; and all the glowing colours of departing day paled, inch by inch, before the sombre night; the scene became a thousand times more lonesome and more dreary than before, and all its influences darkened with the sky. . . .

AN INLET AT NEW MADRID, MISSOURI · 1830

If the coming up this river, slowly making head against the stream, be an irksome journey, the shooting down it with the turbid current is almost worse; for then the boat, proceeding at the rate of twelve or fifteen miles an hour, has to force its passage through a labyrinth of floating logs, which, in the dark, it is often impossible to see before-hand or avoid. All that night, the bell was never silent for five minutes at a time; and after every

VILLAGE OF HERCULANEUM, FROM THE MISSISSIPPI - 1830

ring the vessel reeled again, sometimes beneath a single blow, sometimes beneath a dozen dealt in quick succession, the lightest of which seemed more than enough to beat in her frail keel, as though it had been pie-crust. Looking down upon the filthy river after dark it seemed to be alive with monsters, as these black masses rolled upon the surface, or came starting up again, head first, when the boat, in ploughing her way among a shoal of such obstructions, drove a few among them for the moment under water. Sometimes, the engine stopped during a long interval, and then before her and behind, and gathering close about her on all sides, were so many of these ill-favoured obstacles that she was fairly hemmed in; the centre of a floating island; and was constrained to pause until they parted somewhere, as dark clouds will do before the wind, and opened by degrees a channel out. In good time next morning, however, we came again in sight of the detestable morass called Cairo; and stopping there, to take in wood, lay alongside a barge, whose starting timbers scarcely held together. It was moored to the bank, and on its side was painted, " Coffee House "; that being, I suppose, the floating paradise to which the people fly for shelter when they lose their houses for a month or two beneath the hideous waters of the Mississippi. But looking southward from this point, we had the satisfaction of seeing that intolerable river dragging its slimy length and ugly freight abruptly off towards New Orleans; and passing a yellow line which stretched across the current, were again upon the clear Ohio, never, I trust, to see the Mississippi more, saving in troubled dreams and nightmares. Leaving it for the company of its sparkling neighbour, was like the transition from pain to ease, or the awakening from a horrible vision to cheerful realities. [6]

Saint Louis, Missouri, founded by a Frenchman in 1764, stands at what was once the half-way mark between Canada and Louisiana—an agreeable link between the northern and southern portions of French America. After Missouri became a State in the Union in 1821, Saint Louis acquired new importance as a staging post for the growing emigrant traffic heading West.

When Charles Dickens saw it in 1842 there were still some eighteenth-century French buildings left:

Saint Louis
1842

In the old French portion of the town, the thoroughfares are narrow and crooked, and some of the houses are very quaint and picturesque : being built of wood, with tumble-down galleries before the windows approachable by stairs or rather ladders, from the street. There are queer little barbers' shops and drinking-houses too, in this quarter; and abundance of crazy old tenements with blinking casements, such as may be seen in Flanders. Some of these ancient habitations, with high garret gable-windows perking into the roofs, have a kind of French shrug about them; and being lop-sided with age, appear to hold their heads askew, besides as if they were grimacing in astonishment at the American Improvements.

It is hardly necessary to say, that these consist of wharfs and ware-houses, and new buildings in all directions; and of a great many vast plans which are still " progressing ". Already, however, some very good houses, broad streets, and marble-fronted shops, have gone so far ahead as to be in a state of completion; and the town bids fair in a few years to improve considerably though it is not likely ever to vie, in point of elegance or beauty, with Cincinnati.

Saint Louis, Missouri — *1847*

SKY-LINE, INCLUDING OLD CATHEDRAL AND COURT-HOUSE, FROM THE ILLINOIS SHORE

The Roman Catholic religion, introduced here by the early French settlers prevails extensively. Among the public institutions are a Jesuit college; a convent for " the Ladies of the Sacred Heart "; and a large chapel attached to the college, which was in course of erection at the time of my visit and was intended to be consecrated on the second of December in the present year. The architect of this building, is one of the reverend fathers of the school, and the works proceed under his sole direction. The organ will be sent from Belgium.

In addition to these establishments, there is a Roman Catholic cathedral, dedicated to Saint Francis Xavier; and a hospital, founded by the munificence of a deceased resident, who was a member of that church. It also sends missionaries from hence among the Indian tribes. The Unitarian church is represented, in this remote place, as in most parts of America, by a gentleman of great worth and excellence. The poor have good reason to remember and bless it; for it befriends them, and aids the cause of rational education, without any sectarian or selfish views. It is liberal in all its actions; of kind construction and of wide benevolence.

There are three free-schools already erected, and in full operation, in this city. A fourth is building, and will soon be opened. [6]

Once arrived in Saint Louis it was very tempting to undertake some excursions in the vicinity and to taste—were it only for some hours—adventure in the prairie. Before returning again to the civilised parts of the east and to his native England, Charles Dickens tried to avail himself of this pleasure:

I awoke again at seven o'clock, and by that time the party had assembled, and were gathered round; one light carriage, with a very stout axletree; one something on wheels like an amateur carrier's cart; one double phaeton of great antiquity and unearthly construction; one gig with a great hole in its back and a broken head; and one rider on horseback who was to go on before. I got into the first coach with three companions; the rest bestowed themselves in the other vehicles; two large baskets were made fast to the lightest; two large stone jars in wicker cases, technically known as demi-johns, were consigned to the " least rowdy " of the party for safe keeping; and the procession moved off to the ferry-boat, in which it was to cross the river bodily, men, horses, carriages, and all, as the manner in these parts is.

We got over the river in due course, and mustered again before a little wooden box on wheels, hove down all aslant in a morass, with " MERCHANT

Excursion in the Neighbourhood of St. Louis 1842

TAILOR " painted in very large letters over the door.   Having settled the order of proceeding, and the road to be taken, we started off once more and began to make our way through an ill-favoured Black Hollow, called, less expressively, the American Bottom.

The previous day had been—not to say hot, for the term is weak and lukewarm in its power of conveying an idea of the temperature.   The town had been on fire; in a blaze.   But at night it had come on to rain in torrents, and all night long it had rained without cessation.   We had a pair of very strong horses, but travelled at the rate of little more than a couple of miles an hour, through one unbroken slough of black mud and water.   It had no variety but in depth.   Now it was only half over the wheels, now it hid the axle-tree, and now the coach sank down in it almost to the windows.   The air resounded in all directions with the loud chirping of the frogs, who, with the pigs (a coarse, ugly breed, as unwholesome-looking as though they were the spontaneous growth of the country), had the whole scene to themselves.   Here and there we passed a log hut; but the wretched cabins were wide apart and thinly scattered, for though the soil is very rich in this place few people can exist in such a deadly atmosphere. . . .

PRAIRIE VOYAGERS - 1851

Looking towards the setting sun, there lay, stretched out before my view, a vast expanse of level ground; unbroken, save by one thin line of trees, which scarcely amounted to a scratch upon the great blank; until it met the glowing sky, wherein it seemed to dip : mingling with its rich colours, and mellowing in its distant blue.   There it lay, a tranquil sea or lake without water, if such a simile be admissible, with the day going down upon it : a few birds wheeling here and there : and solitude and silence reigning paramount around.   But the grass was not yet high; there were bare black patches on the ground; and the few wild flowers that the eye could see, were poor and scanty.   Great as the picture was, its very flatness and extent, which left nothing to the imagination, tamed it down and cramped its interest. I felt little of that sense of freedom and exhilaration which a Scottish heath inspires, or even our English downs awaken. It was lonely and wild, but oppressive in its barren monotony. [6]

Quite often European tourists on " one-day safari " encountered wagon trains of emigrants heading West to start a new life. The idea of " no return " frequently had the profoundest effect upon the tourists' imagination, giving a new spiritual dimension to their own travels. But to E. de Girardin, a young Frenchman who went up the Mississippi in 1850, a meeting with a covered wagon was very matter-of-fact :

The " covered wagon " of the emigrants has a canvas top, and is *Emigrants* fitted up inside with tremendous neatness and care, for it will be the *1850* travellers' only home for six or seven long months, and to that end must be as comfortable as possible.

Pistols and rifles, without which nobody ventures into the Far West, hang upon one wall; the cast-iron stove used in camp for baking biscuits stands in one corner; tools and household utensils hang here and there. One nearly always finds a few books on history and geography, and there is always the Bible, that inseparable companion of the American emigrant.

Some emigrants have their name and profession painted on the canvas tilt. On one I saw : " J. B. Smith, dentist from New York. Apply to Wagon Master. " The wagon master was none other than the dentist himself; after unharnessing his oxen and cooking his dinner he would change into a black suit and, like the quacks on the fairgrounds, get his victims into the wagon to have their teeth

DEPARTURE FOR A HUNT - 1851

pulled " painlessly ", charging the modest sum of one piastre [about 28 cents].

I was shown a large wagon with blue and white striped top, hermetically sealed; apparently it is inhabited by six young ladies on their way to the gold-mines in search of husbands and independence. They are said to be extremely pretty and highly " respectable ", the proof of this being that they " lock " themselves in at night by pinning the calico flap. [19]

Before embarking on the second stage of our journey which will take us from Saint Louis to Fort Union, Montana, by the upper reaches of the Missouri, perhaps it may be wise to listen to the advice Black Beaver gave to Baron Balduin Möllhausen, a German who crossed the American continent from the Atlantic coast to that of the Pacific in the years 1853-54. Black Beaver belonged to the Delaware tribe and he had served the United States well during the Mexican War (1846) as hunter and guide. Tired of travelling, Black Beaver passed his days and his evenings regaling foreigners with stories of his adventures and giving them useful advice on hunting bear and antelope, and, of course, buffalo, all duly noted verbatim by Baron Möllhausen:

Hunting Advice 1853

You will not find many buffalo, said Black Beaver. They have gone North because here the sun beats upon their hide, and before the snow drives them back in the Fall you will be beyond the Rockies in a land where no buffalo graze. You may see a few grizzled old stragglers, but these will not repay setting spur to your horse's belly: their meat is tough and has no goodness in it. At best the tongue will be eatable. But beside the thickets and along the waters flowing into the Canadian River you will find turkeys and white-tailed deer.

You must learn to call deer as the Delaware do. As you pass a wood, imitate the cry of the fawn, with a whistle; the father deer, which has already left its young, comes bounding up and is easily taken.

But should one of your people go hunting in this fashion, let him keep his eyes open, for the panther and the jaguar are also misled by whistles, and their charge is so swift that one cannot be sure of placing a bullet in the heart or brain, and these animals are dangerous when wounded.

Antelopes you will find everywhere as far as the Pacific Ocean, sometimes singly, but more often in herds. They are nimble and shy, but extremely inquisitive, so that if one plays upon their curiosity they are amongst the easiest game to shoot. For days on end these tireless creatures will keep pace with the wagon train, seldom coming within rifle-shot. But if you can find some cover such as a bush, a tuft of tall grass, or heap of stones, tie a piece of rag to a stick, set it in the ground and wait. Your patience will not be tried very long. The antelope will come to inspect the strange object, sometimes running, sometimes with caution. You shoot one, and they all vanish; but the noise only inflames their curiosity. You have hardly time to hide before they are back. You shoot another; then a third and perhaps a fourth, before they forsake the place of ill omen.

You should also find black bears along the Canadian River. Shoot to wound; they then rise up on their hind legs and show fight, affording excel-

Bellevue near Omaha, Nebraska — 1833

A FUR-TRADING POST, AND THE OLDEST EXISTING TOWN IN THE STATE

lent sport. You will admire their courage; you will laugh at their antics; but do not go too close, for bears set a high price on their skin and cutlets. If a bear retreats down its hole, make a torch from rags, grass or anything that's handy and go boldly down after him. Blinded by the light, he rears up and covers his eyes with his paws. Shine the torch on his chest and you will see a place where the hair grows in a circle. That is where you must aim, and the beast will fall like a Pawnee lodge when the supports are broken. You can also try smoking him out, but this does not always succeed; he may come up to the opening, scatter the fire with his hand-like fore paws and go quietly down again. . . .

In August and September the buffalo, having eaten their fill of new grass come together in great herds; the plains are covered with them as far as the eye can see. There are far too many to count. One can only guess the number of square miles they occupy and calculate from that. They look like a barbarian host in disorder. They stir up the dust like a whirl-wind, and fill the air with a noise like distant thunder. At this time of year one may roam the prairie for weeks, or even months, without seeing fresh buffalo sign; and if the hunter does not happen to meet with one of the great herds—which can bar his way for several days—he imagines the prairie to be dead, and quickens his pace to regain civilisation and escape from the terrible loneliness.

But in a few weeks the scene changes; the herds break into smaller groups which go off and roam the prairies that were so desolate before. You will find some buffaloes that walk by themselves, their long beards brushing the ground. Some lie and ruminate while their companions play. They are wonderfully agile creatures, leaping around in the drollest fashion. Others set off in close company, following buffalo trails over river and mountain until they come to their favourite camping grounds in the swamps. They are looking for their old " wallows ", and if they do not find these they will make new ones, for the buffalo loves his mud bath.

This is what they do: the leader finds a place that looks suitable, and starts churning up the ground with his horns and fore feet. He throws out the grass and earth, making a sort of funnel that soon fills with water, and plunges in, to escape from the heat and mosquitoes. When he has wallowed to his heart's content and emerges from the bath, he no longer looks like an animal: his long beard and mane are dripping with mud, and only the eyes betray that this is no animated clod but that noble creature a buffalo. All wallow in turn, acquiring a thick crust which clings until washed off by rain or until such time as the buffalo rolls in the grass.

In former times when the buffalo acted, as it were, only as cattle for the Indians their numbers did not diminish; indeed they increased and multiplied. But the white man came and cast covetous eyes upon their hides; the fat beef proved delicious, and commercial instincts were aroused.

The plains Indians were ensnared by the white man's trade goods and liquor; so the war of extermination began. Thousands of buffalo were killed for their tongues or more often for their skins, although in the first few years

INDIANS ON THE HUNTING
PATH - 1851

there was no appreciable lessening of their numbers. The Indians are a feckless race, with no thought for the morrow; and so long as a single buffalo is left alive they will hunt it for its hide. The time is not far off when the vast herds will be only a memory. Deprived of their means of subsistence, the 3oo,ooo Indians—and the wolves—will become the scourge of the civilisation that hems them in, and they in their turn will have to be exterminated.

THE SWISS PAINTER FRIEDRICH KURZ
AND HIS INDIAN GUIDE - 1851

The buffalo has many enemies, but the most dangerous is still the Indian, who has all manner of wily tricks. Buffalo hunting for the Indian is a necessity; but it is also his favourite pastime. Life holds no higher pleasure than to mount one of the handy, patient little ponies that they catch wild on the prairies and gallop into a herd, dealing death and destruction. Everything which might interfere with the movements of man or horse

is flung away. Clothing and saddle are cast aside; all the rider retains is a big leather strap, twenty yards long, which is fastened around the pony's neck and allowed to trail behind. This trail-rope acts as a bridle, and as a life-line too, for recapturing the horse should its rider be dismounted.   In his left hand the hunter carries his bow and as many arrows as he can hold; in his right a whip, with which he belabours his beast without pity.   Indian ponies are trained to gallop close alongside the buffalo, providing an easy shot; the instant the bow-string twangs the pony instinctively dodges to escape the buffalo's horns, and approaches another victim.   Thus the hunt continues until his pony's exhaustion warns the hunter to desist.   The wounded buffalo drop out, and are dispatched by the wives of the hunter, who follow the trail.   The choicest morsels are taken home to the wigwam where the meat is cut into thin strips and dried in the sun, while the hide is tanned, by a process of great simplicity.   Needless to say the rest is left for the wolves, which follow the herd in considerable numbers.

The buffalo has a long mane which gets in his eyes and prevents his seeing very clearly.   For this reason he can also be hunted on foot.   The hunter wraps himself in a wolf-skin, and goes on all fours, grasping his weapons.   If the wind does not betray him by blowing aside his disguise, he has no trouble in stalking and shooting his quarry, for the shots do not disturb the animals in the least.   Their sense of smell, on the other hand, is very keen, but provided a man takes up his stance downwind and well disguised, he can cause considerable havoc amongst a grazing herd.   When a beast is shot its companions feed on as though nothing had happened; they scarcely look up on hearing its death rattle.

Hunting takes place at all seasons, even when snow prevents hunting on horseback.   The Indians put long pattens on their feet, and spear the

INDIANS DEPENDED ON BUFFALO TO LIVE

buffalo while they are floundering in the snow. Thus the work of slaughter goes on, without pause and without mercy. No thought is given to husbandry or preservation. Soon the last buffalo will have disappeared, and with him the last Redskin; and with the last of the Redskins all the poetry will depart from this great North American continent. [20]

The journey from Saint Louis to Fort Union °, at the junction of the Missouri and the Yellowstone, took forty days by steamboat for the 1,620 miles. E. de Girardin, who was going to the Bad Lands of Nebraska, travelled in the IOWA, an American Fur Company ° boat which made one trip to the Upper Missouri each year, stopping at the various trading posts to land new hands and deliver supplies. Progress was slow against a current of two to three miles an hour, and de Girardin was beset by impatience — and fear :

Up the Missouri 1849-50

The river is so tortuous and the current so strong, that it took us four hours to pass the Sioux River junction, although making all possible steam. Our boat shuddered from stem to stern; the decks were awash and the bows sometimes vanished completely under water. We would make a few inches headway, only to drop back again, as the current appeared to redouble its strength. The captain was beside himself. He ordered a barrel of resin thrown into the fire-box — a solemn moment for us passengers, who were torn between fear and excitement. Large numbers of trees are carried down the Missouri by the current; many become embedded in the mud with their tops just below the surface. These are a great hazard to navigation and cause many wrecks. Sometimes the trees become hooked and entangled, forming islands several miles long, and with barely room for a steamboat to thread its way through. Thus it is impossible to travel by night. As soon as the sun goes down the boat is made fast to the bank. As the country is quite uninhabited and no supplies of coal or cord-wood are available, our crew of twenty-four goes ashore with axes, making havoc amongst the poplars and cedars on either bank.

The companies engaged in the fur-trade in American territory are only two in number : the American Fur Company and " the Opposition ". Long-standing and bitter hatred exists between the employés of the two concerns, and they shrink from no means of injuring one another whenever possible.

One day as we were passing a " blockhouse " or winter depot belonging to the Opposition, our captain conceived the charming idea of sending all hands ashore to demolish the houses, forts and stockades. Everything was brought on board and burned in the course of the day.

A CIRCULAR SAW-MILL - 1859

A few days later one of the Opposition boats repaid our captain's little jest with interest by destroying a depot of the American Fur Company. . . .

The nights are stifling. Once the boat is made fast, millions of mosquitoes invade the saloon and state-rooms, and in spite of the heat one has to put on gloves and wrap scarves around head and neck, leaving only a space through which to breathe. [19]

During this same period on the banks of the Missouri Friedrich Kurz, a painter born in Berne, Switzerland, was living out a most European and romantic dream. He had always longed to dwell amongst the Indians, hoping in this way to rediscover Natural Beauty as imagined by the Greeks. For four years, from 1848 until 1852 he lived at several of the great trading posts of the fur companies on the Missouri River, working intermittently as a clerk, notably at Forts Berthold ° and Union, Montana. He thus came into direct contact with the daily life of several Indian tribes :

Life here is much more quiet and peaceful than in civilised countries ; *Indian tribe 1851* the so-called Savage does not argue about religion, the Rights of Man, and other such matters on which mankind should long ago have reached agreement ; he has too much sense for that. What is more, one never hears cursing and quarreling. One notices this when they are playing their favourite game, a sort of mixture of hoop-la [quoits] and darts °. When several darts lie so close together in the target-ring that it is difficult to decide who has won (and they always have bets on the game, often for high stakes), the onlookers are called upon to arbitrate. There is no dispute, and nobody swears because " cuss-words " do not exist; but an insult may have serious consequences. Insults can be wiped out only by blood, and may lead to deadly feuding. [21]

The young Bernese was no ethnographer, but he has some amusing things to say about the effect of his drawings on the Indians, who regarded them as magic :

The Magic Drawings 1851

When the natives came into the office they recognised the portrait of Herr Dennik immediately, calling greetings and offering to shake hands. When it did not answer they clapped hands to their mouths in astonishment. This, they reasoned, was not a live person; but neither was it a

INDIANS OF THE MISSOURI - 1851

looking-glass. It was too much for them altogether. The painting of the dog they also recognised, but they were at a loss to understand why anyone should go to such trouble to honour a mere canine.

The simultaneous arrival of the first painter and the first outbreaks of smallpox and cholera had obviously no connection; but how can one get this into an Indian's head ? This is the third time it has happened; is not that proof enough for superstitious folk? Every time disease has broken out there has been a portrait painter here; the landscape and animal painter (Audubon) brought no such thing. What can one do? [21]

Nature itself provided some wonderful shows: a prairie storm, for example, as described by Friedrich Kurz:

A Prairie Storm 1852

April 13th, 1852. Yesterday we again passed a miserable day; not, this time, on the score of food, for we had goose, but because of a frightful blizzard that whipped across the Plains with a roaring that might have been distant thunder. The sun came out briefly but disappeared again and it grew quite dark, with rain, snow and hail alternately. We had to lash our tents down and weight them with logs; none of us could stand upright outside.

INDIAN BEAUTY OF THE IOWA TRIBE - 1851

Inside we could not hear ourselves speak. There was such a hellish noise, what with the wind roaring, the canvas flapping, the chimney howling, and the creaking and rattling of the tent-poles, that it was all highly uncomfortable. It was freezing cold and we expected the tent to blow away any minute, as in fact that of the La Pierre family did during the afternoon. They came to us for shelter as it was impossible to erect a tent in that

wind. We sent them to the Cadotte's tent as we distrusted the low thieving
creatures and had no wish to share either the goose or our dearly bought
coffee. Antoine was away. The old women were furious, and out of spite
took away the log that was holding our tent down. Fortunately we noticed
in time and were able to put it back.

They had better luck later on. We were all sitting cosily around
eating boiled goose and drinking the broth when a puff of wind, without so
much as a by-your-leave, took the tent from over our heads. We were
left in complete chaos, with everything blowing away—the remains of the
fire, our gunpowder, overcoats, clothes, dresses and all. How could we
have been so trusting? Gone alike were goose and broth. We chased
after our goods and chattels, gathered them up as best we could, and put
weights on the fallen canvas. We beat out that accursed fire, brushed the
ashes from our clothes and salvaged the powder.

There was nothing for it now but to take refuge with the Cadottes in
the only tent still standing; and what a crush it was in that tiny space! We
spent the whole night sitting up, and were heartily glad that no further
impudent gales came to rip away this last refuge. By this morning the wind
had dropped, the sky was a marvellous blue and the sun was shining. [21]

A HAZARD FOR MISSOURI RIVER BOATS · 1833

At this period wild life was plentiful, and it was not unusual to see herds of buffalo :

The sun rose in splendour above the plains, revealing countless herds of grazing buffalo. We often came close to pairs of bulls fighting, so engrossed in their struggles that they took no notice until the sound of our guns set them running, tails up, flanks covered with dust, back to the herd — there probably to resume their battle. I had expected the bulls, at least, to show fight on seeing us, but they all ran away. On the prairies they run as soon as they get wind of man; but on a narrow forest trail they will charge. They also use their horns if one rides very close while hunting. Buffalo never attack man; faced with a bear the bulls are quite brave, the cows less so. It is odd that the buffalo have not been domesticated, as our own bulls at home show far more readiness to attack strangers. [21]

After thirty-two days' travelling from Saint Louis E. de Girardin came in sight of Fort Pierre° South Dakota, founded in 1828 by the Frenchman Pierre Chouteau, one of the heads of the American Fur Company :

At last ... through the morning mist we made out the enormous American flag that flies over Fort Pierre. The river was almost blocked by shifting sandbanks, and we advanced but slowly, taking soundings all

*Fort Pierre
1850*

HERD OF BUFFALOES AT A WATERING PLACE - 1833

the time.   Suddenly a breeze sprang up, and blew the mist away, disclosing a delightful view of Fort Pierre.   We gave three rousing cheers and
fired a salute from our little cannon.   The battlements and white walls of
the Fort itself lay straight ahead.   Around it stood a hundred or so buffalo-
hide lodges, some gleaming white, others gaudily painted with barbaric
designs.   A group of Indians in gala attire leant upon their muskets, watching us uneasily from the bank, as motionless as statues, their faces daubed
with red, yellow and white.   No doubt they were wondering what the great
fire-canoe had brought.   Would it be the cholera, as last year, or some even
more dreadful scourge ?

As soon as we touched about fifty young braves and their squaws
invaded the decks, pushing their way into the saloon, the galley, everywhere, in fact, prodding, prying and tasting everything despite remonstrances
from the Negro cooks; they made short work of a huge pot of hominy that
was on the stove.   The rest of our fare would have gone the same way,
had not one of the chefs taken a whip and driven them out by Force.   Order
was soon restored, and maintained, by a dozen grave warriors, all armed
and wearing the Company's uniform, who acted as police.

Fort Pierre is a huge square, formed by four palisade walls 16 feet
high and 200 yards long; it is defended on the North, the East and the
Southwest by three bastions mounting artillery.   The Company's buildings
run parallel with the palisades; they comprise quarters for trappers,
management, clerks and interpreters, as well as vast warehouses filled with
trade goods and furs; there is a forge where they make hatchets, tomahawks
and knives for the Indians; carpenters' and tinsmiths' shops, stables,
cowsheds and a powder magazine.   The Governor of the Fort received us
most graciously, having his wives prepare an excellent luncheon, consisting
of buffalo tongue, pemmican, and first-rate corn-bread.

Having lived for many years in the Sioux territory, the Governor had
adopted some of their customs, including that of polygamy—not, so he said,
from any culpable motive, but merely for the sake of peace and in further-
ance of his trade.   Surrounded by seven wives drawn from seven separate
tribes of the Dakota Nation, he is assured of the loyal backing of an army
of brothers-in-law, uncles and cousins, which gives him great influence and
greatly facilitates dealings with the natives.   Or so he maintains.

To celebrate the steamer's arrival the Governor gave a great party
followed by a dance.   At the former presents of a bottle of whisky, a

Muscatine, Iowa — 1858

pound of flour and some buffalo-grease were bestowed on each of his guests, who comprised trappers, hunters, guides, Indian scouts, etc. Bonfires were lighted in the compound of the Fort, great heaps of pancakes were made, to be washed down with copious libations. Two fiddlers seated on a barrel, one Canadian, the other Irish, brought back memories of country weddings in my own homeland.

Everyone joined in the dancing: artisans, hunters, half-breeds, Negroes, mulattoes and Indians. Their faces, white, yellow, black, brick-red and bronze, made an almost diabolical show, flushed as they were by the fire-light—and by a second issue of whisky. Heads grew hot, old quarrels flared anew, blows rained down on all and sundry, knives were drawn (by the half-breeds), Indians brandished their tomahawks, and rifle duels were threatened for next morning. Then dancing was resumed, without anyone's noticing that all the women had made off during the fight. Such are the intermissions during a ball at Fort [Pierre] Chouteau. [19]

From Fort Pierre, E. de Girardin struck inland across " the Bad Lands of Nebraska ". Here is part of his log:

The Bad Lands of Nebraska 1850

The landscape is of the most fantastic description: a chaos of tormented buttes and deep ravines that yawn like the maw of some monstrous serpent, disclosing a row of fangs—pyramids of scorched red stone topped with rocks that seem to balance there only by a miracle. Below the soil is blackened as if by fire, fissured in all directions and beset with deep caverns, so many pitfalls for our party's mules. It was here that we lost the wagon, which broke loose and was shattered as we were lowering it by ropes; its fragmentary remains hung suspended between a pair of needle-like crags. Shouldering what remained of our luggage we slithered and rolled to the bottom of the ravine, and there pitched camp for the night. We had eaten nothing since five o'clock the previous morning, and had not slept a wink for two nights; so for the rest of the day we feasted and slept, quite certain that the Indians could not find us. . . .

This morning old Chief Crow accompanied by some of his warriors came to be invited for dinner. When each of them had drunk a litre of coffee and when they had smoked several calumets, they asked us over to their camp, which lay at about a mile's distance on a little hill dominating the river. The camp consisted of five or six cone-shaped lodges made from buffalo-hide, remarkable for their whiteness and cleanliness, and covered with strange barbaric designs in red and yellow depicting warriors smoking the calumet, together with horses, deer and dogs. Many recent scalps were hanging from long poles. Beside each tent stood a tripod of sticks supporting quivers, buffalo-hide shields and lances adorned with brightly coloured feathers. Some young braves were engaged in target practice, piercing a bladder as it was thrown into the air, or rolled down a kind of polished slope like a bowling-alley. They were men of herculean physique, with aquiline noses and sharply chiselled features; but hideously bedaubed with black and white paint.

The chief invited us to be seated upon the buffalo-robes and bear-skins that furnished the interior of his lodge and embarked upon a long colloquy with the interpreter, leaving me exposed to the curiosity of the boys, the squaws and children. The girls were emboldened to go through my pockets, from which they removed my knife, my pencils and my note-book, which passed from hand to hand and seemed to cause great amusement. Finally the boldest and most inquisitive, a beautiful girl with lovely eyes and a magnificent set of teeth, was inspired by my long beard to see whether or not I had fur all over like a bear, and, assisted by her companions embarked upon a too-searching exploration of my person. I was on the point of surrendering some of my apparel when my good friend Chief Crow saved further embarrassment by passing the pipe of peace, whereupon the girls gave back my note-book—but in a sorry state, alas. The unused pages, and the spaces between every line were scribbled all over in the manner one would expect at home from children of four or five. [19]

When Prince Maximilian zu Wied travelled to Fort Union he preferred to go by river, because he thought it might be faster and safer. Here we have a few notes made by His Highness during the voyage up the Missouri between Fort Pierre and Fort Clarke °. The boat was called the YELLOWSTONE :

Between Fort Pierre and Fort Clarke 1833

The following day we saw numerous flocks of prairie hens, thirty or forty birds in each, flying above the river, and we also identified the call of a bull-elk, which, like the stags at home, are sometimes heard singly as late as this. We landed to make breakfast beside a wood, and amongst the bushes comprising the undergrowth we discovered some bearing large clusters of buffalo-berries. These are of a very brilliant red and edible, although like our sloe *(Prunus spinosus)* they only become so after the first frosts. Even then they remain sour and astringent; cooked with sugar they are not unpalatable. We gave some to our bears and to my little pet fox, who found them refreshing and a welcome addition to their diet. We should have welcomed a change ourselves, but although it should have been possible to shoot some game we had so far not succeeded in bagging any.

Traces of beaver were everywhere : trees they had felled, dams, and their characteristically slippery trails. The prairie bushes were full of little titmice *(Parus atricapillus)* and Canadian magpies *(Pica Hudsonica)*. After an unsuccessful shot at a flock of eight splendid white swans and some wild geese we laid up somewhere in the neighbourhood of the White Earth River (so named by Lewis and Clarke) while a hunting-party went ashore. Drift-ice was already floating down into the Missouri from its tributaries, making a great clatter as it split against the drift-wood. The din was increased by a high wind and the slap of the waves against the crumbling banks. My pet animals, who would not eat pork and were very hungry, complained loudly, especially the bears, which was a great nuisance just then. Our hopes were not fulfilled; the hunters had had two shots at game, but missed both. At four o'clock I gave orders to proceed, for my men were dropping from exhaustion. Unless Canadians have a full belly, their endurance cannot be counted upon. [22]

INDIANS OF THE UPPER MISSOURI CARRYING PIROGUES · 1851

This river trip was fraught with troubles for the explorer Prince; at one point he lost some of his precious specimens :

The following morning provided fresh evidence of our rather lubberly seamanship. For some while we had been collecting natural history specimens, which had to be found room for on deck as there was nowhere else to stow them. During the night these hard-won skins, trophies and the like often got thrown overboard, although Mr. Mitchell had imposed a fine of five dollars for any such irregularity. I myself lost a number of extremely interesting specimens in this way, for in our keel-boat it was almost impossible to keep a natural history collection together except by the sheerest good fortune. We did, however manage to preserve our herbarium intact by keeping it in the cabin with us; but it was little enough that we managed to bring safely to Fort Mackenzie °. [22]

The YELLOWSTONE reached Fort Clarke on the 18th June 1833, and left the following day. Prince Maximilian's first stay at Fort Union lasted from June 24th to July 6th, 1833. It was now a year since he had left Philadelphia :

The Fort stands upon a raised piece of alluvial ground or prairie on the north bank of the Missouri and about 1,500 yards from a chain of hills with more prairie beyond. The river flows from West to East immediately in front of the Fort, not more than 50 or 60 yards away. It is very wide just here, and heavily wooded on the far side.

The Fort itself is a rectangle, with sides about 80 yards long. Around it stretches a stockade composed of sturdy square-hewn posts or " pickets " planted close together, their tops crowned with a sort of *chevaux de frise* arrangement to prevent their being climbed. At the southwestern and northeastern corners are blockhouses with pitched roofs and ramparts provided with loop-holes from which small but serviceable cannon peer out. The main entrance to the compound is a well-defended swing gate on the riverside of the Fort. Opposite this on the far side of the courtyard stands the Governor's house, a single-storey structure with four fine glass-windows on each side of the door, a roomy loft above and a big dormer-window. It is an extremely comfortable house, and, like the rest of the buildings inside the stockade, constructed of poplar wood, the usual building material in these parts.

The other buildings contain quarters for the clerks and interpreters. Besides the three who came up with us (Lachapelle for the Arikare lan-

Rondé 1853.

Indian Summer in Iowa — 1853

guage, Ortubize for Dakota and Berger for the Blackfoot dialects) Fort
Union boasted two other interpreters : Halcro for Assiniboine and Lafon-
taine for Cree. Also housed here are the *engagés* [see below] as well as a
powder magazine, and the " stores " (warehouses for provisions and furs),
workshops for blacksmiths, carpenters, and so on, stables and cattle-sheds,
offices and Indian quarters. In the centre of the courtyard are the flag-pole,
and some buffalo-hide lodges belonging to half-breed hunters. There is
also a cannon, with its muzzle pointing at the gate.

The Fort possesses some fifty or sixty horses, a few mules and a so far
not very numerous collection of cattle, pigs, goats and chicken. The cattle
are sleek and fat, and the cows provide adequate milk.

During the daytime the horses are sent out on the prairie, guarded by
armed men on horseback. They are brought in at night, although most of
them have to sleep in the open air. Mr. MacKenzie is having a special
corral made inside the Fort.

Fort Union is one of the Fur Company's most important depots, as it
is the clearing house for two forward trading posts over towards the
Rockies, and controls all the trade in the Rocky Mountain area. Of the
two forward posts, Fort Cass, 200 miles away on the Yellowstone, deals
with the Crow nation, the other, Fort Piëkan (now called Fort MacKenzie)
lies 650 miles down the Missouri, a day's journey below the rapids;
650 miles is the distance by river but a man on horseback can get there in
ten days. Fort MacKenzie handles trade with the three Blackfoot nations.
This post was established a couple of years ago, and as steamers cannot go
far above Fort Union, barter goods are sent on in " keel-boats " which
spend the winter up there, returning to Fort Union in spring laden with
the furs and skins accumulated over the year by trapping or by trade. These
are shipped down to Saint Louis by steamboat during the summer.

Many of the Company's agents in these outlying trading posts take
Indian wives, abandoning them unceremoniously when moved to another
post, or upon returning to the United States. The lower classes of agents,
known as *engagés* or *voyageurs* must be able to act as river guide, steersman,
hunter, etc. as occasion arises. They are often sent on long and dangerous
journeys to trade with the Indians, and every year a number of them fail to
return, killed fighting hostile Indians armed with weapons supplied by the
Whites. Some of the American Fur Company's agents spend the whole
winter in the Rocky Mountains with nothing save a rifle for companion. [22]

*Destruction
of Buffaloes
1833*

The environs of Fort Union were full of game; hunting was both a necessity and a sport. The fresh meat revictualled the Fort and the Indians dependent upon it; the skins and dried or salted meat went down to Saint Louis. Maximilian zu Wied has something to say both about this and about the way the Fur Companies were destroying vast herds of buffalo:

The maintenance of such a large establishment at Fort Union entails frequent hunting sallies on horseback over the prairies, and Mr. MacKenzie has several half-breed hunters who ride twenty miles or more after buffalo every week, bringing the meat home on pack-mules. The flesh of the cow buffalo is extremely good eating, especially the tongues, which are hung up in bunches and smoked, before being sent down to Saint Louis. The enormous marrow-bones are regarded as a great delicacy by the half-breeds and Indians.

The destruction of these great denizens of the West, which are to the Indian what reindeer are to the Laplanders and seals to the Eskimo, proceeds at a dreadful rate. Every year the slaughter increases and the animals are driven further afield. The Fur Company in a recent year sent 42,000 cow-hides down the river to the United States, where they fetch four dollars apiece. Fort Union alone consumes 600-800 annually for its own purposes, and the other forts do likewise. The Indians depend almost entirely on these creatures, selling what skins they do not require for clothing, covering lodges or turning into leather-goods; the Company's agents recklessly shoot buffalo for "sport", often with no intention of using any part of them, except possibly a tongue or two. In some years whole herds perish by drowning in the Missouri or by sinking in the mud. After some floods as many as 1,600 bodies have been counted in one place, and regular dams of corpses build up. From this one can form some idea of the destruction that besets these useful creatures, which are now to be found on the far side of the Rockies, where they never grazed before. [22]

Ten years later, also at Fort Union, Friedrich Kurz, the artist who lived with the Indians, went on a buffalo hunt:

*Buffalo Hunt
1843*

It took us five miles of hard riding to come up with the herd; we thought the Dobbies had spoiled the hunting for us, but as we reached Mackenzie Butte (named after the father of my shooting companion) we unexpectedly came upon a small herd of old bulls and bull-calves. Some lay by the spring at the top of a *coulée*, others were peacefully browsing nearby. We immediately altered course, riding behind the hill and down past the cherry and plum bushes beside the *coulée* to catch the buffalo by surprise; but they had already heard us coming and were up and away, tails angrily waving. We straight away jumped the brook and set off at full gallop,  strung out in Indian file. Our horses entered into the spirit of the chase, vying with each other. I let Mac go ahead so that I could watch him. His practised eye had already chosen its target; he rode up to within two paces, fired—and by the time I galloped past the bull lay dead; he had shot it straight through the heart. It pawed the ground briefly in its death-throes, groaned and rolled onto its side. I thought at first it had died of fright.

We galloped on at full tilt, and I too hoped to get a shot at buffalo. Mac called me and singled out a beast from the herd; I gave chase across the rolling prairie. My bag of sketching materials swung about and got very much in the way, as I had to hold it with my left arm, which was really needed for shooting. I rode up so close to the black bull that I could not miss. My first shot went slightly above its heart, and the buffalo turned away, so that my second shot only hit him in the knee. Mac rode past and put a bullet in the old fellow's head *en passant*. Still keeping up

FORT CLARKE ON THE UPPER MISSOURI · WINTER 1833-1834

with the herd we reloaded our flint-locks in the saddle, letting the bullets roll down on top of loose powder.   Mac made jokes about the way my bull carried on with a bullet " through its heart " : he evidently did not know it was dead.   But in fact it was done for; it stopped and looked angrily around, bleeding from the nose.   I reigned in my " pacer " and turned towards the buffalo, aiming at the eye to finish him off.   But my nag was so excited and out of breath that it would not stand still, and I missed the eye, despite the shortness of the range.   The monster barely shook its head; but then it began to stagger, spreading out its legs to keep its balance; but to no avail; he sank, first upon his knees, then on to his side.   Unfortunately this beast was too skinny for me to use as model for a fine buffalo, so we left it and rode back to the first animal.   We hobbled our horses and let them graze while I drew the dead bull from various sides to the best of my ability. When I had done, Mac cut out the tongue and the stones as titbits for his squaw; then we rode home at a hand-gallop.   What a wonderful life it was, just riding and drawing!   As the second buffalo did not fall to my rifle I had no trophy to take home. [21]

Prince Maximilian went on to Fort MacKenzie, where he stayed from August 9th until September 14th, 1833.   He then returned down the Missouri and wintered at Fort Clarke.   He thus grew well acquainted with life in these outposts :

Fort Clarke
1833

The present Fort Clarke is about a quarter of an hour's sailing below the original Fort established by Lewis and Clarke and roughly 300 paces from the Mandan village of Mih-Tutta-Hangkusch.   It stands on a level

FORT UNION, MONTANA - 1833

plain, about eighty paces from the south bank of the Missouri, which is very steep just here, rising sheer out of the water just below the Indian village. Some 200 yards from the Fort a little stream widens out, that the Indians call Pach-Ohkirussa-Passaha—" The River Where Dishes are Washed ". Two hundred and fifty yards short of the Missouri it divides, one branch flowing southward, and the other winding some 700 paces behind the Fort, emerging on to the level prairie from a ring of hills that block the view from the Fort in this direc- tion. The valley of the stream is grassy, and grows a variety of tall plants and bushes, especially *Syn- genesie* such as solidago and the

HILL WITH STRANGE
CONTOUR ON THE UPPER MISSOURI - 1833

like, the seeds of which, including *Fringilia linaria* and *Emberiza nivalis* are gathered during the winter. In the spring and autumn there are wild duck on this stream, which also has river turtles; a *Unio* * too. When the frost comes, which in 1833 meant November, the duck move to some ponds and marshes a few miles away, there joining other wildfowl including pelicans, swans, wild geese, and cranes, and remaining until those waters freeze. About an hour's sailing below Fort Clarke the Missouri bends east or northeast, passing through forests where the people of Mih-Tutta-Hangkusch have their winter quarters, comprising sixty or seventy huts. Above the Fort a trail leads across the prairie from their summer village to another Mandan settlement, Rohptare, with nothing to break the monotony save a couple of small ravines where prairie hens nest. . . .

The Fort was not badly supplied with feed for the horses, but although there sometimes seemed to be a superfluity of mounts their numbers tended to shrink owing to a local fondness for horse-trading. These animals lead a very hard life; most of them spend the whole winter out of doors, so that on really cold nights they roam the corral with heaps of frozen snow on their backs. In winter they get nothing to eat but poplar-bark from the trees in the forest, and that only when it is not too cold and the snow is not too deep for their daily outings with a young Indian groom called Sih-Sa. The dogs, too, spend their nights in the open.

Fort Clarke possessed no cattle at all, and few other domestic ani- mals, apart from thirty hens, which start laying in March—a breed with yellow legs and a yellow stripe low down across their backs. The cattle were constantly in danger from the Indians, who regarded them as a piece of White Man's Medicine which might upset the buffalo-hunting. There was also a solitary cat, which, however, had no effect on the enormous rat population. These rodents (*Mus decumanus L.*, the Norway Rat) were so numerous and troublesome that nothing would keep foodstuffs from their depredations. It was reckoned that they ate five bushels of corn alone every day, a bushel weighing 5o pounds—in all some 25o pounds daily. There were often stocks of 5oo to 8oo bushels of corn in the store-house.

The rats came on the American steamers; so far none have reached the Monnitarri villages, but Indians have killed seven on the trail thither. It will probably not be long before they become established.

The Indian villages are the Fort's only near neighbours. These villages are surrounded by burial platforms, which present a bizarre appearance and in summer, when the wind is in that direction, exhale vapours which are neither pleasant nor conducive to health. In summer time the prairie looks quite busy, with Indians going to and fro about their affairs, and groups of ponies grazing; but in winter the snowy landscape is dead and desolate in the extreme, with neither man nor beast to break the monotony unless there are buffalo in the region; at most a few scattered wolves, which hang about in sight of the Fort all day long.

On the frozen river there is much more life, for the Indians are continually coming and going between the villages, the Fort and their winter quarters. Women, children, braves and dog-sleighs move about all day long, while, especially on Sunday, people from the Fort go out on snowshoes, and children take toboggans on the ice. [22]

A prudent traveller must now leave Fort Union without further ado if he is to be in Salt Lake City, Utah, before winter.   The way lies up the Yellowstone to its junction with the Powder River, and then follows the latter as far as the country between the Big Horn range and the Rattlesnake Hills. From here on we are in the Land of the Mormons. On muleback one has to ford rivers, cross deep canyons and scale mountains until, after a somewhat anxious journey—but fortunately without mishap—Salt Lake City comes into view. Holy Cities were nothing new to the great British traveller, Captain Richard Burton, who had already visited Mecca and Medina, long forbidden to the infidel, disguised as a Pathan pilgrim:

Approaching
Salt Lake City
1860

At this place the pilgrim emigrants, like the Hajjis of Mecca and Jerusalem°, give vent to the emotions long pent up within their bosoms by sobs and tears, laughter and congratulations, psalms and hysterics.   It is

Ship Yellowstone on the Missouri River — 1833

indeed no wonder that the children dance, that strong men cheer and shout, and that nervous women, broken with fatigue and hope deferred, scream and faint; that the ignorant should fondly believe that the " Spirit of God pervades the very atmosphere ", and that Zion on the tops of the mountains is nearer heaven than other parts of earth. In good sooth, though uninfluenced by religious fervour—beyond the natural satisfaction of seeing a brand new Holy City—even I could not, after nineteen days in a mailwagon, gaze upon the scene without emotion.

The Sublime and the Beautiful were in present contrast. Switzerland and Italy lay side by side. The magnificent scenery of the past mountains and ravines still floated before the retina, as emerging from the gloomy depths of the Golden Pass—the mouth of Emigration Kanyon is more poetically so called—we came in view of the Holy Valley of the West. [23]

The Holy City of the Mormons attracted large numbers of permanent immigrants. Many visitors, too, intrigued by the new religion, stayed for varying lengths of time. The founder of this Church, Joseph Smith, thanks to an angel, had rediscovered the Holy Books, engraved on tablets of gold, which constituted the revelation of Christ to the ancient inhabitants of America. Thought of as heathens, the Mormons were chased from Missouri, Ohio and Illinois successively. Then, numbering 15,000 and led by Brigham Young, the Mormons penetrated to the interior of the Continent in 3,000 covered wagons and after a long march lasting several months, settled near the Great Salt Lake in 1847. There they founded a theocratic State. A Frenchman, Jules Rémy spent a month at Salt Lake in 1855 :

Salt Lake City 1855

We made our entry into Salt Lake City on the 25th of September, 1855, at a quarter past three in the afternoon, fifty-eight days after leaving Sacramento. We made for the centre of the city, advancing along one of the principal thoroughfares—a street bordered on either hand by gardens and orchards, whose trees, especially the peaches, were laden with fruit. The inhabitants mistook us for the courier operating the monthly mail service, and for this reason our passage excited little remark. We directed our steps initially to the town hall, where Haws wished to ask the President to recommend us some lodgings. His Honour was not at home, and so, on the advice of the clerks, we made our way to the Union Hotel, situated near the northern extremity of the town. A short stoutly built man, neatly dressed and of respectable mien, was smoking a long china pipe by the front door of the hotel. This was the proprietor, the Hon. Kinney, Supreme Judge of Utah Territory in the name of the Federal Government. He introduced himself most charmingly and bade us enter his abode, placing the best rooms at our disposal; he even made us free of his own large drawing-room. Before tea, which meal was taken at six o'clock, we were regaled with port-wine and American brandy. George we dispatched to find quarters at the Deseret Hotel, kept by a Mormon named Townsend.

Judge Kinney's house was of some size and, indeed, quite well appointed. By contrast with the desert, it seemed a veritable palace. Inside, we found a young mountain sheep, which looked more deer than sheep, playing with a large local bird. The latter resembled an African ostrich in size, but differed from that creature in having a long beak. The presence of these animals, whose tameness contrasted strongly with the immense solitudes of Utah which had given them birth, added an original touch to our apartment, which we found highly agreeable.

Shortly before nightfall that same day a party of English Mormons pulled up in Union Square outside our hotel, where they were greeted by the band of the Mormon church. The new arrivals pitched their wagon camp right there, pending the allotment of quarters and land.

We saw a number of Utah Indians about the town, and they seemed to be extremely well treated by the inhabitants.

That evening we were called upon by General Burr, head of the United States Topographical Engineers in Utah Territory, an old man whose intelligence was in keeping with his position. There also called a Dr. Hurt, the assistant Indian Agent; he was a most likeable man, although, alas, not enjoying the best of health. We were thus fortunate from the first in enjoying the society of persons of refinement and education.

JUNCTION OF THE YELLOWSTONE RIVER WITH THE MISSOURI - 1833

These Federal Government officials were far from belonging to the cult of Joseph Smith, and spoke at length upon the state of the country as they saw it. They led us to believe that we should not be long in discovering the hidden sores that prey upon Utah Mormons, who might behave decently enough in public, although things were very different behind the scenes. They spoke warmly of Brigham Young, the first President, but were unable to comprehend how a man of his intelligence could so strangely delude his poor fanatical followers. They added, furthermore, that several Mormons from the Old World were murmuring against the despotism of the Church, citing amongst others the case of a well born and eminently respectable Frenchwoman who had been deserted and left destitute by her husband because her faith in Mormonism had collapsed upon contact with the Saints in Utah. From what follows it will be seen that we were not able completely to share the opinions of the worthy cartographer and doctor, being unwilling to judge so considerable a society upon a few isolated, and indeed, inconclusive occurrences.

Peter Haws and the two Shoshone Indian chiefs whose services had proved so valuable during the last stage of our journey remained several days before returning to their distant abodes weighed down with tokens of our gratitude. It was most extraordinary how the two Indians not only failed to demand the slightest recompense for their long journey and hard

VIEW OF THE ROCKY MOUNTAINS · 1833

work, but remained completely impassive at the sight of our gifts. What a contrast with the savages in Oceania, whom we could never satisfy, and who would cheerfully have accepted the very shirts from our backs !

The day following our arrival was spent in exploring the city. The streets are all 40 metres [131 feet] wide and run north to south and east to west. Beside the streets run streams of clear water ingeniously brought down from the mountains. Each of these brooks is adorned with a double row of cotton-woods. The roads intersect at right angles to form squares or " blocks " measuring 202 metres [219 yards] a side. Each dwelling is set back at least twenty feet from the road and has a cultivated yard around it. This arrangement not only imparts a countrified air to the city but vastly increases its area : from corner to corner it measures three English miles. The great majority of the houses are built of adobe, in a style that is usually simple, often elegant and always clean. Certain of the dwellings are very grand, including that of Brigham Young, which is like a palace. This edifice measures 3o metres [98 feet] long by 40 [131 feet] wide, and is built of various kinds of stone, including some superb granite brought from the mountains at great expense. The tall jutting ogival windows in the upper story rise beyond the roof, conferring upon this Mormon masterpiece the aspect of a crenellated diadem. Thirty Sultanas are to inhabit this harem which, although still far from complete, has already cost the Mormon pontiff 15o,ooo francs. The latter's private fortune, the result of fortunate speculations, is said to exceed two million francs. The house in which Brigham Young lives at present with his seventeen wives, stands alongside this palace, with a bee-hive on the roof, symbolising the industry and innocence of the people of Deseret. Close by are the office of the President and the *bureau des dîmes,* or " Tithing Office ".

Not far from the President's palace is the Court House. A library established by the Federal Government in Washington and continually added to by donations, is attached to the Court House for the use of the public. A little beyond is the Social Hall. . . .

The temple, which is to have six great many-sided belfries and will, according to the Mormons far surpass in splendour and architectural magnificence every monument in the world, is being built of excellent local granite. The architect of this prodigy is a Mormon Englishman named T. O. Angell. There is a drawing of the Temple in the President's office, which he allowed us to copy. The Mormons do not say whether God gave the

The White Castles on the upper Missouri — 1833

OUTCROPPINGS IN WESTERN MONTANA WHICH REMIND VISITORS OF CASTLES ON THE RHINE

dimensions and proportions of the Temple of Sion at Salt Lake City as he gave those of the Temple of Nauvoo in the beginning to Joseph Smith. . . .

We were struck by the cleanliness of the town and by the general prosperity evinced by the style and upkeep of the houses. We could but admire the order, peacefulness and industry apparent upon every hand. . . .

The members of this little community perform their functions like the worker-bees in a hive, thoroughly justifying the emblem which the head of the Church has placed upon the summit of his palace. They are the masons and carpenters, the gardeners, the smiths, the furriers and the gatherers of the harvest. Theirs are the children who thresh the corn and it is they who mind the flocks and herds, bring stone from the mountains, dig irrigation canals and so on. Tailors, shoemakers, brickmakers, potters, chemists manufacturing gunpowder, millers, sawyers, gunsmiths making and repairing rifles; in sum, artisans and workers of every kind. There are no idlers or unemployed. Every person, from the humblest believer to Bishop or Apostle, is engaged in manual tasks. One has only to see Mormons at work to realise why their colony, which was not founded until 1847, is now so flourishing and progressive. Nor is this activity, admirable and productive as it is, the result of organised toil on the lines dreamed of by certain European economists; each man works for himself and his family under the triple incentive of need, self-interest and well-being. The poorest, who are usually the latest arrivals, go and work for the wealthy; should they not find work they apply to the Church, which always has tasks to be done, and makes payment in clothing, foodstuffs and firewood.

There are no bar-rooms, gambling-saloons or houses of ill-fame. These do not exist amongst the Mormons. The only public meeting-places are the Temple, the schools, the military parade ground and, from time to time, the Social Hall, where they hold dancing and singing and theatrical entertainments, and also give courses in science and history. One never hears trouble in the streets, there is never a sign of a brawl. For this reason prosecutions are rare, and almost the sole function of the Courts, according to the magistrates, is the settlement of overdue debts.

Although there are no bar-rooms or drink-shops of any description, this does not mean that the Saints have renounced the use of liquor in moderation. No commandment compels them to reject certain productions of Nature or certain products of the arts. It is true that Joseph Smith in his sermon entitled Word of Wisdom pledges the true believer to abstain from fermented liquors and tobacco, and recommends such abstinence as a means to perfection; the most devout do abstain for this reason, but they are not above drinking in moderation when opportunity offers. Many of them are beer drinkers, for which reason hops are grown in the valleys; others drink wine when they can get it; a few even permit themselves whisky, which they distil from potatoes. Families generally spend their evenings at home in conversation, preaching, and reading from the Scrip-

MORMON CARAVAN ON THE WAY FROM CALIFORNIA TO GREAT SALT LAKE CITY - 1860

tures and other religious writings, or the periodicals published by their leaders. Not a woman is to be seen on the streets at night, a remarkable fact in a population where there are more women than men and where the practise of polygamy might be expected to bring greater freedom of behaviour.

The spectacle of this hard-working and sober community is not without its entertaining side when one considers the diverse elements that compose it and the classes from which it is predominantly drawn. There are at Great Salt Lake City—to list them in order of numbers—representatives of the following nationalities: English, Scotch, Canadian, American, Danish, Swedish, Norwegian, German, Swiss, Polish, Russian, Italian, French, Negro, Hindu, Australian. We even saw one Chinese. Of diverse origins and often conflicting beliefs, most of them are completely without education, and drawn from utterly different backgrounds, some righteous, others indifferent, the majority perhaps a prey to the basest instincts; they have come together notwithstanding differences of climate, language, customs, laws, nationality and tastes, they dwell in harmony— living indeed better than their fellows—in the midst of the American continent. They form almost a nation within a nation, and one, be it said, which abides as little by the decrees of the United States Government as by the *firmans* of the Grand Turk *.   One almost begins to believe in the possibility of universal fusion, a future in which all peoples shall coalesce into a single republic.   Such is certainly the hope and aspiration of this people, who call themselves the favoured children of Abraham. . . .

We stayed a whole month in Salt Lake City, exploring the neighbourhood by day, passing the evenings in lively discussions with our Mormon and Gentile guests, and part of the night in setting down our impressions and checking our notes. . . .

Looking back, it seems to me that men have never been busier, nor has time passed more swiftly.   We were content with four hours' sleep *per diem*, thanks to habits contracted in Indian country.   Our health did not suffer in the least from this crowded life, the best proof being that Mr. Brenchley and I each regained five pounds of the weight we had lost on the outward journey (19 pounds in his case, 17 in mine) in the space of 31 days.   This rapid recuperation was certainly not due to high living, for our host, the great Judge Kinney, subjected us to an invalid's or penitent's diet that was very far from strengthening.   We practically died of hunger, in other words, and although we were paying more than we should have done at the Café Anglais, we did not like to complain, especially as the others seemed satisfied ; we tried to tell ourselves that our appetite was unreasonable. However, if the diet did more to irritate our stomachs than satisfy them, the regular routine, the absence of worry and of exertions comparable with those we had undergone while crossing the desert, did much to maintain us in good health.   We also contrived to come by a drop or two of wine, at vast cost, to make up for the lack of solid food.   The kindness of our host in other directions more than made up for the meagreness of his table.   The Judge's helpfulness and good humour, as well as the recollection that Utah was in a state of famine, gave us patience to endure our fasting.

Amongst a number of excursions that we made within a radius of 15 to 20 leagues [50 miles], we must mention several visits to the Great Salt Lake itself, a huge sheet of water which reminds the Mormons of the Dead Sea and leads them to think that God created it as a latter-day American replica of the Judean original.   We never visited the lake without bathing in it, although prompted more by curiosity than inclination ; and we were much amused at the astonishment of our men, who were convinced that such highly saline water must be harmful, especially to the eyes and ears.   On one occasion we managed to persuade a Negro to join us in a swim.   Afterwards, for a joke, he allowed himself to dry in the sun without brushing the water off, becoming covered with a whitish crust so that he seemed to have turned into a pillar of salt like Lot's wife.   The whitened black declared that his new skin gave him torture, as though needles were prodding at every pore.

BRIGHAM YOUNG - 1855

We believed him, for we too prickled painfully all over until we had rinsed in fresh water.   Mr. Brenchley, who insisted on diving in the hope of finding madrepores [a sort of porous coral] despite the density of the water, also complained of sore eyes; but these effects soon disappeared.   We generally went to Black Rock, some 15 miles out of town, travelling in an excellent two-horse *char à bancs* which conveyed us there and back for the sum of 25 francs.   We seldom devoted more than five hours to such outings, including the journey and the bathe.

We also went walking and riding in the Wasatch Mountains, where the people of Salt Lake obtain firewood and timber for building.   There are more bushes than trees proper, the latter consisting mainly of conifers, maple, small oaks, poplar and sumac.   We met abundance of the Camash onion that the Indians prize so much, and in the most secluded spots we came upon small hop gardens, so well disguised as to hint at clandestine breweries.   The woods harbour thousands of squirrels, but intensive hunting over the past few years (the flesh is eaten in Utah) has made them timid and very hard to kill.   Gentiles had described how the Mormons lured their enemies to these valleys and murdered them : the ground was supposed to be strewn with skeletons. We saw no bones of any sort, only honest woodmen carrying faggots, felling trees and mending bridges.   We counted seventeen wooden bridges over a stream in one valley; it is part of the city's water supply. . . .

Our studies and excursions did not keep us entirely out of society. We went to a number of parties, and these too proved instructive.   We were bidden one evening to an all-male supper-party by two prominent shop-keepers named Gilbert and Gerrish. Not many official people were there, but our fellow guests proved to be cultured and amusing. They included Dr. Hurt, the assistant Indian Agent, an excellent talker, endowed, like most medical men, with the gifts of eloquence and observation. He gave us a vivid picture of the savage tribes with whom he was in daily contact, telling us of the diplomatic shifts and ruses to which he was driven in dealing with these children of nature, their strong sense of justice, their pride, their natural dignity. Indian chiefs were great sticklers for protocol, he said, and described their manner of speaking: so grave, so well reasoned and so grand. He spoke too of their high-mindedness—and of their blood-thirsty instincts. The Redskin is indeed a strange mixture, hard for Pale-faces to understand.

Mr. Gerrish presided over the feast with an urbanity that was quite European; we heard as much wit and impromptu punning as one would find in the middle of New York or Paris.

We were introduced to sparkling Catawba, a wine that reminded us, in its sparkle, its colour and indeed its flavour, of that nectar which grows

THE MAIN STREET AT GREAT SALT LAKE CITY - 1860

upon the slopes of Rheims and Epernay. This Catawba wine, which we sampled later upon its native soil at Cincinnati, is grown from vines transplanted from the banks of the Rhine to those of the Ohio. Two kinds are made : Catawba proper, which is colourless or slightly golden, and Isabella which is pink in colour, sweeter, and more popular with the ladies. American sparkling wine is just as exhilarating as ours, but stronger and more intoxicating. In short it is inferior to good French Champagne. All the same it is preferable to the doctored wines too often exported by dishonest shippers, and is therefore a threat to our own white wines in this part of the world. Frenchmen abroad must be ashamed and dismayed by the stuff exported as Champagne, and often bearing highly respectable labels. [24]

At the end of his stays in Salt Lake Jules Rémy drew up some very instructive accounts —though it should be remembered that the costs he talks about involved a party of four men and twelve animals :

Expenses in Salt Lacke City 1855

Our expenses for the thirty-one days came to 13,000 francs [equivalent to the yearly salary of a French official of the highest rank]. This fabulous figure requires some explanation before it can be understood. First of all it is no reflection on Mormon hospitality, because our principal suppliers were Gentiles. Secondly, out here everything brought from the United States or Europe costs its weight in gold. Apart from this there was something like famine in Utah at the time, owing to a plague of grasshoppers —grain, bread and vegetables were fabulously dear. Feed for our animals, on which we dared not economise in view of the long and difficult journey home, came to 19 dollars a day. This was exorbitant but inescapable. The purchase of a wagon, harness, two mules and a few bits of clothing accounted for a sizeable sum ; presents for the Indians and supplies for the journey also took some of the needful. There remained our own food and lodging, which the Judge rightly considered could not be put at less than that of our animals and raised accordingly by an amount proportionate to our respective positions. However, if the Judge's hospitality did come rather expensive, the rest of the tradespeople treated us very decently ; which cannot be said of certain more accessible countries to which fate or fancy has led us.

On the morning of Friday October 26th, 1855, we bade a tumultuous farewell to Judge Kinney. In all we mustered twelve saddle and draft animals, of which four were ridden by ourselves and the men and four were harnessed to the wagon. The remaining four, whose turn would come, followed *en liberté*. Our turn-out was magnificent for those parts, and we felt as proud as any farmer driving to market. The gleaming new wagon and harness, not to mention the spotless new awning, made a brave and splendid show; and our sleek and well-groomed mules seemed quite conscious of the fact, and positively coquettish. Djelmi had not grown, but she was prettier than ever, and put on the airs of a regular aristocrat. Campora too was rather *grande dame* in the way she sailed along. Jack, the most intelligent of all the mules, had eyes as soulful as ever and stuck to his master like a dog; he seemed to lack only the power of speech. Riley retained a wicked eye and rebellious nature despite his increased portliness; at bottom he was less malicious than he looked and one learned to laugh at his baleful gaze after a minute or two. Our other beasts, including two gigantic new mules, looked equally healthy and smart, but all their good points were physical; useful creatures, but dull. The most insignificant member of our party was a Mormon dog. One could not say what variety he was, except that he looked like a mixture of everything. Nor was he any better than he looked; he was the most apathetic and dull dog imaginable. We had hoped to use him as a watchdog at night, but he was the soundest sleeper in the party, and the most craven. His voice never made itself heard. He was christened Tiger in token of his office; and when his true nature appeared the name was retained out of irony. [24]

MAIN STREET OF GREAT SALT LAKE CITY - 1853

A STATELY RANCH-HOUSE NEAR SONOMA, CALIFORNIA - 1858

CHAPTER THE FOURTH

In which the Reader,
having traversed the Deserts of Utah and California,
arrives safe and sound at Los Angeles;
whence he embarks for San Francisco
—not to make his Fortune
but to make the Acquaintance
of the Country and its People.

" California is beginning to take shape " proclaimed the famous Parisian weekly *L'Illustration* in its issue of 31st August, 1850. The cautious note in *L'Illustration*'s headline was even more justified at the time. Modern visitors to California know that, even today, this American State, which is almost a country in its own right is still in process of taking shape. But until 1849, when the Gold Rush brought a great influx of visitors from all continents, few European travellers had set foot in this part of North America. From that moment onwards, California became " news ", and frequent advertisements appeared in the European press inviting investors to put money into gold-mining companies. Many responded to the call. Some, of course, were content to take only a financial or commercial interest in the new country, but others engaged their persons as well. Unhappily, few if any of these " merchant venturers " set down a record of their failures or successes in the Gold Rush and it is to more detached observers that we must turn for a description of that land which in 1850 was admitted to the Union as the State of California.

Jules Rémy, whom we have already encountered in Chapter III, traversed California in both directions in 1855, in his travels to and from Salt Lake City. He seems, surprisingly, to have been little interested in gold-seekers and what may be called the Forty-Niner Mystique. On the outward journey, he was absorbed mainly by a study of the Mormons. On the way home, his only desire was to draw clear of the mountains before winter closed in. Rémy's description of Las Vegas, where he arrived hungry and dead-beat, may surprise those familiar with that city in its later and more hectic manifestations. In his day it was no more than a fortified farm operated by Mormons in the hope of attracting the Indians and giving them some training in agriculture. Los Angeles, too, made little impression when Rémy passed through. A tumble-down place, though pleasantly situated, he notes, adding " there is nothing angelic about it, in fact quite the reverse ". Three other Frenchmen, Alexandre Achard, Patrice Dillon and Louis Simonin travelled in California between 1849 and 1860.

Of Alexandre Achard little is known except that he visited the famous Murphy mine near Sonora in 1849. He has, however, left vivid impressions of San Francisco in the first year of the Gold Rush, when, to his astonishment, it cost far more to have a shirt laundered than to buy a new shirt, and playing the piano in a saloon offered a surer means of livelihood than prospecting for gold.

Patrice Dillon reached San Francisco twenty months after the discovery of gold by James W. Marshall, a man then employed by John A. Sutter. Dillon had just been appointed French Consul at San Francisco, and the country was in a ferment when he sent off his dispatch to the *Revue des Deux Mondes*. His article is packed with information about the cost of living—from the price of eggs, which often fetched a dollar apiece—to the surprising intelligence that a hard-working family of six persons, acting together, could earn as much as 4,000 or 5,000 dollars in six months. This despite the number of new-comers arriving in San Francisco, which Dillon estimates at 2,000 a day during the last months of 1849. He told his readers, too, how Californians admired anyone who stood up for law and order, and recounted how a local judge acquired popularity by sentencing to be hanged all who were brought before him, regardless of their alleged offence or of their guilt, thus frightening away all the thieves, vagabonds, gunfighters and other riff-raff that would otherwise have infested the district.

The same pragmatic trait in the American character is mentioned by Louis Simonin. Writing some ten years after Dillon, he explains that the present peaceful state of the community was due to the energy of the citizens themselves, illustrating this with the story of the trustful saloon-keeper who eventually recovered his money by posting the names of his debtors and the sums they owed, along with a forceful notice which read: " Be a Man If You Want Your Name Taken Down. " Pressure of public opinion had replaced the Six-Shooter.

Visitors to this turbulent and colourful California of the Fifties noted, too, that although the local mosquitoes were vicious to both sexes of mankind, the men-folk there, as elsewhere in the United States, treated the ladies with the greatest respect. At the same time Louis Simonin remarks that his travelling companions used to gulp down their meals in a mere ten minutes, and that, however much one might admire the Americans for their kindliness and thrift, in 1859, their table-manners took some getting used to.

Leaving Salt Lake City, Utah, on October 26th, 1855, Jules Rémy's little expedi-tion advanced southward at a brisk pace, hoping to reach Los Angeles, California, before winter. They stopped for the night at the small Mormon town of Lehi near Utah Lake, and promptly found themselves set upon by urchins. Later after crossing the desert they were brought news of a major victory for French Forces in the far distant Crimean war :

We settled down in the middle of the road, without troubling to look for an inn that we should probably not have found. Our men purchased wood, forage and grain and, once the animals had been hitched to the fence rails of a garden and given their feed we lighted a fire, on which Victor cooked supper while we wrote our notes by its light. We had not been there more than an hour before the whole town knew it. Inquisitive crowds came flocking; I think some people got out of bed specially, and we were literally assailed by a troop of small boys who, the following day being Sunday, showed no inclination to go early to bed. I do not know whom these onlookers thought we were, but they evinced a singular desire to be informed of everything concerning us ; and the sleepiness that weighed upon our weary eyelids rendered us little disposed to satisfy their curiosity. However, the more we thrust them away the more anxious they appeared for conversation. Our every movement was spied upon and it was impossible to utter a word without its being overheard and our remarks discussed. We could not move a step without being followed. I would recommend all governments who find the upkeep of a police force too expensive, to rely for this service upon small boys ; they can count on their zeal, if not their perspicacity. We were still being plagued by these idlers at two o'clock in the morning. We decided to go to bed as a polite means of hinting that they should withdraw; several of them lay down beside us and started to snore in a way that we found the more deplorable as it

Leaving
Salt Lake City
1855

prevented us from sleeping ourselves. Others, seeing that we were awake, continued to ply us with questions, to which we framed monosyllabic replies. We were tempted to order them away in no uncertain terms, but that would have scarcely been right : the highway belongs to everyone, and they had every bit as much right to be on their own road as we had. At dawn the grown-ups arrived, and we were again assailed with questions, so that finally we took refuge in silence. Intelligent curiosity I can appreciate and

YEDRA, TYPICAL
CALIFORNIAN PLANT - 1847-1851

enjoy, but the cloddish sort I absolutely detest ; the former is pleasant, and may even be instructive ; the latter does nothing but bore and infuriate. Some of them asked why we lighted our pipes with brands from the fire instead of using our matches ; others continually asked the time for the sake of seeing us take out our watches. Others wanted to know whether it was our expenses that we were writing in our diaries, how many pens we used up in a year, and how long it had taken us to learn to write. God, how infuriated we were that night ; it would have been better to have had mosquitoes !

When daylight returned and the desire for sleep no longer oppressed us, we laughed heartily at our late ill humour and agreed that our visitors had not been really bothersome and stupid, but merely naïve. An old fellow of Welsh origin brought us a large jar of milk as a present ; another gave us some eggs. The man in front of whose house we had camped, an Englishman, showed himself most obliging and his wife or, I should say rather, one of his wives, placed her ovens at our disposal and urged us to accept some potatoes. The small boys were now so respectful that we were sure that they had not intended to annoy. We took the road again at half-past seven, convinced that they had come to spend the night with us out of politeness : examples of civility which prove more embarrassing than civilised may be met with in every country. [24]

The journey continued without incident, save for the normal inconveniences attendant upon travelling through almost waterless desert. A halt at Cedar City, Utah, provided Jules Rémy with a glimpse of Mormon pioneers at work :

Cedar City
1855

Towards midday we came to Cedar City. A troop of Indians galloped across our front and stopped at their encampment under the walls of the

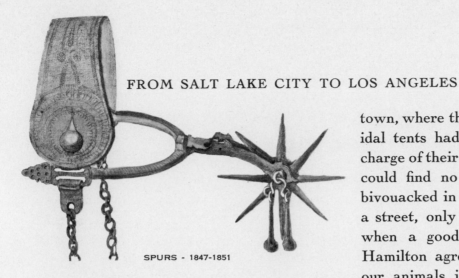

SPURS - 1847-1851

town, where the tall pyramidal tents had been left in charge of their squaws. We could find no lodgings, so bivouacked in the middle of a street, only too delighted when a good man named Hamilton agreed to house our animals in his corral.

The town of Cedar is situated on Coal Creek, 270 miles from Great Salt Lake City. It was founded in 1851 by a company of thirty-five Mormons whose capacity for work has become almost proverbial. First of all they erected a fort to protect them against attack from the aborigines, then they put up palisades to enclose an area of 500 acres, dug canals, sowed vast fields; then they commenced the exploitation of rich iron deposits lying a mile or two from the settlement. The city is imposing and well situated. The high mountains at whose foot it lies present a bizarre appearance; the rocks are of a reddish colour, and give rise to strange optical effects when the mountains are capped with glistening snow, as at the time of our visit.

As we spent two whole days at Cedar we had time to make excursions into the surrounding country-side. First we inspected the large plant that has been constructed for extracting the iron. We could see that the ore was indisputably rich, yielding from 25 to 75 *per centum* pure iron. The mineral rights for fifty years have been granted by the Utah legislature to a joint-stock company known as the Deseret Iron Company. The furnaces now produce around thousand kilogrammes [one long ton] of iron every twenty-four hours. The coal used in this plant is taken from what is said to be an inexhaustible seam in the mountain four or five miles above the town. This coal is excellent, but contains so large a proportion of sulphur that it is deemed best to purify it by moderate heating before use. Coal and iron are not the only minerals found in the neigh-

OX-CART - 1847-1851

bourhood of Cedar; there are also sulphur and lead mines, and certain indications suggest that cinnabar may also be discovered.

When the foundations of Cedar City were laid, less than ten years ago, the settlers imagined themselves to be tilling virgin soil, and that they were the first human beings to found a society in these wild surroundings. They were mistaken : many centuries before, the soil they now tilled had supported numerous generations. Quantities of coloured potsherds have been discovered, establishing that the Mormon city is built upon the site of an important Aztec town, the Aztecs, though now extinct, having been at one period the most highly civilised people in the two Americas. Certainly the fragments of pottery we have been able to examine display a perfection of colouring that is not present in the *huacas* [sanctuaries] of Peru. Unfortunately no complete article has been found, and the fragments so far unearthed have been so broken as to permit of no reconstruction being made. Notwithstanding this it is already evident that the ceramic arts had been brought to a high state of development by the ancient peoples of the New World, although in purity of form they do not approach the magnificent Etruscan vases from Corneto now housed in the Vatican. Ruins of ancient manufactories, too, have been found in this part of Utah, including recognisable kilns used by the potter. [24]

In these parts the Indians appeared to be at peace with the Mormons, whom they looked upon as a special sort of Paleface, superior to " Americans "—by which they meant all other white men. Jules Rémy took due precautions, however :

*Journey
through the Desert
1855*

The Moody is deep, and although the water is clear and limpid it is not easily drinkable, being tepid and rich in alkali. We had to fill a barrel with it however for use on the road. We followed the river banks for several hundred yards before crossing. Only two Indians followed us to the ford, and then they promptly made off. We felt that their departure had lifted a great burden. . . .

The country-side was exceedingly dry, and the hills as far as we could see were all sandy, without a trace of vegetation. On emerging from the valley a little before nightfall, we set off across a vast undulating desert which we resolved to cross in one stage, thus sparing our animals the tortures of thirst. About ten o'clock however, when the moon went down, the darkness was so intense that we had to abandon this idea and suspend our march. We tethered the animals to the wagon so as not to lose sight of them ;

LANDSCAPE SOUTH OF LAS VEGAS - 1849

we still had some grain left and it was pleasant to feel that, thanks to our forethought, they would suffer no pangs of hunger while standing thus close to the expedition's household goods. The desert traveller is like an ocean mariner; just as the latter regards the ship as another homeland, so does the former cleave to the wagon, his terrestrial ship; each trusts his star and places himself in God's hands, whence alone cometh salvation. We lay on the sand, lulled to some extent by the sound of our animals munching their corn, and congratulated ourselves on having crossed the valley of the Moody where so many emigrant trains had been wiped out by Indians. At length, having rendered thanks to Heaven, we fell asleep. [24]

What a relief to arrive at Las Vegas! Man and beast could shelter at last in the confines of the little mud-walled Mormon fort:

The Spanish name *Las Vegas*, which signifies " fertile fields ", was bestowed upon this spot by the Mexicans because it is a sort of oasis in the desert. The Mormons have established a farm here to attract the Indians, with the idea of converting them and teaching them agriculture. This settlement, which stands on New Mexican soil, is one of the latest founded by the Sect. It is safe to predict that it will attain much importance, for only a very

*Las Vegas
1855*

LANDSCAPE ON THE COLORADO RIVER - 1849

narrow tract of land is cultivable and the desert extends for a considerable distance in every direction.   However, Las Vegas has its uses, one must admit, as a caravanserai at which the U.S. mail and desert travellers can replenish their supplies.   The fort at present possesses one house and a barn. We found thirty-three Mormons there, nearly all priests, and not a solitary woman.   They grow cereal crops and vegetables, which do well.   The corn they sold us was of very good quality.   They treated us with indifference and showed little disposition to oblige, but this coolness was a normal condition with them, not a sign of ill will. [24]

RANCHER'S HUT NEAR LOS ANGELES - 1847-1851

The crossing of the Mojave Desert between Las Vegas and San Bernardino, California, took about ten days.   Beyond it lay softer, more welcoming country, where law and order reigned once more :

The Mojave Desert
1855

When night fell there still remained a small wood to be crossed before arriving in San Bernardino.   We became separated in the pitch darkness and for a moment felt lost.   I made my way towards a light, which proved to be that of an outlying house, and there learned that the town lay only a few steps farther.   After wandering through deserted streets I at length found our wagon, unharnessed, standing before the house of Bishop Crosby, to whom we had a letter of introduction.   The bishop's wife received us in the absence of her husband.   She was a large " comfortable " body who did the honours of her inn most affably, and seemed quite upset when we insisted on sleeping in the street rather than accept her much-vaunted beds, but we found the latter too short and too shut in.   She sold no wine, for reasons of Temperance, but she offered us tea and coffee, and volunteered the information that, should we be set upon securing some wine of the country, we could obtain it from the schoolmaster. Victor [the cook] did not arrive until two hours after me, and Huguenot [Rémy's servant] was later still, because of Riley, who would keep lying down in the road.

It froze hard during the night. At seven o'clock next morning the Bishop's wife served us an excellent breakfast, and we were joined by Mr. Philips, who was waiting to complete the journey with us. While we were eating dessert a Mormon missionary arrived from Los Angeles, bringing the news that Sebastopol had fallen on the 8th September*. We celebrated the occasion as good allies should, with patriotic sentiments and all the solemnity that the circumstances allowed. After the cold of early morning came the burning sun of day, and it seemed to us that the sky had suddenly lightened as though to bid us welcome.

San Bernardino is an entirely Mormon creation, and therefore very recent. In acquiring a large tract of land on Californian soil only a short distance from the sea the Mormons' aim was to establish a *pied à terre* for emigrants arriving via the Pacific. The plan speaks well for the Church's foresight. It does in fact serve a triple purpose in the Mormon economy : supplies can be obtained there on advantageous terms for the journey from California to Utah; people coming from hot countries who find Salt Lake too cold for them may remain in or return to San Bernardino; and Brothers may be relegated there whose turbulence or lack of zeal might otherwise compromise harmonious relations in Utah itself. At the time of our passage San Bernardino counted a population of 1,400 Mormons, answerable in temporal matters to the State legislature and in religious matters to a resident Apostle. As the Californian Constitution does not tolerate polygamy, the Saints who live here must renounce the plurality of wives. [24]

Los Angeles was reached on November 29th, 1855, that is to say after thirty-four days' march, during which it was hot in the daytime, but freezing cold after sundown. The stay at Los Angeles ought to have been very agreeable to the tired travellers, yet it was far from being so. The natives were hostile, but in a very special way :

We spent ten days or so at Los Angeles waiting for the steamer that was to convey us to San Francisco. It was not a particularly pleasant stay. The country itself was hardly prepossessing, and although we regained our liberty after it had been threatened at one point, it was not hard to see that we were regarded with suspicion in many quarters. There were even some

*Los Angeles
1855*

who paid the French authorities the compliment of taking us for police spies or *mouchards* as they called them, sent over by the Emperor to discover what the miners thought of his Government. In such circumstances, however great one's contempt for public opinion, it may be imagined that life was filled with unpleasantness, not to say humiliation. However, these insulting suspicions did not bother us unduly and in no wise deterred us from studying the country with the calm detachment born of a conscious superiority over our vulgar detractors.

The town which the Spaniards, for what reason I know not, baptised with the name of " The Angels " is anything but angelic —quite the contrary; and I fail to see what the most fervent well-wisher could find remarkable in it. Ill-planned and ill-built, the place looks dirty and poverty-stricken. Most of the houses are single-storey buildings in the Mexican style, built of adobe bricks and provided with flat roofs, the latter being not tiled but covered with a coat of bitumen, taken from a spring not far away. Alongside these filthy and miserable habitations, the strangers attracted to California by the discovery of gold have erected dwellings that are more comfortable, more seemly and better built. The situation of Los Angeles, however, is better than the building. The flat plain on which the city stands stretches to the sea on the south and west; on the east, or mountain side, the eye is greeted by hills, most of which present a very arid appearance. [24]

LOS ANGELES, WITH THE PLAZA CHURCH AND SQUARE IN THE MIDDLE DISTANCE - 1855

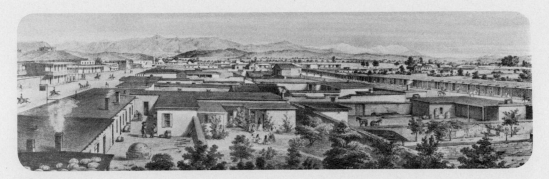

LOS ANGELES LOOKING NORTH, WITH MAIN STREET AT LEFT · 1857

It is usually the master who gives " references " to servants when they leave his employ. But it was otherwise with Jules Rémy, who received the following strange testimonial from the faithful Huguenot. It was composed by a schoolmaster and set down by a letter-writer, since the author of the sentiments could scarcely name the letters of the alphabet :

Dear Sir,

    As one who has, in the dual capacities of Guide and Man-Servant, crossed the Plains from Great Salt Lake City to California in your Company, pray allow me to express my Thanks for all the Kindness that you have shown towards me. Permit me also to bear witness of my Admiration for your Intrepidity and Hardihood during our journey through Hostile Indian Tribes, whom you managed to win over by your manly Bearing, which was at the same time Affable and Audacious. Indeed, you conducted yourself in the Desert and Mountains as though you were Native of those Parts. My warmest good wishes go with you, my Brave and Noble Friend, wherever you may be, whether under tropic Sun or in your home Country.
    With Affection and Respect,
        Yours,   Huguenot. [24]

*Unusual Reference
1855*

    Bent on visiting San Francisco, Jules Rémy and his companion, J. L. Brenchley, M.A., left Los Angeles for San Pedro, their point of departure which served as seaport for Los Angeles, remarking that the place had only three houses, the shore was too steep and the landing-stage bad :

At nine o'clock that evening we boarded the SENATOR, the big steamer which was to carry us to San Francisco. Once more we had occasion to appreciate the advantages enjoyed by travellers in a free country : no formalities were required in obtaining a passage, and nobody asked for a pass-

*To San Francisco
1855*

port, that costly, humiliating, vexatious and ineffective encumbrance, which is quite unworthy of this century and of our civilisation. Passports, octrois, and Customs constitute three veritable plagues for the travellers; they not only reflect upon the dignity of man, but also occasion a great waste of precious time. When will the civilised nations renounce these miserable, out-moded and insulting institutions? Is it not better to let one rogue pass than to bedevil a thousand law-abiding people? Would it not be preferable to allow a pair of gloves or a bottle of brandy to be smuggled than to go through people's pockets and turn their trunks upside down? If states and municipalities need the revenue and cannot obtain it elsewhere it would surely be simpler to levy an individual landing-charge than to insult people by prying into their effects—a procedure which would appear odious and revolting had not long custom inured us to it. None of these inconveniences awaited us in California, a fact which occasions the above reflections.

The SENATOR put to sea at two o'clock in the morning on December 9th. The sea was calm and we made good progress, never losing sight of the coast. At ten o'clock we put in at Santa Barbara to pick up and set down passengers. For all that we were aboard a republican ship, Equality, that chimera of modern political thinking, by no means held undisputed sway. Not that we had occasion to complain! We were first refused permission to sit at the First-Class table, on the reasonable ground that we were not properly dressed. However, when it was realised that the clothes we stood up in were the only ones we had left, we were suffered to remain amongst those who had the good fortune to possess the correct wardrobe.

On the 10th, around 11 o'clock in the morning we called at Monterey, in a huge bay where the fronds of giant seaweed could be seen waving below the surface. The coast-line was picturesque, with pine-covered hills making a delightful background to the township.

At nine o'clock that evening we cast anchor in the Bay of San Francisco, that Queen of the Pacific Coast, so young and yet already so well-grown; a marvellous city the rapidity of whose development has surpassed every historical precedent, and destined perhaps to be the capital of a new republic—if it be true that the great United States Republic is not in a position to satisfy all factions despite her prestige and unrivalled prosperity. [24]

The history of San Francisco and California in the mid-nineteenth century was so astonishing that *L'Illustration*, "the universal journal" published in Paris, had this to say in its issue of August 31st, 1850: "California is beginning to become a fact. For

The Presidio of Monterey, California — 1826-1827

A FORMER SPANISH GARRISON FLYING THE MEXICAN FLAG

the past two years so many strange, exaggerated and contradictory reports have assailed our ears from this unknown and mysterious Eldorado that one has feared to give them credence. Today all doubts are set at rest. Europe has seen and handled—nay turned to advantage—gold from the overflowing mines in whose existence she refused to believe ; emigrants who left our shores in poverty have returned home wealthy ; traveller's accounts, of unimpeachable veracity, have appeared in every language. ''

Among these reports figured that of Patrice Dillon, who was French Consul at San Francisco towards the end of 1849 :

Yerba Buena, otherwise San Francisco, lies on the right as one enters the Bay, a little beyond the old Spanish fort. Today it is a town of 50,000 souls, which bids fair to become, within the next few years, the capital of the Pacific. The forest of rigging that extends in every direction, reminds one of Le Havre and Marseilles. At the present time there are 340 merchant ships moored off shore, not counting brigs and schooners. Every ship, without exception, has lost its crew, and from many of them even the captain has deserted. A corvette of the United States Navy flying the flag of Commodore Jones, keeps solitary watch over this silent fleet.

We went ashore unhindered at an improvised landing-stage below the old fort. There were no customs men to turn out our pockets, or plunge a questing blade through parcels and trunks. The octroi, that clumsy device for universal hindrance that is at last disappearing wherever some spirit and enlightenment exist, is utterly unknown to the Americans. For them, time has just as much value as merchandise, and anything that robs them of it without demonstrable cause is an infringement of their rights as free men. True liberty consists, in American eyes, not in being allowed to pour forth philosophical extravagances to an audience starved of material benefits, but in being allowed to get on, without let or hindrance, with the jobs for which they consider themselves most fitted.

At San Francisco, where fifteen months ago there was nothing but half a dozen rude cabins, they now have a stock exchange, a theatre, churches of every Christian denomination, and a large number of quite handsome dwelling houses. A few of these are stone built but the majority are of wood or adobe. The fronts of the houses are whitewashed or painted, the streets are well laid out and the whole effect is quite pleasing. On each side of the town, lines of tents extend far along the beach, forming a new kind of town that is not without originality. Here are to be found emigrants from both Worlds, as well as Chinamen, Malays, and a raggle-taggle crew from all the South Sea islands, sailing out of Botany Bay ; they

*San Francisco
1849*

pause here before heading for the gold-fields.   In their ranks may be found the sometime Minister of Justice to King Kamehameha of the Hawaian Islands, now the most formidable gunman in California; he it was who composed the famous legal code that Bible Societies in Great Britain and America hailed as a masterpiece of human wisdom.   In these tents you find murderers, parricides, road-agents and the like upon whom the hand of God's justice

PRESIDIO OF SAN FRANCISCO - 1816

has yet to fall.   Comedy and drama—especially the latter, are found here in abundance : incredible escapes and adventures that the most fertile imagination of the novelist has not yet dreamed of, here await the historian.

San Francisco buzzes with activity like a vast beehive.   Carriages, carts and wagons drive haphazardly about the streets, creating confusion and running into one another.   I pity any absent-minded professor who may chance to find himself in San Francisco, for he is likely to be run over without anyone so much as crying " Get out of the way! "   Tall raw-boned fellows in sugar-loaf hats tear about, thrashing their horses without sparing a thought to people on foot.   The side-walks are thronged with silent, pre-occupied crowds hurrying to the Assay Office, an ill-proportioned structure at the bottom of the town, or to the Stock Exchange, an edifice standing between two gambling-saloons, and always besieged by groups of speculators.

Every country on earth has financial interests in San Francisco but, as is only to be expected, the American element leads.   American law permits people to set up in business in any way they choose. Everyone, therefore, is broker, shipping-agent, banker, money-changer, auctioneer, or, indeed, several of these professions at once. Whether the ship-owners and merchants of Le Havre who consign goods to San Francisco make their fortunes I know not; but I am positive that the agent at this end does not lose money. The extent of his charges under the head of brokerage,

PASSAGE INTO THE BAY OF SAN FRANCISCO FROM THE TELEGRAPH - 1847-1851

exchange, and warehousing would be an education to his *confrères* in Europe; without any exaggeration they may be reckoned at 5o to 1oo per cent on the net amount of each transaction.

It is only fair to add that the consignee in San Francisco has heavy expenses to meet. Thus, apart from the material cost of living in a country where an egg may cost as much as five francs and a potato as much as three, rents run from 15o,ooo francs [$3o,ooo] to 3oo,ooo francs [$6o,ooo] a year. There are quite a number of houses which bring their proprietors 8oo,ooo francs or so *per annum* [the equivalent of $16o,ooo today and of course a great deal more in buying power]. . . .

One of the factors responsible for the unreal and exaggerated rentals of buildings in San Francisco is the large number of gaming-houses which have sprung up. Every exile from the *maisons de jeu* at Frascati, and in the Palais-Royal, or from kindred establishments in London, Paris and Vienna seems to have foregathered in this promised land of the gambling fraternity.

The moment a house falls vacant the gamblers leap upon it, regardless of rental, and move in with their roulette-wheels. At the present time there are one hundred gambling-houses in San Francisco, each one of them crammed every night with vagabonds of every kind and colour—Sandwich Islanders, mulattoes, Chinamen, and Malays, besides white men—if they may be called that—of every nationality—and every man Jack of them a ruffian of the deepest dye. Every country in the world seems to have poured its detritus into this human sewer.

There is no stranger spectacle than these gambling-houses after eight o'clock of an evening. Outside, an immense crowd blocks the doorways; within, the gamblers force their way to the *monte* tables, often coming to blows in the process. Elsewhere, quarrels of this sort may be settled by blows and kicks. In California an insult, or sometimes even the merest nudge is a signal for knives or pistols to be used. "Quiet, down there", shouts the Bank when shots ring out, "you're making too much - - - - - din, you - - - - - s!" Someone else cries "I'll drill a hole in you, Devil take me if I don't!"; such are the terse but strenuous comments to be heard on every hand. When all go armed such fracas must have serious consequences.

Once he reaches a table, the new-comer—usually fresh from the mines—unstraps his tan leather belt, places one end on the green cloth and gives it a slight shake. Several gold nuggets roll out. The "head manager" [*sic*] extends a large bony hand, picks them up and weighs them on a balance at his side, paying out their value at the rate of eighty-five francs an ounce. The customer places his stake and the same bony hand rakes it in; he plays again, with like result. After fifteen or twenty minutes the belt is again unstrapped. It is seldom indeed that a gambler goes home without

THE GOLDEN GATE. ENTRANCE TO THE BAY OF SAN FRANCISCO - 1855

being stripped, in a single night, of everything he has earned by several months of toil and privation. . . .

The population of San Francisco is daily swelled by sea-borne emigrants flocking from all parts of the world. The Sandwich Islands, Tahiti, and the Fiji Islands, as well as New Zealand and Sydney, have voided themselves of their white population, and all these heterogeneous elements have merged into the great mass of gold-miners. They are all away at the moment, but when winter comes they will head back into town for shelter; the only ones here are shop-keepers, ships' captains, and men who have made money at the diggings and are now in town to squander it on gambling and debauchery. The population is almost entirely male, so that the few decent women who have come out here with their husbands scarcely dare venture out of doors. However, there has been some improvement in this respect. Since the purely American element secured the upper hand in San Francisco no woman can be insulted with impunity, for, as is well known, nowhere in the world are women treated with greater respect than in the United States.

On the other hand, those industries which in Europe would incur the strongest moral censure are here in full swing, and hardly a week goes by without some Chilean or American brig chartered by speculators discharging a cargo of females into the town. It is this traffic, I am told, which at present shows the quickest returns.

Were one to analyse the elements of the San Francisco commercial population one would find some odd ones indeed. Every New York store-keeper who has gone out of business, every fraudulent bankrupt wanted by the authorities, every confidence trickster and adventurer in the Union has descended upon this promised land. " See that man over there ? " remarked

SAN FRANCISCO FROM GREEN STREET, TELEGRAPH HILL LOOKING SOUTH - 1859

SAN FRANCISCO, MISSION DOLORES, NOW CORNER OF 16TH AND DOLORES STREETS - 1860

my cicerone, himself a U.S. citizen, " he's one of the greatest geniuses in the country.   President of the biggest concern in Baltimore.   He had the idea of " cornering " all the fresh meat in the U.S.A. and refusing to sell it except at his price.   He had gotten hold of three-quarters of the cattle in the States and was just getting his hands on the rest, when another American — guess he is a genius too—started bidding against him.   The struggle between them was terrible and went on a long time.   The public, who just love anything big, were tickled to death.   In the end both fellers went broke." " Still ", added my friend, " they've pulled through all right.   The feller you just saw arrived here six months ago without a cent and he's now worth 100,000 dollars ; the other one's done even better.   They're aiming to have a real show-down any minute now. . . . "

The most surprising thing about San Francisco is the scarcity of thefts, despite the enormous opportunities and the extremely rough population. Everywhere you look—in people's gardens, outside the houses, in the streets and public places—you see heaps of merchandise from all over the world lying around apparently unguarded ; yet none of the thieves and professional bad men so much as look at it.   The reason is that California, like every other country, has its code, a code universally recognised and respected.   Thus, it is quite in order to shoot a man or stick a knife into him during a quarrel or to get one's own back ; but taking someone else's gear is the lowest crime of all, and a thief can expect twenty bullets to fly in his direction from the nearby tents and cabins.   Store-keepers, miners, and boatmen would drop what they were doing and give chase, for it is in everyone's interests to suppress theft since there are neither police nor military to safeguard the public. Such a state of affairs must immediately arouse feelings of astonishment and even indignation in the European breast; one cannot conceive how any Government can be so lax in its essential duty as not to extend direct and official protection to a Territory that has placed itself under the national banner; but many things that appear strange to a European seem perfectly natural to the Americans. To them society is merely an association of free and intelligent elements in which people find their proper niche by a process of natural affinity. Any intervention by the authorities, save in extreme circumstances, it is felt, would only upset this balance, and it is better for the citizen to take the ordering of certain matters into his own hands than to leave it to the Government, thus placing himself permanently in thrall. One cannot altogether blame the Americans for being built this way. . . .

One exceedingly odd thing strikes me about San Francisco, and that is the popularity earned by those who display firmness and courage in defense of law and order. Outside Sacramento when I was there, there was an *alcade*, or sheriff, whose territory had previously been a rendez-vous

CROWDS LINED UP FOR MAIL
AT THE OVERWORKED SAN FRANCISCO POST-OFFICE DURING THE GOLD RUSH - 1849

for all the gunmen and desperadoes from miles around. Crimes were frequent, misdemeanours even more so. For each and every offence the good Judge had only one punishment. A terse " Hang him! " was the invariable verdict when an accused came before his court. The local populace, who themselves acted as lictor, required no second bidding : he was " hung ", then everyone went quite happily back to work. Whether it was a stabbing, or the theft of a pipe or pocket-handkerchief the verdict was always the same : " String him up! ", carried out literally and without pity. If anybody ventured to remark that the accused might not be guilty, and it would be well to hear his defence, the sheriff would say " Hell, you all know there ain't nobody innocent around here. If he ain't done *this*, he's done some other thing either here or some place else. String him up! " Everyone would grin, and go cheerfully off to the hanging.

At that time the old Spanish system applied, in which all power was vested in the *alcade* without a jury. Later this was altered because Americans have an invincible objection to dispensing with the only safeguard that prevents justice from turning into despotism. It is true that in conditions then prevailing trial by jury served only to render the proceedings more grotesque. How often has one seen a jury of twelve inebriates empanelled to judge another of their ilk! The verdict of Guilty (it was almost invariably Guilty) would be followed by the sheriff's usual " Hang him! " Then would follow the oddest scene imaginable. The foreman of the jury, himself far gone in liquor, would drag a Bible from his pocket and read a chapter to the condemned man. Then all the jurymen would clap him on the back and assure him that the verdict had been arrived at solely from a sense of duty. Then " Come on, feller, cheer up! You've still got a quarter of an hour while they're fixing the rope. What'll you have? " Whereupon everyone would go off and get drunk.

A young Frenchman of good family opened a saloon in those parts and quickly made a fortune. He found only one difficulty. Amongst his customers was an American, a deserter from the navy, who was always coming in and demanding drink at the point of a pistol, and rarely if ever paying for it. The Frenchman grew weary of this and applied to the sheriff. The good officer was just writing out a sentence of Death that he had just pronounced. He listened to the complaint without taking his eyes from the paper. Still without looking up he reached out and took a double-barrelled pistol from the right-hand side of his desk and handed it to the plaintiff.

San Francisco, California — 1849

FLEET ABANDONED BY GOLD-HUNGRY CREWS, SEEN FROM RINCON POINT

" But, Monsieur, what is zees for ? "   " Take it ", said the sheriff with his usual terseness.   " You've let yourself be insulted, so you evidently don't have no pistols.   Take it, and bring it back afterwards. "

The young saloon-keeper returned to his tent, packed everything portable and left the district for ever.   " I have 60,000 francs ", he said when telling me this story, " and I still have a head on my shoulders.   To H - - - with the sheriff and his deputies and the whole primitive country. I'm off to France on the next mail-boat. "

During the first days following the discovery of gold a group of Americans, Frenchmen and British formed themselves into a band known as the Hounds.   Their avowed object was to raise funds by voluntary subscription so that any member who lost his money and was unable to work, might have his passage paid home.   Every member wore a stripe on his sleeve for purposes of identification.   To start with one heard nothing but praise for the Hounds, who were the sole means of preserving law and order, often coming to the help of the authorities.   But gradually quarrels broke out between them and the Chilean miners, who understood gold-mining and, working together in gangs, had prospered exceedingly.   The Hounds thereupon served notice that the Chileans must get back to their own country, and declared war.

Worsted in several encounters the Chileans left the workings and took refuge in San Francisco.   The Hounds followed and blood shed became a nightly occurrence.   There was never any peace because miscreants of every nationality, scenting trouble and pickings rushed to join in. Houses were sacked, liquor-stores looted, all with complete impunity. Whereupon the San Franciscans, turning their backs upon the whole affair went straight to the Excise Office for their liquor, in short minded their own business and behaved as though they had nothing whatever to do with either side.   Only the British, accustomed to proper protection from the authorities and the soul of discipline as usual, showed indignation, protesting against the culpable negligence of the Federal Government.   Matters rested there until rumours reached San Francisco of frightful excesses committed by the Hounds the previous day at a Chilean camp.   They had massacred several women after outraging them before their husbands' eyes, and then set fire to the tents and burned the bodies.   The news reached San Francisco one evening.   First thing next morning a man named Brennan, leader of a sect known as the Mormons that had recently arisen in the neighbourhood, marched to the main square ringing a bell. People followed him to see what was afoot. Brennan climbed upon a table and harangued the crowd, which by now was large and close-knit. His language was crude, terse and to the point. Were they a lot of cowardly scum, he demanded, willing to stand around with closed eyes and folded arms while a bunch of gunmen committed atrocities that cried out for vengeance ? Did they want the same thing happening to their own wives and daughters ? Yesterday it was foreigners ; tomorrow it might be their turn, the turn of American citizens ! He was ashamed of them all, he said ; they were selfish lily-livered wasters. For his part, he added, he was fetching his pistols right now and as sure as God made little apples he would drill a hole through the first Hound he met, and the rest of his hearers should do the same.

His cry was taken up all over town. Everyone joined the crusade : French, British, Germans and Americans. By evening all the Hound leaders had been taken. The good *alcade* out at Sacramento gave them short shrift, with his usual " String 'em up ! "

The number of immigrants arriving daily in California by sea can be set at 2,000, with every European nation represented. American ships can be recognised by the lively cheers from passengers and crew when the vessel docks at El Dorado. Unskilled labourers earn 150 dollars a month, cooks easily make 300 a month, while artisans such as carpenters, blacksmiths and so on receive better wages still. Servants do not exist ; men worth several million dollars clean their own boots and carry out the multiplicity of household chores that elsewhere are done by maids.

The cost of living is not especially high for the working classes. Fresh meat is still plentiful, and sells for 1 franc 25 centimes the half-kilo [25 cents a pound] ; salt meat and biscuit, with which the market is flooded, are hardly dearer than in Europe. I can say the same of ardent spirits, which are at present quite hard to dispose of ; a few weeks ago this was true of claret, stocks of which were lying around on the side-walk because people would not buy any more. Then all of a sudden gold-miners swooped down and bought every bottle, because some interested party had started a rumour to the effect that spirits induced fevers, which could be avoided only by limiting oneself to red Bordeaux. . . .

In San Francisco the only ties that count are those of family. A united family of half a dozen hard-working boys or girls may earn 20 or 30,000 francs [up to 5,000 dollars] in six months. Life is not enormously dear for the working man.   Biscuit and bacon cost no more than they do in the United States.   Rents are exorbitant, it is true, but one can always sleep under canvas in one of the innumerable tents which surround the town, forming, so to speak, the suburbs of San Francisco.   Until recently monopolies had rendered certain goods exceedingly dear.   A can of sardines cost seventeen cents an ounce and a bottle of brandy twenty dollars, but now all kinds of provisions can be had very reasonably, thanks to the easy transportation facilities offered by the steamers using the Bay.

At the gold-fields prices vary a great deal from place to place, depending upon demand, so that it is impossible to provide any yard-stick for the guidance of French exporters.   Taking the number of miners as 200,000 and their average daily earnings as 12 dollars, we arrive at a figure of 240,000 dollars a day, that is 12 million francs.   This figure, I have absolutely no doubt, is far higher than the sum actually being earned.   The gold-mining fraternity, drawn for the most part from the lower orders, manifests that irresistible craving for drink that is characteristic of the Anglo-Saxon race.   It is unusual for them not to abandon work for days on end in order to give free rein to this predilection, the moment they are in possession of a few thousand francs.   It is after these orgies, as a rule, that they fall victim to the fevers that prevail up there; these fevers are due not so much to the climate as to the intemperate habits of the emigrants.

MERCURY MINES OF NUEVA ALMADEN, SANTA CLARA COUNTY · 1847-1851

The country is far from unhealthy, and the climate at San Francisco is so bracing that only woollen clothing can be worn. The almost invariable costume of the miners is a red or blue flannel waistcoat, and trousers of coarse cloth or canvas. [25]

SMALL RANCH AND CORRAL IN SAN MATEO COUNTY - 1847-1851

At the beginning of 1850, that is to say six months after Patrice Dillon's remarks were written, another Frenchman, Alexandre Achard, landed at San Francisco and found the city in a notably less prosperous phase than that described by Dillon. His report, date-lined Murphy, June 1st 1850, appeared in the Parisian *Revue des Deux Mondes* on the 15th August following :

San Francisco
1850

On the 26th March, after a day's stop at Acapulco, our " steamer " put into San Francisco and the five or six hundred passengers in the CALI-FORNIA disappeared like a flight of starlings. Here was I at last setting foot in the fairyland to which so many eyes are turned : California, the realisation of dreams for a few, a land of bitter disappointment to many.

Seen from the ship as we docked, San Francisco had the appearance of a ruined city. No trade, no commerce ; the harbour, quays and warehouses clogged with unsold merchandise. Movement and activity were apparent only around the saloons and gambling-houses ; but there was no lack of movement there. Speculation in real estate, in which everyone, from labouring man to banker had plunged headlong, had swallowed up what had seemed the most solid fortunes. There could be no revival in trade or commerce, I was told, until the rainy season drove the miners back from the diggings, their money-belts stuffed with gold dust and nuggets.

San Francisco, as everyone knows, stands like a vast amphitheatre, half-way up the steep hills behind the Bay where the Pacific rollers break. Behind the town stretch other hills, destitute of vegetation. The houses, doomed to perish in the great fire, are almost all built of wood. The streets running parallel with the water-front are broad and straight and level, whereas those at right angles to it appear very steep and difficult, impassable indeed for wheeled traffic. Road-building in California is not yet in its infancy. The streets remain as chance has made them; they are never mended or swept and the trash thrown out of the houses is never cleared. In summer the dust and stench are intolerable; in winter the streets become swamps in which pedestrian and mule alike sink up to the ankle. In some quarters there are quagmires so deep that men and even mules have disappeared, with no hope of succour. To be perfectly truthful I should add that nobody in this gold-crazed city seems to mind very much. These quagmires look quite disgusting, and a pestilent stench arises from the stagnant black water and the debris floating upon it—half-gnawed bones, filthy old underclothing and the rest. No part of the town is free from them, even the centre and down-town districts. As for the weather, it is probably the most capricious in the world. From nine o'clock until midday it is oppressively hot; from then until seven there is a terrible wind which stirs up whirlwinds of dust. The evening brings mist, making everything damp, and the nights are intensely cold. It is the weather of Algiers, Avignon, London and Stockholm all in the same day.

The town is perfectly orderly, and despite the hotchpotch of nationalities and emigrants there is no danger to life or property. Stacks of merchandise lie upon the docks and no one amongst that motley crowd dreams of turning it to his own use. Is this due to honesty? I think not. Justice is swift in the Californian capital, and the ordinary working population are prepared to enforce respect for private property, knowing that the city's prosperity depends upon the maintenance of law and order. What is more, many of the rougher elements scarcely come into town; they make straight for the " placers ", which here govern everyone's thoughts and actions. With the bolder spirits gone, the rest soon find lucrative employment, or at least a means of scratching a living until something better comes along.

It is very difficult, with the best will in the world, to set down the whole truth about San Francisco. Everything can change utterly in a couple of weeks; prices move up and down to an extent that is terrifying:

OUTSKIRTS OF SAN JOSÉ - 1856

a bottle of brandy costs 3o dollars one day; a week later it is 20 francs [4 dollars]. A singer at the Opera House, Monsieur Barroilhet, has a brother, who by a stroke of luck made 250,000 francs overnight on a cargo of timber. When he arrived there was a shortage of wood; a month later those very planks were worth next to nothing. This is really an astonishing place. Side by side with riches from the Arabian Nights, there is abject poverty; houses furnished in Chinese lacquer, like that of Dr. Oliveira, stand cheek by jowl with filthy hovels made of straw and mud.

I have already mentioned that San Francisco was in the grip of a depression when I arrived. Its first effect was to drive down prices of consumer goods, especially articles of European manufacture, such as textiles, sheets and clothing. One could live at a pinch on three dollars a day. A room—completely furnished—could be rented for 200 francs a month .[4o dollars] — the same room a month before had cost 200 dollars. On the other hand a leg of mutton still cost 27 francs [5 dollars 5o]; a pound of butter 15 [3 dollars]; a litre of milk 7 [1 dollar 5o], and if one wanted radishes he had to pay 5 francs [a dollar] the half-dozen. In conditions such as I describe, when business has been brought to a standstill, the only emigrants assured of making a reasonable fortune are the artisans. A carpenter, wheel-wright, cabinet-maker, or blacksmith can always find work at an ounce of gold-dust a day, that is 8o francs [16 dollars]. As their food and living expenses do not come to more than 20 francs [4 dollars] they can put aside 6o dollars a day with no hardship. Laundry is something virtually unknown in San Francisco, for a very simple reason: one has to pay 3o francs, or very nearly, to have a dozen shirts, handkerchiefs or pairs of socks washed and ironed, while the same shirts can be bought new at the hosiers for 24 francs a dozen. It is the same story—*at present*—with all manufactured articles. A pair of sheets cannot be laundered for less than 5 dollars; and so sheets and pillow-cases are a luxury few can afford. . . .

Anyone who can scrape a fiddle, blow a *cornet à piston* or troll a ballad— any itinerant musician in fact, however unskilful, can disembark at San Francisco without fear. However meagre his talents may be he will find a dozen saloon-keepers eager to utilise his services at 80 francs a day. The night session pays at least two ounces of gold-dust, or 160 francs. Having heard one or two of the most sought-after artists in San Francisco, it seems to me that the poorest tenor from the *cafés chantants* in the Champs-Elysées, or the worst player in any small theatre orchestra at home, could make mountains of money out here. The saloons where these indescribable players are to be heard never lack patrons, and it is the same with the gambling-houses that stand on every street corner. Everybody here gambles and the play never stops. What the prospectors make during the mining season they lose during the rains. A few lucky ones—clever ones if you prefer—have amassed fabulous fortunes in these hells. These gaming-houses, with their crowds of hangers-on, present a most animated spectacle, but one that frequenters of casinos in the Rhineland or at Frascati would scarcely recognise. They consist of large halls, open day and night, with tables for *roulette*, *trente et quarante* and *monte*, which is the most popular game. Heaps of gold in the form of coin, dust and nuggets are constantly changing hands across these tables. The players are clad mostly in the picturesque garb of the miner, comprising red or blue jacket with blanket or striped cape thrown over the shoulder and an enormous hat made of straw or felt. Some of them have clothing made from skins. The sums lost at the tables are incalculable; the ruined miners go back to the " placers ", wash some gold out of the sand, and start again.

MAIN STREET OF SAN JOSÉ, FROM THE CITY HALL - 1858

One of the most picturesque things about San Francisco is the extra-ordinary way in which the classes are intermixed. Everybody does every-thing. There is no such thing as a shameful profession or a degrading occupation. The only criterion is money. However, if any distinguishing characteristics are observable amongst the ranks of the male population of California, I would say that it is the lower classes of emigrants who affect the greatest ostentation when they have made money, and they are most concerned with outdoing their neighbours. Contrariwise, people who belong by birth and education to the cultured classes of European society, devote themselves feverishly to toil of the harshest description. There have been tales of a wagoner-marquis, and a hunter-viscount. Nothing could be truer : I came across a man, lately secretary to a French nobleman and politician, working as waiter in a saloon ; he made eighty francs a day at this occupation, sufficient to sustain him in hopes of the " lucky break " about which all Californians dream. [26]

Ten years later, on June 2nd, 1859, another Frenchman, Louis Simonin, disem-barked at San Francisco. In California Simonin started a great travelling career and regularly furnished accounts of his journeys to the French magazine *Le Tour du Monde*. Later, in 1874, he again visited America and crossed the continent from Washington to San Francisco. His report on California makes an astonishing contrast with those of Patrice Dillon and Alexandre Achard :

San Francisco
1850

During the drive from the water-front to my hotel I took stock of this busy and astonishing place. There was no doubt about its being an Amer-ican city : wooden houses, for the most part well built, broad streets running parallel to one another or at right angles, on the chequer-board plan ; huge stores ; enormous sign-boards ; spanking turnouts thronging the cobbled streets ; omnibuses picking up and setting down bustling passengers ; frantically busy people. It all reminded me of the cities I had just been visiting on the Atlantic seaboard. But here and there the old-time San Francisco of Gold Rush days, the San Francisco we dream about in France, was to be seen sticking through : a broken-down hovel beside a fine house, a board-walk with boards so loose that people fall through ; many unpaved streets, which the rainy season will swiftly turn into a bog.

Such contrasts are inevitable in a town that has grown so fast ; and the costumes to be seen in the streets are equally striking and disparate. The Americans, first of all, in their serried ranks looking very much at home, as is only natural. The French, British, Irish, Germans and Italians

California — 1851

PLACER OPERATIONS AT FOSTER'S BAR

convicts, American " loafers " and bad men from every clime ran wild through the four corners of the town, pillaging and murdering. Gone too is the era of notorious fires, not all of which were accidental, that wiped out in a few hours towns it had taken months to build. They have also closed down the famous gambling-saloons, where revolver shots used to punctuate the shouts and imprecations of the players. Law and order have been re-established, thanks to the violent methods of enforcement which had to be adopted, so that for some years past San Francisco and, indeed, California generally, has compared quite favourably with the most peaceful and civilised countries. This is why, gentle Reader, my law-abiding host cared little about the latches on his doors and windows, and the reason, also, why I, having omitted to purchase a revolver, rifle and Bowie knife *chez* Devisme or Lepage before leaving Paris, failed to remedy this deficiency in San Francisco, contenting myself with peering through the gun-smiths' windows at Colonel Colt's six-shooter, the best revolver made. All this lacks picturesqueness, I agree. It would be nice to pose as a Forty-Niner with a whole museum of artillery round my waist; but I must beg Readers to remember that it is the California of 1859 that I am describing, not that of the Forty-Niners. Ten years is a century to these energetic Americans. . . .

The majority of the houses are of wooden construction, as being easier to move about. I saw some being transported on a low cart with extra-strong wheels, and sometimes the occupants did not even bother to quit their dwelling, but went about their business in the usual way. Other times it was a question not of transporting the dwelling but of raising it off its foundations and realigning the floors by means of a powerful screw-jack under each corner. A huge hotel underwent this operation, without one of the numerous customers evincing the least concern. . . .

The houses may still be mainly of wood, but San Francisco today is well protected against those nameless disasters that so tragically marred the city's early days. An excellent fire-fighting service has been organised. Two watchmen keep the city permanently under observation from the top of the City Hall tower, and sound the tocsin at the first glimmer of fire. At this fire-pumps converge upon the conflagration from every quarter, there being constant rivalry between the various volunteer fire-companies as to who shall arrive first and display the greatest courage. The fire is quickly extinguished, but the enthusiasm with which the pumps are manned is so great that the jets of water prove as destructive as the devouring element itself. I am greatly struck by the zeal which San Franciscan firemen bring to their calling. Some of the bravest and most daring fire-fighters in the city are of French origin—the Lafayette Company in particular.

In each company the engine itself is cosseted like a spoilt child. Once the fire is out the pump is brought back, to be housed in a shed built for the purpose, where a faithful fireman mounts guard night and day. Around the walls are inscribed the " battle honours " of the company, or rather of the engine in which it is personified. [27]

SAN FRANCISCO BEFORE THE GOLD RUSH - C. 1840

But Louis Simonin " wished also to see the interior of this interesting country ". In following his narrative and his journey through California in the year 1859, it is well to keep in mind that important changes had taken place since the early days of the Gold Rush. Simonin boarded the steamboat with the intention of sailing up the San Joaquin River as far as Stockton :

To Stockton
1859

The interior appointments of the ship were in excellent taste, and the state-rooms beautifully kept. There was a luxuriously decorated *boudoir* reserved for the use of the fair sex, who in California as elsewhere in the United States, are treated with the utmost respect. We passed through the Golden Gate and steamed close in to some of the islands in the Bay. Here vast flocks of sea-birds, cormorants, pelicans and the like, after gorging themselves with fish, come to bestow the products of their laborious digestive processes, thus instigating the manufacture of what is now called

STOCKTON, ON THE SAN JOAQUIM RIVER - 1855

guano.   In a short while we entered the Bay of San Pablo, which is next
to that of San Francisco.   Here the water became quite clear, and as we
passed between the rising banks we could imagine ourselves on one of the
Swiss lakes, the rounded mass of Devil's Peak on our right rising to
4,000 feet, as we threaded our way past little white-sailed boats.

From the bay of San Pablo we passed through the narrows into a bay
called Suisun, after the Indian tribe which used to' frequent these shores.
We passed Mare Island on our left, with the biggest Federal Navy yards
on the Pacific Coast and soon we beheld Benicia, given over to the Army,
and the dockyard belonging to the Mail Steam Packet Company.   Benicia,
known as the Venice of California, is one of twin sentinels guarding the
entrance to Suisun Bay, the other being the agricultural town of Martinez.
We now entered the marshy lower reaches of the San Joaquin, with its
low, swampy banks and bulrushes.   The San Joaquin comes out at almost
the same point as the Sacramento River but the two issue from exactly
opposite directions, the former from the south, the latter from the north;
thus we see the extraordinary phenomenon of two opposite currents practically sharing the same estuary.

Reaching Stockton at day-break on June 18th, P. . . and I went ashore
to look at the town.   It seemed to be a place of some 10 or 12,000 inhabitants, and has great commercial importance because the bulk of the Californian wheat is shipped from here.   It is a place of fragrant gardens, and
fertile plains growing mainly cereal crops.   The town is well laid out, and
has several fine buildings; there is also a remarkable artesian well supplying
water to the entire population.   It boasts a number of hotels on the American plan, together with a French restaurant, called the Lafayette.

Throughout the day we were in Stockton we were its most faithful customers, and we were only sorry they could not offer us rooms. We went to the American hotel to be devoured by mosquitoes, which the proximity of the San Joaquin River furnishes in abundance. They are of the very first quality; even in the Tropics I have not found their equal. [27]

Between Stockton and Coulterville Simonin travelled by stage-coach, stopping for luncheon at Knight's Ferry:

The stage, which was admirably upholstered and very well sprung, made not less than eight to ten miles an hour. We were, as they say " quite full up ": three ladies, two farmers, a prospector, a store-keeper, P... and myself. It was stiflingly hot, we were covered in dust and every so often the coach ran over tremendous bumps, which set us all laughing heartily. The interior panelling and ceiling of the coach carried vivid paintings of extremely *décolletées* nymphs, among other things, while the landscape outside was quite new to me. But we paused hardly long enough to change horses, and for my part I should have preferred a more leisurely progress. On arriving at Knight's Ferry we alighted, not merely for a change of horses but also for luncheon; we had covered twelve leagues [24 miles] in three hours. . . .

Set upon a table with a distinctly grubby cloth were little plates of boiled vegetables : here a turnip or carrot, there an onion or potato. We each speared the sample in front of us with a fork. Soon the main course was brought in and handed round, roast beef or roast mutton; we finished with a dessert, the choice being pies made with rhubarb or fruit. Everything

By Coach in California 1859

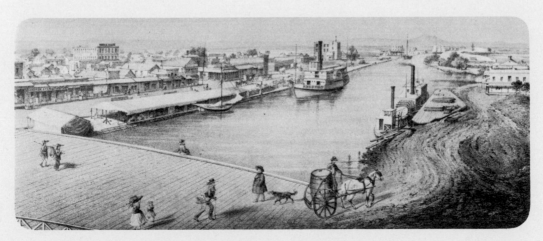

BRIDGE AND RIVER TRAFFIC IN STOCKTON - 1855

was eaten from the same plate, and in less than ten minutes, for, as they
say in America, " time is money ". No table-napkins, of course, each
guest doing the best he could with a handkerchief or the hem of the table-
cloth. Americans do not object to putting elbows on the table ; but, this
apart, your American is a reasonable table-companion, whatever his walk
in life. There is never the slightest argument—never indeed a word of any
kind—to break the silence during the *table d'hôte*.

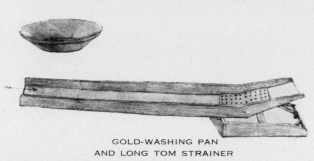

GOLD-WASHING PAN
AND LONG TOM STRAINER

After this Spartan repast,
at which water is the drink
at midday, and tea or coffee
in the evening, one goes into
the bar, where everyone pays
his share. The Yankees are
in the habit of drinking spirits
to assist digestion. I have
the greatest admiration for the
States in general, and for California in particular, but I must confess
that I have never grown used to the American way of eating. [27]

Coulterville was a mining centre that may be taken as typical of its period.
Here is Simonin's description :

Coulterville
1859

The population of the " camps " as mining districts are called in
California is somewhat different from that of the " placers " [see below].
Here for instance is how the population was distributed in Coulterville
in 1859. There were about 200 Americans, who kept hotels, bars, cafés,
pool-halls, stores, etc., and carried on various trades ; fifty Italians, most
of them gardeners, although a few kept stores ; thirty Frenchmen, comprising laundrymen, butchers, blacksmiths, and bakers ; forty German Jews
with ready-made clothes shops etc. ; and about as many Irish, Mexicans
and Chileans, variously employed, if employed at all. Finally a few Negro
cobblers, barbers, bath-attendants or washermen ; and a few Chinese
gardeners or cabinet-makers. Most of the year about a hundred Italians
were encamped around the town, subsisting on what they could filch. Five
hundred yards away, living like outcasts in a village of their own were
nearly three hundred Chinese. Altogether this came to about 800 persons,
forming a pretty odd mixture. All Californian mining camps have much the
same composition, although naturally varying in size. Some are very

populous, others even less so than Coulterville, which corresponded to a French *commune* or English-speaking parish, with its single magistrate, a policeman and other local officials. A doctor and pharmacist are also to be found in the township—if one may so describe the place, and Coulterville would be unlikely to disclaim the title, in view of the importance of its hotels and saloons, and the smart villas along the river-front. [27]

In contradistinction to a " camp ", a " placer " meant a claim being worked by one or several prospectors. Here is Alexandre Achard's description of one that he saw soon after his arrival, at the beginning of 1850 :

Gold-workings are always situated in a ravine hemmed in by mountains ; a stream runs down, and it is beside this stream that the prospectors pitch their tents. The land belongs to the first occupant. As soon as digging begins the ravine is named after the man who first drove his pick into the virgin soil. . . .

Gold-Miners
1850

When an emigrant finds a ravine that shows promise, either from the prospecting point of view or as a site for setting up shop, he cuts down a dozen or so pines, trims them and carries them down to the placer to build a tent. This will take him a week or ten days ; he can then turn to and work the gold or spread out his stock-in-trade. Everyone out here does his own manual labour, for the laziest workman costs at least an ounce of gold a day. Emigrants cook their own food, do the dishes and wash their clothes in the stream, living a sort of Robinson Crusoe existence, except that they work rather harder and have more to do. His tent erected and his claim staked and registered with the local sheriff—which confers a legal title to the site—the prospector waits for the rainwater to disappear from the hollows ; if this takes too long to go, or the claim does not yield richly enough, he leaves his tent and goes looking for gold elsewhere.

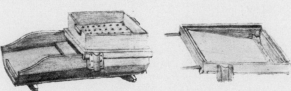

CRADLE-STRAINER FOR GOLD

When I reached Murphy camp, the nearest pine-trees were two or three miles up in the hills ; in another six weeks there would probably be none within five miles. You can imagine that there's not much " comfort " in this sort of camp. Anyone with Sybaritic tendencies beds down on pine-boards covered with pine-needles, but most people sleep on the ground, wrapped in a blanket that serves as mattress by night and top-coat by day.

Owing to the speculative activity that has taken possession of California, there is no lack of the necessities of life on the diggings, but everything costs two or three times more than it would in San Francisco itself. I paid ninety francs for an abominable pair of boots, and was congratulated. [26]

Life in the diggings was very rowdy, only quietening down with the passage of time or the exhaustion of the gold deposits. It was one wild adventure after another, ending, in most cases, in death by violence :

*Placer's People
1850*

The workings are the scene of frequent murders, which threaten to become a daily occurrence. At Sonora the other day a gambler who had lost his money got drunk, mounted his horse and rode it into a bar-room brandishing a gun. When they offered to turn him out he " shot the place up ", killing two poor devils who were having a drink in a corner. Drunken scenes of this sort occur almost daily, especially on Sunday when they are continuous, for the miners take a day off and come into town to gamble away the gold found during the week. They then drink themselves into a fury on hard liquor and run through the streets and saloons threatening, insulting and striking people, and letting off guns at random. Anyone attempting to stop them is shot down like a dog. All American-born, these men cling together and come to each other's aid. To resist one of these bandits is to have the whole crew against one. They detest all foreigners, but their hatred is directed especially against Mexicans, whom they treat as a conquered race. And what a business *that* was, by God, the conquest of New Mexico ; and what stories could be told ! [26]

Among other oddities, Louis Simonin's travels in the interior brought him into contact with a fellow-Frenchman, whose rough and ready adaptation to frontier life is a commentary not only on how Californian miners lived in that period but on contrasts between European and Yankee customs in general :

*A French
Gold-Miner
1859*

Without enumerating cases of individuals who came down in the world during the Gold Rush, I feel I may make mention of several notable eccentrics amongst the Coulterville miners. One of the oddest, who comes to mind through his commanding stature and big black beard, is Vermenouse, a Frenchman from Auvergne [in the centre of France] ; a mighty slayer of rattlesnakes, whose rattles he takes home to his hut, and the terror of Chinese chicken-thieves. As he keeps chickens and Chinamen hereabouts share the fox's reputation for laying waste the farmyard, he mounts guard with his gun, occasionally bringing down a squirrel as proof of his marksmanship to daunt the citizens of the Celestial Empire. He refuses to make

Sacramento, California — 1849

RIVER BOATS AND THE VIEW FROM THE FOOT OF J STREET

babbling brooks and the song of birds.   Ahead, we could see the snow-capped peaks of the granite Sierra Nevada on the horizon, some of which rise to several thousand metres.   This range marks the boundary of California, separating it from Utah Territory, and that strange polygamous sect, the Mormons who builded their New Jerusalem in this wilderness.

YOSEMITE FALLS · 1855

On our first day out we stopped at Marble Spring, a grotto situated, as its name implies, amongst the marble hills. A clear spring issues gently from the calcareous rock, running down into a transparent lake at the bottom of the gorge, accessible by steps. The walls are covered with stalactites and it is deliciously cool below. We chose this spot for dinner. We sat under a shady elm by the entrance to the grotto; the dogs, after quenching their burning thirst at the little lake, came and demanded a share of our picnic. That evening we pitched our tents in the forest, and lit a huge wood-fire.

The following day and the day after we met with some Indians, who sold us fish.   They wore ornaments of bone in their noses and ears, and some of them sported singular adornments around the neck. Long thick black hair hung untidily over their foreheads and down to the shoulders.   They walked proudly, the head held high, grasping their lances, bows and arrows, silently following a feather-bonneted chief. Behind came their squaws, carrying the baggage and the children on their backs in long rush baskets.   These Indians, all clad in rags, presented a pathetic spectacle. Neither men nor women were good-looking; their faces showed few signs of intelligence and their thin and puny bodies looked anything but healthy. These, like other desert Indians live on roots, herbs, acorns and grasshoppers together with game and fish when they succeed in catching any. The language they speak amongst themselves is made up of strange sounds; a few muster some words of Spanish, having picked them up from elders of the tribe who were converted to Christianity by the Franciscan fathers. For in days gone by, when California belonged to Mexico and the latter country belonged to Spain there were twenty or more missions run by Spanish missionaries, and it is estimated that there were 100,000 Indians in California, of whom one quarter had been converted. Today all have reverted to savagery, and there are only 50,000 left, even this number dwindling before the American invasion.

My friend, who had come to know the Indians well, by frequently travelling through their country and staying in their villages, told me a good deal concerning their customs, dances and domestic habits. They are so skilful at plaiting rush baskets that these vessels will hold water. They even use them as cooking-pots. To boil water for cooking some of their food they heat stones and throw them into the pot. I have seen something similar in Corsica, where the shepherds boil water in wooden pots.

Some of the Redskins we met proved willing to accompany the Pale-faces and act as guides. On the way they killed a little game, which we did ample justice to, and they came with us as far as the Yosemity [*sic*] Falls. On the way thither we passed through the forest of giant trees

THE YOSEMITE VALLEY - 1855

(Sequoia gigantea) [the Giant Redwood] which Nature seems to have planted on purpose beside the falls, as though to bring together the two greatest natural wonders of America.

Picture, if you can, four hundred cedar, pine or cypress trees, more than half of which measure between twelve and thirty metres in circumference—that is to say that it would take the same number of persons to encircle them. One such Colossus, now overthrown by either age or tempest, once reached to a height of more than 450 feet (eight times the height of a five-storey house) and 40 metres around—122 feet. This is probably the tallest and largest tree that has ever been; and by counting the concentric annual rings its age has been established as no less than 4,000 years, so that it was upon this earth before the Flood. My companion told me that the bark of one of these trees had been taken to San Francisco and re-erected. When it was set up, a piano was installed and there was still room for more than twenty persons to dance. It is also used as a little bazaar. In Calavera County, which is next to Mariposa County, there is another forest of giants that the Americans call " mammoth trees ". These trees are to the vegetable kingdom what the now extinct mammoth is to the animal. Some of them have been given whimsical names : we have the "Father of the Forest", and "Mother and the Daughter", together forming the " Family Group "; next come the " Three Sisters ", "Husband and Wife ", the " Old Bachelor ", " Uncle Tom's Cabin ", and the " Miner's Hut ". The latter, having recently been struck by lightning, now lies on the ground beside the " Father of the Forest ", although the latter's fall was due to an age approaching fifty centuries.

From the forest of Big Trees we went on to the Yosemity Falls, whose rapids fall sheer, in three steps, from a total height of nearly 2,500 feet [*sic*! but the reality is 620 ft.]. Niagara Falls are only 300 yards wide and the drop does not exceed 160 feet, although the volume of water passing over them is greater than that of any other Falls, and it is in this respect that they are so remarkable. However, Yosemity too, is one of the foremost natural wonders of America, and the falls are the highest in the world. I could not drag myself away from the splendid and picturesque landscape. At the foot of the Falls, a lake; this lake spills over to form the lower reaches of the river, which flows peacefully down between high walls of rock to a valley shaded by oaks, poplars and firs. We surprised some elks drinking at the waters' edge, and observed some Indians in a little rowing-

Marysville, California — 1855

AT THE JUNCTION OF THE FEATHER AND YUBA RIVERS

need I add, there is the indispensable W.C., a commodity that our European railroads would do well to provide. It is possible to walk—at one's own risk and peril it is true—from one car to the next; it is also permitted for intrepid lovers of scenic beauty to stand in the open on the gangways joining one car to another.

By means of a cord running the whole length of the train it is also possible for the conductor to communicate instantly, should necessity arise, with the engineer. There is only one class of accommodation for all passengers, apart from Negroes and Chinamen, who are piled into a little car of their own on wooden benches. Here the "coloured people" as the Americans disdainfully call them, enjoy the only freedom they are allowed— that of waiting patiently for the journey to be over as soon as possible. . . .

Coming into Folsom we crossed a humid low-lying plain, whose unhealthy vapours bring on fever in the summer. This plain, and that of Tulares in Southern California, are the only swampy districts in the country. Accusations that the climate of Eldorado in general is fatal to Europeans are quite unfounded. California offers the finest climate in the world, it is the healthiest country on earth. In summer, the heat, though intense, is easily bearable, thanks to breezes morning and evening, and the dryness of the air. In the autumn come the rains, causing the ground to be covered with lush herbage, which springs up on response to this beneficent watering. There is scarcely ever any snow. The rains, which are often torrential, last for several days; but once the clouds have disappeared the sky becomes as clear and bright as in the summer, and it is deliciously warm. This, then, is the climate that awaits the emigrant in the Land of Gold; the much-

BUSY SACRAMENTO - 1857

vaunted skies of Nice and Naples are nothing to it. If there have been a few cases of miners dying of fever in Eldorado, these have been due to illness contracted in Panama or at sea. The newly turned sod, also, especially on virgin soil, develops unhealthy emanations, and many a prospector must have perished mainly from the effects of this fever, which is known to the medical profession as " navvies' " fever. One thing that particularly struck me at Folsom was the incalculable quantity of stage-coaches that waited to meet the train.

Folsom is the centre for all services to the northern gold-fields, as Stockton is for the south. I took the Grass Valley stage. It was eight o'clock in the morning, so we started in the cool of the day. This " stage " was similar to that which had carried me from Stockton to Sonora. In imagination I allowed myself to travel on beyond the Rocky Mountains to the Atlantic States. There I saw stage-coaches like the one in which I was riding, railways like that which I had just left; the same kind of towns, the same people, the same customs. I fell to reflecting that although so much uniformity in a country as big as Europe might well drive the tourist to despair, it was also not without its droll side.

While I was buried in these reflections we crossed the splendid suspension bridge over the American River, and were soon bowling through woodlands of oak and pine. The road was no more than a trail, in the normal Californian fashion; levelling and consolidation are work left to the passing stage-coaches. Furthermore, as the land belonged to no one, not even the Government since the State laid no claim to it, the coach drove indiscriminately on the right or left, according to the whim of our Jehu. The result was a national—one cannot use the word Imperial or Royal—highway whose width put our finest French roads to shame.

In the distance, the first outlying foot-hills of the granite Sierras raised their jagged pine-clad slopes against the sky. On the plateau over which we were passing trees hugged the trail closely, so closely indeed that now and then branches would thrust their way through the windows, like inquisitive passers-by anxious to see what was inside. These episodes, like the bumps, provided our principal amusement, for in the United States there is little conversation, and we arrived at Auburn at noon, nine of us in the stage, without having uttered a word. . . .

We pulled out of Auburn at one o'clock and travelled all day, oppressed by the heat and thickly covered with dust. Californian roads are fast, and

" open " in more ways than one—carrying much traffic but entirely un-maintained : metalled roads and macadam are unknown and watering unheard of. It may be imagined what they are like after six months of drought; in winter, on the other hand, several days' torrential rain turns the dust into liquid mud, into which carriages sink up to their axles. But there is a good and a bad side to everything : if more heed had been paid to building the Californian roads, not so many would have been made —and none at all, probably, if the Government had taken a hand. After

THE TOWN OF AUBURN, PLACER COUNTY - 1857

all, one cannot have everything all at once—the finest climate in the world, miraculously fertile soil, bushels of gold *and* roads as smooth as city streets. Anyway the Americans themselves do not complain, and as it is their country it would be ungrateful for a visitor to do so.

At one of our wayside stops, the kind-hearted saloon-keeper had formed the habit of giving credit to all and sundry. Stage-drivers, carters, prospectors and the rest would swallow their whisky at the bar and pro-mise to pay " next time ". The unpaid bills attained enormous proportions, and the bar-keeper could hardly pursue his debtors all over the West. But he hit upon an excellent plan : he stuck the defaulters' names on a post in letters a foot high, together with the sum that each owed. On top was a huge sign saying "BE A MAN IF YOU WANT YOUR NAME TAKEN OFF".

The saloon stood just by a bridge, so the tall post attracted immediate attention : and in a country where public opinion is everything the punish-ment soon took effect. A large proportion of the names had gone by the time I was there, and I could only read two or three because our driver, who probably knew several of the bad payers, whipped up his horses as we crossed the bridge. J. Freeman was down for four dollars, W. Ball for three, F. Wheeler for five, " Irish " McLane for three and a half. A dollar is worth five francs, so that the thirty or so names on the post represented quite a tidy sum, even in the Land of Gold. . . .

We reached Grass Valley that evening after a long day's drive. Its approaches looked like the outskirts of any Californian mining town : nothing but holes and hummocks, ditches and banks where the ground had been turned over. There was not a spot anywhere in the ravines, on the

GRASS VALLEY SETTLEMENT - 1858

hills or along the streams showing alluvial sand that had not been attacked by the miner's pick and shovel. The place looked as though it had been overwhelmed by an avalanche.

In my eagerness to study America at first hand, I took rooms at the Hôtel de Paris, which, paradoxically, was kept by an American, instead of at another hotel kept by a Frenchman. This was a mistake. I was literally skinned at the Paris. Although I almost never took meals in the hotel I still had to pay my two dollars fifty a day the same as Americans who sat down to four meals. Every time I wanted my boots cleaned it cost 25 cents. The Gold Rush price. By the time I was in California the fee had gone down by half in the main centres ; but apparently Grass Valley still held to the old tariff, much to shoe-shiners' delight.

Grass Valley is not only the mining town *par excellence*, but a charming place in its own right, with houses in excellent taste. Lola Montez*, the famous adventuress who recently died in poverty in New York, spent part of her time in California at a villa in Grass Valley—and she had been around " some" in every country on earth. [27]

The Grass Valley plateau, with its famous Gold Hill, Lafayette and Massachusetts mines had been the scene of deadly shootings during the good old days of " Forty-Nine "; a fact, along with the growing destruction of timber, in California, remarked by Louis Simonin as he continues his story :

Grass Valley 1859

The famous Allison Ranch lode, the richest gold-seam in California, lies just outside the town. Its name has become a byword : the quartz is so full of gold that it yields more than one franc per kilogramme—about twelve cents a pound. The three Irishmen who own the mine discovered it in 1851, but only started working it in 1855, as it was thought that quartz deposits were not worth working. Having left Ireland with no money they are now millionaires several times over; and their fabulous profits increase every year. Each has built himself a pleasant little house, and, as good Catholics, they have erected a chapel in gratitude to God. They look after their employés exceptionally well, and every Monday, by way of entertainment, they take it in turns to go down to San Francisco with the gold brick representing the week's output.

I stayed several days at Grass Valley, visiting mines, amalgam plants, and even placer deposits. Every known method of gold working was here to be seen, a conspectus of Californian mining. Beside the stream into which the quartz mills discharge their residue I happened upon a couple of Frenchmen washing for gold. They told me that they had been doing this now for four years and the amount recovered showed no sign of diminution. The sands they were washing had already passed through the crushers and amalgam plants; but their simple flume, consisting of a wooden channel for the water to pass over with a little mercury in the bottom, extracted gold that had eluded the more complicated machinery, proving that the simplest arrangements are sometimes best.

The Grass Valley plateau where all the mines and crushers now stand was once richly wooded with cedars and gigantic firs. Most of these trees

MARYSVILLE - 1856

have now gone, swallowed by the miners' unceasing demands upon timber for building, and even for feeding the boilers of their steam-machinery. In California there are no laws or regulations controlling the exploitation of forests. They cut and fell just as they please, each man taking the tree that suits him; the axe spares nothing and never rests. Nobody thinks of conservation, still less of re-planting. The result is a general depopulation [*sic*]; the climate of California has already been altered by the continental

FORT SUTTER NEAR SACRAMENTO - 1849

deforestation, which adversely affects rainfall, the wind pattern, and the humidity of the soil. The landscape has been changed, too. The once wooded Grass Valley plateau displays nothing but naked hillsides, with a few forlorn stumps to mourn the trunks and branches of yore. The view now is anything but attractive and picturesque, so that the eye strays to the distant Sierras, whose flanks have not yet been denuded of their black pine trees, probably because the distance is too great.

Such thoughts will no doubt be considered unnecessary and ridiculous by any American—and particularly Californian—reader who may chance to see this travel article. But it is quite permissible to express regret at the mounting flood of materialism that everywhere tends to engulf us. Industrialism squeezes our hearts dry, and the very landscape is butchered in the name of progress. My companions, the Messrs. C. . . being by now true Californians, did not share my views; but they were so friendly and cordial that we always avoided the subject. . . . [27]

After several days in Grass Valley and around, Louis Simonin went to Marysville, California, where he stayed one night only, having to catch the next day's boat for Sacramento, and connect with the steamer that was to take him back to San Francisco :

From Marysville to San Francisco 1859

The wagon that was to carry me to Marysville made no difficulties about taking me—except that it turned into a stage-coach when the road became less hilly and tortuous—and we set off at a gallop. The bumping and shaking that I now had to endure far surpassed all previous tortures of this nature that we had undergone. Was it perhaps a visitation of Providence because I was travelling on Sunday? I would not know; but I do know that at one point I came within an ace of abandoning the accursed vehicle. I leaned out of the window and shouted to the driver: "Is there much more of this devilish road?" Sitting there calmly on the box, controlling his cattle with a firm and experienced hand, he looked down at me in astonishment: " It gets a bit better, bye-and-bye ". The " bye-and-bye " seemed to be interminable, and I was all for getting out, consigning my baggage to some carter on the road, and hiring a mule to carry me to Marysville. Only obstinacy kept me aboard; I was very nearly sick to my stomach, for not only was I suffering from a painful malady, but the vehicle came very close to turning turtle. The road was so cambered at one point that the whole machine tilted on one side. "Never mind! " cried my three Yankee fellow-passengers. Alighting from the wagon, they seized hold of its flanks and, exerting all their weight on one side succeeded in restoring its equilibrium. Incidents of this sort are frequent in California. The usages of self-government accustom the citizen to rely on no one but himself, and he is never at a loss. . . .

Marysville is the prettiest and " cutest " place I saw in California. Situated at the junction of the Feather and Yuba rivers, it is beautifully laid out, with broad streets and sumptuous public buildings. Some of the houses are built of brick, and can compare with dwellings at San Francisco and Sacramento for style, luxury and comfort. The town's exceptionally favourable situation renders it an important trading and commercial centre, serving, like Sacramento, most of the northern mines. There are at least 15,000 inhabitants, and the country around may truly be termed the garden of California. Taking a stroll on the evening of my arrival I witnessed an impromptu boxing-match. Two Americans had had a difference of opinion, and were settling it with their fists, each seeking to black the other's eye or dislocate his jaw. A large circle of spectators surrounded the warring

Sutter's Mill, California — 1849

VIEW OF THE SOUTH FORK OF THE AMERICAN RIVER WHERE THE GOLD RUSH STARTED

The latter indeed was one of our happiest and most delightful journeys. The low-lying banks of the river reminded me of the Saône, bordered for the most part by fine trees, with delightful glimpses here and there of a smiling countryside. Occasionally we saw cattle drinking but they promptly fled in panic at the sight of the on-coming steamer noisily belching smoke and steam from its funnels.

INDIAN VILLAGE ON THE FEATHER RIVER - 1847-1851

It is on the Feather River that Captain Sutter, " the General " as the Americans call him, has taken up residence, on a large ranch in the county that bears his name. This veteran of pioneer days in California has derived very little profit from the discovery of which he was, virtually, the author. He was practically driven away from the land on which Sacramento now stands, although that land belonged to him, and ousted from the placers in the neighbourhood of his fort. He intended to build a town there, to be called after him. But Sutterville is now derelict, having been replaced by Sacramento. In short the old Captain, although a rich man, has not profited as he deserved from discovering the gold, and he has withdrawn from unjust humanity to his ranch beside the Feather. Truth to tell, the role of soldier-farmer is far more in keeping with his noble character; the miners have the gold-fields, which feed no one, while he has fields of wheat to feed humanity. *

Arriving safely at Sacramento after six hours' steaming, we just had time to change from our boat to the ANTELOPE, in which I had travelled before to the Californian capital. We descended the Sacramento as safely and pleasantly as we had the Feather; we entered the Bay and by midnight I was knocking on the door of the International Hotel at San Francisco, having covered by steamer nearly 80 leagues [195 miles] in less than eighteen hours. [27]

In 1850 Alexandre Achard concluded the narrative of his travels thus :

Every adventure-seeker, remittance-man and bandit throughout the two Americas and Mexico—everyone in short who is at odds with the law or desires to escape notice, sets out to seek his fortune, or at least find freedom of action, in California. It will be a long while before the law succeeds in regularising these movements, and guaranteeing the safety of travellers. But does the United States Government care ? They have placed a duty on the export of gold; the Treasury is satisfied, so nothing else matters. The Federal Government allows matters to take their course, and makes no attempt to enforce order in the diggings, or suppress the gambling and drunkenness. It is realised that a day will come when prospectors no longer roam the hills, and the gold-fields will at length grow crops. The rough elements will then fade away, giving place to yeomen of sturdy stock like those Pilgrim Fathers and stolid Dutchmen who laid the foundations of the American Republic. [26]

Conclusion in 1850

By 1859 the picture has indeed altered. From the conclusion of Louis Simonin's account we can see how rapidly the rowdy California of Gold Rush days had vanished, to be replaced by peace, prosperity and Chamber of Commerce prose :

I am most anxious to remove the false impressions concerning California that are still current abroad, especially in France, based on unfortunate accounts of the early days. It is not yet realised how quickly California has become a model State. Although the flood of French emigrants dried up some time ago, there is no lack of Germans, Irish—and above all Americans of the California Trail, so that each year the population increases by 20,000 souls. California to the Yankees is the Promised Land, offering an exceptional climate, inexhaustible mines, and rich and fertile soil. Wages are higher than elsewhere, affording the hard-working emigrant a chance to make his fortune in short order. Extensive commercial relations exist with the world at large : on the seaward side commerce with India, the Dutch East Indies, China, Japan, the South Seas, and the Pacific colonies of Spain, while overland there is daily contact with the Atlantic States : the Old World, in short, and the New. What young country ever enjoyed a more favourable situation ? What rival can stand beside this youthful and vigorous State, that has minted one more Star to adorn the Star-Spangled Banner ? [27]

Conclusion in 1859

RICHARD F. BURTON

PHILIPPE SUCHARD

HENRI HERZ

ELISÉE RECLUS

BASIL HALL

INDEX
TO
NAMES
OF
TRAVELLERS

FRANCOIS-ANDRÉ MICHAUX

CHARLES DICKENS

FREDERICK MARRYAT

JEAN-JACQUES AMPÈRE

1 GELONE, M. F. D.
Manuel-Guide des Voyageurs aux Etats-Unis de l'Amérique du Nord.
Paris, 1818

The author describes himself in the title of his book as a " sometime student of engineering " and this is all that we know about him. Published and printed in Paris, his book was " addressed especially to merchants, farmers and persons of every profession and trade on the Continent of Europe ". It is filled with miscellaneous information : addresses of banking-houses, hotel prices, the cost of land and of other necessary articles. . . .

2 SUCHARD, PHILIPPE
Un voyage aux Etats-Unis d'Amérique.
Notes d'un touriste pendant l'été et l'automne de 1824.
Boudry (Switzerland), 1947

For Philippe Suchard (1797-1884), an enterprising young Swiss with liberal ideas, the United States was *the* country of liberty and freedom. He had just founded the famous chocolate factory which still bears his name at Neuchâtel in Switzerland, when at the age of 27, he made his first trip to America to find out about the New World. In 1834, he established the first steamer service on the Lake of Neuchâtel. In the course of a second visit, in 1843, he founded the Swiss settlement of Alpina in the State of New York where blast-furnaces were constructed. This settlement lasted for five years. In 1873, when he was seventy-six, he made a trip round the world.
The diary of his first journey to the United States was only published forty years later.

3 MONTLEZUN, Baron de
Voyage fait dans les années 1816 et 1817 de New York à la Nouvelle-Orléans.
Paris, 1818

The Baron de Montlezun—in all probability the French aristocrat whose full name was Barthélemy-Sernin de Montlezun de la Barthelle—first seems to have become acquainted with the New World when he served in the American War of Independence. A pronounced snob and political reactionary, the Baron does not appear to have relished the restored Bourbon monarchy which followed the fall of Napoleon at Waterloo in 1815. In that year or the next he set off on a long voyage to America and the West Indies. He vented his spleen in derogatory accounts of the countries, institutions and individuals with whom he came in contact.

4 HERZ, HENRI
Mes voyages en Amérique.
Paris, 1866

Henri Herz (1806-1888) was born in Vienna but completed his musical studies in Paris and took out French naturalisation papers, becoming a brilliant pianist and composing some agreeable pieces. Although not written until twenty years after his return to France, his memoirs of his American concert tour (1846) are precise and full of good stories, as well as shrewd but kindly comments upon life and manners in the U.S.A.

5 HALL, BASIL
Travels in North-America in the Years 1827 and 1828.
London & Edinburgh, 1829

Captain Basil Hall (1788-1844) of Edinburgh, had already retired from a successful career in the British Navy when he made his 13-month visit to America. He did not think much of American democratic institutions as they then were; but he took with him a *camera lucida*—an optical device that foreshadowed the present-day camera—and with its aid made many drawings. Forty of these were published separately in 1830 by Cadell & Co., Edinburgh, and in London by Simpkin, Marshall, Moon, Boys & Graves. A few are reproduced here (see pp. 70 bottom, 79, 84, 85, 86 bottom, 97, 98, 111, 112, and 117).

6 DICKENS, CHARLES
American Notes for General Circulation.
London, 1842

The famous English novelist (1812-1870) celebrated his thirtieth birthday on American soil during a four and a half month visit in 1842. As a writer he was apt to see things in black and white, and as reporter he was not always kind towards emergent America. On his return home he drew upon his American experiences while writing *Martin Chuzzlewit* published in 1843.

7 AMPÈRE, JEAN-JACQUES
Promenade en Amérique ; Etats-Unis, Cuba, Mexique.
Paris, 1856 (nouvelle édition)

Jean-Jacques Ampère (1800-1864) was the son of the famous French physicist André Ampère, who gave his name to the unit of electric current. Jean-Jacques spent about five months in the U.S.A. in 1851-1852, as he put it, " in order to see something entirely new ". He was especially interested in studying American literature, the Temperance Movement and Protestant religious sects. He brought a cultured and intelligent mind to bear upon the transatlantic scene, and was an indulgent observer of American foibles. He was on the Faculty of the *Collège de France* and a member of the *Académie Française*.

8 BEAUVALLET, LÉON
Rachel et le Nouveau-Monde.
Promenade aux Etats-Unis et aux Antilles.
Paris, 1856

Léon Beauvallet (born in 1828), French actor and playwright, played juvenile leads in the company which the great tragic actress Rachel took to the United

States mostly to perform Racine, Corneille and Molière in French. Since very few Americans, then as now, knew French, the French company not surprisingly enjoyed only limited success. Their season of thirty-one performances in New York took in only 97,595 dollars, whereas the famous Swedish singer Jenny Lind took in 512,303 dollars for the same number of performances and at the same period.

9 MARRYAT, FREDERICK
A Diary in America, with Remarks on its Institutions.
London, 1839

Captain Marryat (1792-1848) retired after a distinguished career in the Royal Navy in 1830, immediately after writing the first of his famous sea-adventure stories, " The Naval Officer, or Scenes and Adventures in the Life of Frank Mildmay ". His most famous book, " Mr. Midshipman Easy " appeared in 1836. The following year he made a long tour through the North East and North West of the United States " to ascertain what were the effects of a democratic form of government and climate upon a people which, with all its foreign admixture may still be considered as English. " On the whole Marryat found the effects were " exclusively degenerative " in nature. Serving in the Burma War of 1824, he was the first to suggest the employment of a steamship (H.M.S. DIANA) on active service in the Royal Navy.

10 FERGUSON, WILLIAM — F.L.S., etc.
America by River and Rail or Notes by the Way on the New World and its People.
London, 1856

Apart from this account of his journey in America, William Ferguson seems to be quite unknown. His main interest was in studying the technique of the American railways.

11 MICHAUX, FRANÇOIS-ANDRÉ
Voyage à l'ouest des Monts Alléghanys, dans les Etats de l'Ohio, du Kentucky et du Tennessée et retour à Charleston par les Hautes-Carolines, entrepris pendant l'an X-1802, sous les auspices de son excellence M. Chaptal, Ministre de l'intérieur.
Paris, 1804

François-André Michaux (1770-1855) was a tireless French botanist who spent sixteen months (1801-1803) in the U.S.A., travelling widely on foot and on horseback. He also descended the Ohio River by dug-out canoe. His main concern was studying plant-life with reference to possible cultivation, but he also had a good deal to say about stock-raising, industry, the economy in general and matters of scientific interest.

12 GRASSI, GIOVANNI, SJ
Notizie varie sullo stato presente della repubblica degli Stati Uniti dell'America settentrionale scritti al principio del 1818 dal padre Giovanni Grassi della Compagnia di Gesù.
Milan, 1819

Giovanni Antonio Grassi (1775-1849) was an Italian Jesuit who lived in Russia, Portugal, England and the United States, where for five years he served as President of Georgetown College (c. 1812-1817). He died at Turin after spending some years there as Confessor to the exiled King Felix of Sardinia. His book is devoted mainly to a description of various religious movements in the U.S. It was widely used as a general introduction for clerics visiting North America.

13 BARBAROUX, CHARLES-OGÉ
Voyage du Général Lafayette aux Etats-Unis d'Amérique en 1824.
Paris, 1824

Charles-Ogé Barbaroux (1792-1867), a French politician and diplomat, held the office of *Procureur Impérial* (Public Prosecutor) first at Marseilles, then at Pondicherry in French India, next on the island of Réunion and finally in Algiers. He accompanied General Lafayette (then age 67) throughout the latter's triumphal return to the U.S. some 47 years after Lafayette had first placed his sword at General Washington's disposal in the War of Independence. At the time of his death Barbaroux was a Senator under the Second Empire (Napoleon III).

14 CASTELNAU, FRANCIS DE
Vues et souvenirs de l'Amérique du Nord.
Paris, 1842

Francis de la Porte, known as Comte de Castelnau (1812-1880), was a great French traveller who made extensive journeys through North America (1837-1841) and South America (1843-1847). He served as French consul at Bahia, the Cape of Good Hope, Singapore, and Melbourne, where he died. His book is somewhat impersonal and makes rather dry reading, especially in large doses.

15 POUSSIELGUE, ACHILLE
Visite aux grottes de Mammoth dans le Kentucky, 1859,
in : " Le Tour du Monde ", Paris, 1863.
Quatre mois en Floride, 1851-1852,
in : "Le Tour du Monde", Paris, 1869 vol. I ; 1870 vol. I

Achille Poussielgue (1829-1869), attaché to the French Embassy in Washington, was extremely keen on travel and natural history. He presented the Museum of Natural History in Paris with an important collection of zoological specimens collected during his visits to Florida and to the Mammoth Caves in Kentucky.

216

Nevertheless his most exciting discovery in the New World was a pretty girl held prisoner in a lighthouse off the Florida coast. The *Tour du Monde*, a French weekly magazine was popular from 1860 to 1914 and went in heavily for accounts of trips in the then touristically fashionable United States.

16 RECLUS, ELISÉE
Fragment d'un voyage à la Nouvelle-Orléans, 1855,
in : " Le Tour du Monde ", Paris, 1860 vol. I et II

Elisée (or as we should say, Elisha) Reclus (1830-1905) was a Frenchman, but after studying in Berlin he was exiled from France for his anarchist activities. He then travelled in England, the United States and Colombia, and became a famous Professor of Geography, teaching this subject at the University of Brussels, in Belgium where he died. This account, amounting to a few pages only, gives his impressions of the Mississippi delta and the town of New Orleans.

17 EYMA, L. XAVIER
in : " L'Illustration " Paris, 1848

L. Xavier Eyma would be unknown except for the fact that the famous French magazine *L'Illustration* published his travel articles about the United States. He is especially good on New Orleans, on the river steamers and on American railroads.

18 BERNHARD KARL, HERZOG ZU SACHSEN-WEIMAR-EISENACH
Reise Sr. Hoheit des Herzogs Bernhard zu Sachsen-Weimar-Eisenach durch Nord-Amerika, 1825 und 1826.
Weimar, 1828

All through his boyhood Bernhard Karl, Duke of Saxe-Weimar-Eisenach in Thuringia (1792-1862), wanted to visit the United States. But it was not until he was thirty-three that he was able to realise his dream. In order to do so, he had to get a special leave of absence from the King of Holland, whom he was serving as an officer in the Dutch army. The Duke spent some six months in the U.S. and travelled more than 7,136 miles. He was delighted with his trip and wrote : " To my great regret, the hour at length arrived when I was constrained to leave this happy and prosperous land, in which I had seen and learned so much, and in which *much* more still remained to be seen and learned".

19 GIRARDIN, E. DE
Voyage dans les mauvaises terres du Nebraska 1849-1850,
in : " Le Tour du Monde ", Paris, 1864, vol. I

Apart from this article in *Le Tour du Monde*, nothing is known about Girardin. One thing is certain though, translated as *les mauvaises terres*, the Badlands of Nebraska sound very bad indeed.

20 MÖLLHAUSEN, BALDUIN
Tagebuch einer Reise vom Mississippi,
eingeführt von Alexander von Humboldt.
Leipzig, 1858

Impelled by fondness for science and travel, Balduin Möllhausen left his native Germany at the age of 24 after completing his studies in topography. On arrival in the United States he joined the expedition of Prince Paul of Württemberg, whose aim was to explore the Rocky Mountains. The expedition was a failure, and Möllhausen spent several months living amongst the Ottawa and Omaha tribes of Indians. Then, thanks to an introduction from the famous scientist Alexander von Humboldt, he was able to join Lt. A. W. Whipple as topographer and draftsman, on a survey of the tributaries of the Missouri, Rio Grande and Colorado rivers for the U.S. Government. The aim of the survey was to plan the route of a transcontinental railroad from the Atlantic to the Pacific. Altogether Möllhausen made three trips to the United States. Apart from his travel books, he published a number of novels and short stories. He spent his later years in Germany where he died in 1905.

21 KURZ, FRIEDRICH RUDOLPH
Aus dem Tagebuch des Malers Friedrich Kurz über seinen Aufenthalt bei den Missouri-Indianern 1848-1852.
Bern, 1894

Primarily a water-colourist, Friedrich Kurz (1818-1871) was born at Berne, Switzerland. He landed at New Orleans at the beginning of the year 1846, when he was 28, and travelled from that town to Saint Louis, Missouri, a journey that took seventeen days. He then went on, by short stages interspersed with stays amongst the Indians, as far as the Upper Missouri, where he made his home amongst the Indian tribes for four years. " From earliest childhood, " he wrote, " I have been fascinated by Indians and primeval forest. . . . In depicting Indian life in these pages I do but set the stage for a greater work, the culmination of a lifetime, although the two objects are in fact one. I had to find a setting for my Adam and Eve, a primeval Paradise in some warm and friendly clime ; it was essential to familiarise myself with the life and customs of primitive peoples, before I could render them truthfully. " Kurz had spent twelve years preparing for this professional tour which was to be the fulfilment of his childhood dream. His ideal of beauty was that of ancient Greece which he tried to retrace in the Indians ; this is revealed by the sketches and drawings preserved in the Berne Historical Museum. Kurz helped to found the first Arts School in Berne and was its first director. He died in Berne in 1871.

22 MAXIMILIAN PRINZ ZU WIED
Reise in das innere Nord-Amerika in den Jahren 1832-1834.
Coblenz, 1839-1841

Maximilian Alexander Philip, Prince of Wied-Neuwied, in Prussia (1782-1867) was fifty when he arrived in the United States. He remained there two years, and travelled up the Missouri as far as Fort Union, Montana. The Prince's great work is concerned mainly with natural history and anthropology, making no concessions to the Romantic or the Picturesque ; but he was accompanied by the Swiss artist, Karl Bodmer, who produced 81 magnificent engravings for his book (see pp. 109, 128, 136, 137, 144, 145, 146, 147, 148, 150, 151 and 152).

23 BURTON, Sir RICHARD FRANCIS
The City of the Saints and Across the Rocky Mountains to California.
London, 1861

Captain Richard Burton (1821-1890) was not only one of the great explorers of the nineteenth century but one of the most bizarre and controversial figures in Victorian England. Born in Hertfordshire, he spent much of his childhood in France and Italy, before going up to Trinity College, Oxford and into the Indian Army in 1842. A brilliant linguist with a mastery of some thirty-five languages and dialects, he did much Secret Service work, being able to pass as a native in the bazaars of India and the Middle East. In 1853 he made a pilgrimage to the Holy Cities of Medina and Mecca, forbidden to non-Muslims, and it was a desire to see " the newest Holy City of all " that led him in 1860 to visit the Mormons at Great Salt Lake, Utah, where he had a long interview with Brigham Young, the Mormon Leader. He explored Somaliland in 1856, then served in the Crimean War, after which he embarked with John Hanning Speke on his greatest expedition, in the course of which they discovered Lake Tanganyika. Speke and Burton quarrelled, and Burton's reputation suffered but he nevertheless received the gold medal of both the French and British (Royal) Geographical Societies, and was knighted by Queen Victoria in 1868. Ironically he is best known not for his explorations but for his monumental and piquant translation (with copious and provocative notes) of the Arabian Nights (1885-1888).

24 RÉMY, JULES
Voyage au pays des Mormons — relation, géographie, histoire, théologie, mœurs et coutumes.
Paris, 1860

Jules Rémy seems to have left no traces apart from this book. His account is highly interesting for the details he gives of how people travelled across the Plains and Mountains and desert country of the West, either in wagons, on mule-back or in the sort of travelling carriage which Richard Burton assures us was called an " ambulance ". In addition to numerous botanical notes Rémy's book relates conversations between the author and Brigham Young, the Mormon Leader, and describes religious life in Great Salt Lake City, Utah. Although he did not really have much fondness or sympathy for the Mormons, Rémy succeeds in remaining objective, and his book may be regarded as a reliable document on Mormon life and customs.

25 DILLON, PATRICE
La Californie dans les derniers mois de 1849,
in : " La Revue des Deux Mondes ", 15 janvier 1850,
Paris.

Patrice Dillon seems to have served in the French diplomatic or consular service at San Francisco. Apart from this article in a well-known French literary journal, which shows he was an excellent journalistic writer with a sharp eye for local colour and the gift of turning a precise phrase, he has left little trace.

26 ACHARD, ALEXANDRE
Voyage de Paris à San Francisco, scènes de mœurs en Californie.
Les Américains et les Français dans les Placers.
In : " La Revue des Deux Mondes ", 15 août 1850,
Paris.

No other work by this writer is known.

27 SIMONIN, LOUIS
Voyage en Californie, 1859,
in : " Le Tour du Monde ", Paris, 1862

Louis Simonin contributed a series of travel articles to *Le Tour du Monde* magazine, of which this was the first. Subsequent numbers related to the French island of Réunion in the Indian Ocean (1862), Great Britain (1865), the Far West (1868), the Chincha Islands of Peru (1868) and a journey from Washington D.C. to San Francisco (1874). His Californian piece shows him to be a lively, thoughtful and conscientious reporter.

EXPLANATORY NOTES

CHAPTER I

Page 8

It is very difficult to express the prices quoted by nineteenth century travellers in terms of today's money. There are a number of reasons for this: first of all the fluctuations in national currencies during the century, then the very different values placed upon specific goods and services on each side of the Atlantic both then and now, and finally the differing rates at which the standard of living has risen in European countries and in the United States. In 1818 a dock labourer on the Atlantic seaboard of the U.S.A. earned about $2.50 a day; in France around the year 1830, the most that a French workman could hope for was the equivalent of 50 cents a day, U.S. money. In order to make valid comparisons it would be necessary to know the prices of identical articles of food-stuffs on both sides of the ocean — and to assume that these prices were uniform throughout the whole of France and the United States respectively, which was far from being the case.

In 1818, a United States dollar was worth roughly 5 French francs, as it is today; but in terms of wages a dollar represented half a day's labour for an American workman, while in France it took a man two days to earn his 5 francs. Evidently no real comparisons are possible, and those we have given in the text must be regarded as very tenuous.

Page 21

This remark of Philippe Suchard's remains obscure. It probably refers to contemporary politics in Spain, where a group known as the Apostolic Party was formed after the Revolution of 1819 by absolutists wishing to overthrow Queen Isabella and place Don Carlos on the throne.

Philippe Suchard, holding extremely liberal views and coming from a Protestant country, probably disapproved strongly of Apostolic methods, and of the exploitation of Catholicism for political ends.

Page 26

Elisa Felix, who acted under the name of Rachel, was born in Switzerland on the 28th February 1820, of French parents. After difficult beginnings she joined the *Comédie Française* on the 12th June 1838. She made a considerable name for herself, particularly in *Phèdre*, the tragedy by Jean Racine (1639-1699). Upon her return from the tour of the United States and Havana in which she had hoped to make her fortune, her doctors advised complete rest. She died at Cannes, at the age of 37, in January 1858.

CHAPTER II

Page 95

Léon Beauvallet is here alluding to a celebrated scene in Racine's *Phèdre* (Act V, scene 6). The young Hyppolitus, having been cursed by his father, Theseus, is devoured by a sea-monster before the eyes of his preceptor and confidant, Theramenes. The latter, still afflicted with the horror of the scene, hastens to Theseus to pour forth an account of Hyppolitus' tragic fate. The tragedy of *Phèdre* (or, in English, Phaedra) was one of the plays in Rachel's repertoire during her American tour.

CHAPTER III

Page 132

Fort Union, Montana, was a very important post situated at the junction of the Yellowstone and Missouri rivers. Erected in 1829 and completed by the American Fur Company in 1834, it became the Company's most important station on the Upper Missouri. The post was sold to the United States Government in 1867.

Page 132

The American Fur Company was one of the first giant commercial undertakings in the United States. Founded by John Jacob Astor in 1808 it played a large part in American history by opening up the unexplored or unexploited regions to white settlers. Most of the fortified trading posts on the Great Lakes, in the Middle West and in the Rockies were founded or maintained in the early days by the Company. In his " Journey through the Bad Lands of Nebraska (1849-1850) " the French traveller E. de Girardin described the American Fur Company as the most enterprising concern in the American fur-trade on the American continent, although he did speak also of " the Opposition " without, however, mentioning any rival concerns by name. The centre for the fur-trade at this time was Saint Louis, Missouri, which handled trade to the tune of $300,000—500,000 a year between 1847 and 1860.

Page 133

Fort Berthold, North Dakota, was founded by Bartholomew Berthold, one of the proprietors of the American Fur Company, about midway between Fort Clarke and Fort Union, Montana.

Page 133

Here is the description of the game given by Friedrich Kurz : " The Herantsa are fond of the so-called billiard game, which, when weather permits, they practise constantly in and about their village. They play the game with a billiard wand that they throw with full strength toward a hoop rolling along the ground. This wand or cue has four markings indicated with leather and at the end a pad made of leather-strips, scraps of cloth, or, for want of something better, even bunches of grass. The winner starts the hoop, both players run along beside it and throw their wands, the flight of which is retarded by the pads, called idi by the Herantsa, so that they do not take too wide a range over the smooth course. To be sure the ground is not as smooth as a floor ; it is uneven, but cleared of pebbles and filth. According to that mark on the cue or wand on which the hoop in falling rests, they reckon the game. Oftentimes the players throw their wands so uniformly that they fall one upon the other, making it impossible for the contestants themselves to decide which wins.
Whereupon, without wrangling or the least suggestion of contention, they appeal at once to the older spectators, whose decision is accepted. Although they always put up some small or trifling objects, at the beginning of the game, the stakes are steadily increased in value until not infrequently they mount quite high ; for instance, from bows, arrows, knives, mocassins, to buffalo-robes, ornamented leggings, richly adorned leather-shirts, tobacco pipes, guns, horses, tents, and it sometimes happens that the players even venture their elder wives. Some members of the Herantsa Tribe devote themselves exclusively to this game — never take part in the hunt ".

Page 137

Fort Pierre was the name of a fortified trading post at the confluence of the Bad River and the Missouri in what is now South Dakota. Originally built by Joseph La Framboise in 1817, it was reconstructed in 1822 under the name of Fort Tecumseh. In 1828 Pierre Chouteau, one of the heads of the American Fur Company established a third fort, which became widely known under the name of Fort Pierre between 1832 and 1856. It stood on the right bank of the Missouri, opposite the present city of Pierre, S. Dak.

Page 140

Fort Clarke, like Fort Pierre, was situated on the right bank of the Missouri, standing above the present city of Stanton, N. Dak., and below Washburn.

Page 142

Fort Mackenzie, Wyoming, was originally called Fort Piëkan when it was founded, at the point where the Marias River flows into the Missouri, in 1832. It was later moved to a site on the Missouri farther upstream. The Fort lay one day's journey from the great rapids of the Missouri. In 1832 it was the most advanced of the trading posts in the direction of the Rocky Mountains.

Page 148

Hadj, Hadji or Hajji is the name or title given to Mohammedans who have made the pilgrimage to Mecca or Medina. The word means " holy ", and signifies that its bearer has fulfilled one of the conditions of entry to the Paradise of Allah.

Page 155

Under the Turkish Empire a *firman* was the sovereign's formal edict, grant, licence or passport in writing, issued with a certain amount of ceremony.

Page 147

A species of mollusc.

CHAPTER IV

Page 169

The siege of Sebastopol, in Russia, lasted from October 1854 until September 1855, and was one of the key operations in the Crimean War, by which the united British, French and Turkish forces sought to prevent Russia's expansion into the Eastern Mediterranean. This war was, in fact, just another episode connected with what contemporary politicians called " the Balkan question ".

Page 205

Lola Montez, or more correctly, Maria Dolores Eliza Rosanna Gilbert (1818-1861) was an Irish adventuress, dancer and singer who became the mistress of King Ludwig I of Bavaria. For some time she could be called the ruler of that country, but she was driven out of it by the Revolution of 1848. She reappeared in the United States in 1851, settling finally in New York, where she busied herself with good works.

Page 210

Johann August Sutter (1803-1880) was born at Rünenberg in Switzerland. He went to California in 1839-40, where he was granted territories by Mexico which included the land on which Sacramento now stands. He bestowed the name of New Helvetia on his estates, in memory of his native land, and built a fort to protect his mills and saw-mills. In 1845, still under the aegis of Mexico, he owned 150.000 acres of land and even enjoyed the title of Military Governor, with the rank of General. When the first discoveries of gold were made on his land he was invaded by gold-seekers of every nationality and colour who paid no regard whatever to his territorial rights. His lands were laid waste, and by 1852 he was ruined. Unfortunately for Sutter the original deeds by which he had been ceded the land by Mexico perished in a fire that devastated San Francisco, so that he had no written evidence of ownership. After a long series of fruitless lawsuits, Johann August Sutter died in Washington D.C. while engaged in a final attempt to obtain recognition of his rights.

ACKNOWLEDGEMENTS

COLOR-PLATES

Anonymous
page 180
The I.N. Phelps Stokes Collection of American Historical Prints, New York Public Library

Anonymous
page 200
The Robert B. Honeymoon jr. Collection of Western American Art, University of California, The Bancroft Library, Berkeley

BEECHY, Richard, British (1808-1895)
page 172
The Robert B. Honeymoon jr. Collection of Western American Art, University of California, The Bancroft Library, Berkeley

BENNETT, William James, British (1787-1844)
page 80
The I.N. Phelps Stokes Collection of American Historical Prints, New York Public Library

BODMER, Karl, Swiss (1809-1893)
pages 128, 148, 152
Northern Natural Gas Company Collection, Joslyn Art Museum, Omaha, Nebraska

COOPER, George Victor, American (1810-1878)
page 196
The I.N. Phelps Stokes Collection of American Historical Prints, New York Public Library

GARNERAY, Ambroise-Louis, French (1783-1857)
pages 12, 18, 40, 104
from : " Collection générale des vues des ports de mer dans l'océan et dans la Méditerranée, 1842-1843 "
Bibliothèque Nationale, Paris

HYDE DE NEUVILLE, Baroness Anne-Marguerite-Henriette, French (c. 1779-1849)
page 72
Musée de Blérancourt, France

LATROBE, Benjamin Henry, British (1764-1820)
pages 32, 76, 100
Collections of the Maryland Historical Society, Baltimore

LEWIS, Henry, British (1819-1904)
page 124
The I.N. Phelps Stokes Collection of American Historical Prints, New York Public Library

LITTLE, John
page 208
The I.N. Phelps Stokes Collection of American Historical Prints, New York Public Library

NARJOT, Ernest Etienne de Francheville, French (1827-1898)
page 188
The Robert B. Honeymoon jr. Collection of Western American Art, University of California, The Bancroft Library, Berkeley

RONDÉ, Philippe, French
pages 138, 142
from : Philippe Rondé, " Voyage aux Etats-Unis, " Paris, 1826
Bibliothèque Nationale, Paris

SVININ, Pavel Petrovich, Russian (1787/8-1839)
pages 26, 60
from : " Voyage Pittoresque aux Etats-Unis de l'Amérique par Paul Svinin en 1811, 1812 et 1813 "
The Metropolitan Museum of Art, Rogers Fund 1942, New York

TODD, William
page 96
The I.N. Phelps Stokes Collection of American Historical Prints, New York Public Library

BLACK AND WHITE ILLUSTRATIONS

Anonymous
pages 64, 65
Musée de Blérancourt, France

BARTLETT, William Henry, British (1809-1854)
pages 29, 34, 35, 39, 42
from : N.P. Willis, " American Scenery from Drawings by W.H. Bartlett ", London, 1840
Bibliothèque Cantonale et Universitaire, Lausanne

BENNETT, William James, British (1787-1844)
pages 10, 48, 82, 179
The I.N. Phelps Stokes Collection of American Historical Prints, New York Public Library

BIRCH, William, British (1755-1834)
page 15
The I.N. Phelps Stokes Collection of American Historical Prints, New York Public Library

BODMER, Karl, Swiss (1809-1893)
pages 109, 136, 137, 144, 145, 146, 147, 150, 151
from : Maximilian Prinz zu Wied, " Reise in das innere Nord-America in den Jahren 1832-1834 ", Coblenz, 1839-1841
Bibliothèque Cantonale et Universitaire, Lausanne

BUFFORD, J.H.
page 44
The I.N. Phelps Stokes Collection of American Historical Prints, New York Public Library

CASTELNAU, Francis de la Porte, known as Comte de Castelnau, French (1812-1830)
pages 86 top, 87, 89, 92, 93
from : Francis de Castelnau, " Vues et Souvenirs de l'Amérique du Nord ", Paris, 1842
Bibliothèque Cantonale et Universitaire, Lausanne

CHASSEVENT
page 154
from : " Le Tour du Monde ", Paris, 1862

CHORIS, Ludovik, Russian (1795-1828)
page 174
from : " Voyage pittoresque autour du Monde, " Paris, 1822
Bibliothèque Cantonale et Universitaire, Lausanne

COLLOT, Georges-Henri-Victor, French (c. 1751-1805)
pages 52, 54, 55
from : " Voyage dans l'Amérique septentrionale ", Paris, 1826
Bibliothèque Nationale, Paris

COOPER, George Victor, American (1810-1878)
page 207
The I.N. Phelps Stokes Collection of American Historical Prints, New York Public Library

PORTRAITS

CONTENTS

The Editor would like to express his thanks to all those Curators and Librarians
of institutions on both sides of the Atlantic who have given assistance in
the compilation of this book, and especially to Doris Coffin, of Time-Life
Books, and Timothy Foote, European Editor of the International Book Society.

Devised and compiled by an Edita staff team
composed of Ami Guichard, Joseph Jobé, Charles Riesen,
Anne Bioley, Ursula Claren
and Max Thommen, who designed the cover

Photogravure printed by Héliogravure Centrale, Lausanne,
on matt satin antique wove paper
specially made for this book
by the Papierfabrik « Sihl » an der Sihl, Zurich

Colour plates by Offset Jean Genoud, Lausanne

Bound by Maurice Busenhart, Lausanne

Printed in Switzerland